EYEWITNESS COMPANIONS

Dogs

DR BRUCE FOGLE

"WHEN WE ARE WITH OUR DOGS
THERE IS NO LONELINESS OF
SPIRIT. WE ARE CONNECTED."

Baffin Island Inuit saying

LONDON, NEW YOR...
MUNICH, MELBOURNE...

Project Art Editor	Maxine L...
Project Editor	Rob Hou...
Editorial Assistant	Miezan v...
Managing Editor	Liz Whee...
Managing Art Editor	Philip Ormerod
Publisher	Jonathan Metcalf
Art Director	Bryn Walls
DTP Designer	John Goldsmid
Production Controller	Linda Dare

First published in 2006 by
Dorling Kindersley Limited
80 Strand, London WC2R 0RL
Penguin Group

Produced for Dorling Kindersley by

studio cactus ltd Ⓒ

13 SOUTHGATE STREET WINCHESTER HAMPSHIRE SO23 9DZ UK
TEL 00 44 1962 878600 FAX 00 44 1962 859278
EMAIL MAIL @STUDIOCACTUS.CO.UK WEBSITE WWW.STUDIOCACTUS.CO.UK

Senior Editor	Aaron Brown
Designers	Dawn Terrey, Laura Watson, Sharon Cluett, Sharon Rudd
Editorial Assistant	Jennifer Close
Creative Director	Amanda Lunn
Editorial Director	Damien Moore

2 4 6 8 10 9 7 5 3 1

A CIP catalogue record for this book
is available from the British Library

ISBN-10: 1 4053 1264 5
ISBN-13: 978 1 4053 1264 6

Colour reproduction by Colourscan, Singapore
Printed and bound in China by
Leo Paper Products Ltd

Discover more at
www.dk.com

Introduction 10

STORY OF THE DOG

THE DOG'S ORIGINS 14

THE DOMESTICATED DOG 28

CONTENTS

FOR MILLENNIA, DOGS HAVE BEEN OUR MOST TRUSTED ANIMAL COMPANIONS. THEY MAY COME IN AN ASTONISHINGLY DIVERSE RANGE OF SIZES AND LOOKS, BUT THEY ARE ALL ALIKE IN THEIR SINGULAR SUCCESS AT READING OUR INTENTIONS. THIS UNIQUE ASSET EXPLAINS THE SUCCESS OF OUR RELATIONSHIP WITH DOGS.

ANCIENT ORIGINS

Traditionally, it is said that our relationship with dogs began around 15,000 years ago when, with the development of agriculture, our ancestors became more sedentary. Anthropological evidence of the wolf evolving into the dog – a reduction in the size of the brain, teeth set more closely together – dates from that era. But recent genetic evidence puts the date much earlier (*see* pp.22–23). Although the date is uncertain, genetic

Dogs as pets
In North America, Europe, Japan, Australia, and New Zealand, there are over 100 million canine companions – a dog in one out of three households.

tests confirm that the dog evolved from Asian wolves. A line of wolves that felt at ease in close proximity to humans survived and multiplied. This adaptation proved to be immensely successful for both parties, and eventually some of their descendants, living in human settlements, no longer mated at will: their matings were controlled by people. For the first time, dogs were selectively bred to perpetuate attributes of their parents that people found advantageous.

Care for your dog
Grooming a dog is good for the dog's skin, hair, and circulation, but it also satisfies our inherent, lifelong need to nurture.

BREEDS AND THEIR USES

The original values of dogs remain cardinal virtues today. Because they are as gregariously sociable as we are, and because, when raised from birth in a human environment they consider their human family to be their own, from the first, dogs have co-ordinated their activities with ours. They naturally protected the territory they lived in by barking warnings of approaching strangers, and defended the settlement when necessary. They accompanied human "pack" members on the hunt and, with their superior speed and scent-trailing ability, and their unique facility for knowing what we want them to do by reading our hand signals and even our eye line, they actively contributed to successful hunting. No less important was the dog's social position within the human family. Young pups were

Breed diversity
Selective breeding enhances or diminishes traits that exist within the dog's genetic potential. Body shape and coat texture vary, but all dogs share a similar palette of potential coat colours from white through brown to black.

playthings, a source of entertainment for the family. Pups and small dogs were bed-warmers on cold nights. Dogs were also a reliable source of nourishment when preferred forms of food were not available. Selective breeding to enhance certain characteristics grew, and by 5,000 years ago all the shapes and sizes of today's dogs – dwarfs, bantams, giants, and brachycephalics (flat-faced dogs) – existed. It is only in the last 200 years, however, that selective breeding for size, shape, and skill has grown into a true industry, with kennel club standards written for hundreds of different breeds.

CARING FOR A DOG

People who choose thoughtfully the type of dog best suited to the way they live, and then invest a little time sensibly training their new companion, are rewarded with all the values that come from sharing your home with a dog – comfort, honesty, constancy, entertainment, friendship, and unfeigned affection. Unfortunately, there's a flip-side. An unwise choice, random training, and haphazard care lead to anxiety, distress, and finally failure. The following pages describe how easy it is to build a successful, mutually gratifying relationship with a canine companion.

Working dogs
Assisting on the hunt has long been a vital dog job, and many of today's breeds come from hunting dogs. This Schillerstövare is rare in still being able to fulfil his hunting role.

STORY OF THE DOG

THE DOG'S ORIGINS

The species we call the dog is, both by intent and by accident, our invention. It is also one of the most prolific land-based predators ever to have existed, vastly surpassing in numbers the wolf from which it descends. The dog is a success story in so many ways because of its ability to fit effortlessly into an ever-evolving human environment.

DOGS – THEN AND NOW

The dog's ancestor, the Asian Wolf, chose to live in proximity to humans. Proximity developed into an intimate association – an association that began almost 15,000 years ago, according to archaeological records. In fact, when people first set foot in North America, they arrived with their dogs. Today, new genetic evidence suggests that their migration occurred 20,000 years ago, so our relationship with dogs is even older than we thought.

While a number of breeds, such as the Siberian Husky, Chow Chow, Shar Pei, Japanese Akita, Shiba Inu, and the Pekingese, are truly ancient breeds, genetically close to their Asian Wolf origins, the great majority of the world's 400-plus breeds of dogs have been "created" by us within the last 200 to 300 years. Through selective breeding, we have optimized both the dog's size and appearance, as well as its ability to hunt, herd, guard, and defend us.

The hunt is on
This painting shows what hunting hounds looked like in 16th-century France – remarkably similar to today's Greyhound.

Whatever role we ask of them however, dogs unfailingly lavish upon us a quality few other animals can: companionship.

If numbers of pet dogs throughout the world – estimated to be around 140 million in Europe and North America alone – are an indication, whatever the origins of the curious partnership between man and canine that evolved all those millennia ago, the dog's position at the centre of our lives is assured.

Dogs through the ages
A close-up of the Bayeux Tapestry, chronicling the Norman conquest of England by William the Conqueror in 1066. Full of animal imagery, the tapestry depicts 35 hunting dogs.

The trusty husky
One of the most ancient of dog breeds, the agile, athletic, and tireless Siberian Husky has historically been used as a draught animal by the Arctic Chukchi tribes.

Meet the ancestors

The statement "Your dog is a wolf in disguise" has been repeated so often that it's often taken for immutable fact. Lurking under your pet's fine coat, so it is said, is a primitive wolf, waiting to escape and revert to nature. The truth, however, is not quite that straightforward.

WHICH WOLF ANCESTOR?

When we think of wolves we usually picture the majestic North American Timber Wolf or the more independent European Grey Wolf, the "baddie" in Little Red Riding Hood. It's easy to forget that these are but two of the many races of wolf that once existed or still exist today. Is the dog a Timber Wolf or a Grey Wolf in disguise? The question isn't simply rhetorical because, while these are the subspecies of wolf we are most familiar with, each has its own unique set of behaviour patterns. The Timber Wolf is a true pack hunter, coordinating hunting and sleeping activity with other members, while the European Wolf is much more self-reliant, hunting on its own or only with its immediate family.

OUT OF ASIA

In fact, the modern dog shares little of its ancestry with North American or European wolves. Recent evidence indicates that the dog evolved in east Asia. Throughout all of Asia, and extending as far west as the Arabian peninsula, there existed and still exist races of relatively small, sociable, and

King of the canines
Wolves are the most successful members of the Canidae family, which is named after its members' large, gripping canine teeth. Until recently, the European Grey Wolf (*above*) – an especially large and powerful predator – was believed to have been the direct ancestor of all dog breeds.

A black Canadian Wolf
The variation in coat colours we see in dogs is nothing new genetically: dog's wolf relatives are also diverse.

Grey Wolf with cub
Wolves retain a lifelong exuberance – a continuing enjoyment in playing, particularly with younger wolves.

Evolution of the wolf

Wolves are members of the Canidae family, which also includes jackals, foxes, and African Wild Dogs. The canids' immediate ancestor, *Leptocyon*, lived seven million years ago. All domestic dog breeds are believed to be descendants of an Asian wolf, such as the Arab Wolf shown below.

LEPTOCYON

FOXES

AFRICAN WILD DOGS

JACKALS

WOLVES

adaptable wolves. In both appearance and behaviour, Asian wolves differ considerably from their larger European and North American relatives. The large wolves specialize in capturing and killing big game; their shorter-coated Asian relatives evolved as efficient scavengers and survive by preying on smaller animals and living off carrion. However, although there are obvious physical similarities between Asian wolves and modern Asian pariah dogs, the exact origins of the dog remain controversial. While today's Asian wolves may be the direct ancestors of the dog, it's equally possible that an extinct type of wolf provided the founder stock.

PERSECUTED TO EXTINCTION

During the 19th and 20th centuries, hunters decimated wolf populations. Only 100 years ago there were over two million wolves in North America alone. Today, only one per cent survive. We have been ruinously successful at killing off isolated races and in the last century alone at least seven races of wolf became extinct. One of these, the Japanese Wolf, was the world's smallest wolf. Standing only 39cm (14in) high at the shoulders and less than 84cm (2ft 9in) long, it became extinct in 1905.

JAPANESE WOLF

Howling wolves

All wolves are sociable. They communicate with other members of their family by using scent or, like these Timber Wolves, by voice.

Taming the wolf

Pet dogs are "domesticated" wolves in the sense that they are wolves that successfully acclimatized to living under our terms and our management. But what is it exactly about wolves that made them so willing to do so? And why do we find their behaviour so appealing?

A NEW ECOLOGICAL NICHE

The story of the domestication of the wolf differs from that of most other domesticated animals because we didn't actually tame it – the wolf *chose* to live in close proximity to us. It *chose* to become tame. Wolves found the area around human campsites – effectively a new ecological niche – to be a fruitful habitat. They scavenged from human waste, fed off rodents attracted by human food, and were safe from other large predators that had already been cleared from the region by humans. No doubt young wolves were captured by locals: wolf pups were as appealing to humans then as they are now. Some were raised to adolescence, then eaten. Others, probably the most sociable, survived into adulthood

Primitive partnership
This prehistoric cave painting from Ennedi Plateau in Chad reveals dogs' early role in the human community, probably assisting in the hunt for large animals. Wolfdogs that helped and protected the tribe survived and bred, establishing themselves as the first pet dogs.

A working relationship
Humans soon discovered that, just as dogs protect the human family from danger, they would do the same with livestock if they were raised from puppyhood with the animals. In Namibia today, Anatolian Shepherd Dogs still protect goats from cheetahs, continuing an ancient role.

and were able to breed. It was a case of "the survival of the friendliest", those with the most playful and most juvenile characters survived. The wolfdog's pack instinct allowed it to fit in with the human family group, with its familiar hierarchy of dominant and submissive members. Its superior hearing and keen sense of smell made it a useful sentinel, alerting its human pack to outside dangers.

FIGHT, FLIGHT, OR FRIENDSHIP
In terms of adapting to human life, a modern-day equivalent of the wolf is the fox. During the last 20 years this rural, secretive, nocturnal animal has changed its habits dramatically, integrating itself into bustling urban environments and emerging as a confident daytime hunter and scavenger. And like its wolf ancestor thousands of years earlier, the fox's "flight distance" – the distance within which it will allow an "enemy" to approach before fleeing – has diminished considerably.

THE TAMING OF THE FOX
Fascinating work by a Russian geneticist, Dmitry Belyaev, that started in the 1950s showed just how easily and quickly behaviours in animals can be changed. From new litters of fox cubs on Russian fur farms, Belyaev selected individuals that showed the least fear when handled and were most likely to lick him or approach him voluntarily. In other words, he selected from foxes that retained juvenile behaviour characteristics. Within fewer than ten generations, many of the descendants behaved as "domesticated" individuals, eager to meet strangers, lick their keepers, and whimper when left on their own. Selectively chosen for docility, Belyaev's foxes also developed other characteristics, including blue eyes and piebald (black and white) coats. The full-body wag of puppyhood and the submissive raising of their paws to strangers were retained. Belyaev had produced what were, in effect, lifelong juveniles. And that's exactly what dogs are.

Part of the family
Keeping a pet dog isn't just the preserve of Western cultures. Here, a Yanomami Indian family living in the Amazon rainforest of South America is pictured with a domesticated canine companion.

Conquering the world

Dogs emerged out of Asia, accompanying humans on trade, conquest, and migration routes. They moved north to Arctic lands, south to SE Asia, Papua New Guinea, and Australia, west via India to Africa and Europe, and east to the Pacific Islands and the Americas.

ARCHAEOLOGICAL CLUES

The first dogs, which were physically identical to wolves, formed a loose, scavenging association with ancient humans. We can only assume this because their fossils can't be differentiated from wolf fossils. There are certainly wolf bones, found with human fossils, dating back some tens of thousands of years, but it can only be guessed whether these wolves were prey or primitive companions. In parts of Asia and even in Europe, however, archaeological evidence exists that suggests humans

An early partnership
This woman and her dog were buried together around 12,500 years ago in Ein Mallaha, northern Israel.

and wolfdogs may have formed a bonding relationship long before our ancestors settled into permanent agricultural sites. Researchers at the British Museum confirmed that a jawbone, found in a cave in Iraq occupied by people 14,000 years ago, was that of an equally ancient domesticated dog. Israeli archaeologists discovered a 12,500-year-old human grave in which a dog pup was held in a seemingly warm embrace by its female owner. In Spain, an even older burial site was excavated, revealing the

The distribution of the dog
Genetic evidence confirms that the first wolfdogs emerged in Asia between 40,000 and 100,000 years ago before rapidly spreading throughout the world. A land bridge in the ancient region of "Beringia" allowed land migration of people and dogs from Asia to North America around 20,000 years ago. The descendants of the first Asian wolfdogs still exist today on all continents except Antarctica.

→ **TRADE, CONQUEST, AND MIGRATION ROUTES**

---► **LAND BRIDGE**

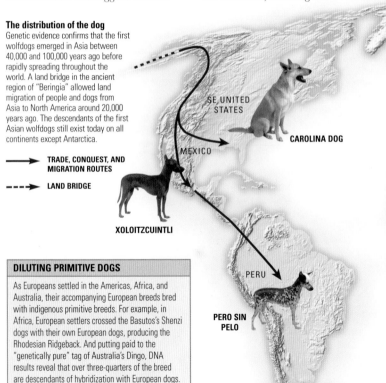

SE UNITED STATES

CAROLINA DOG

MEXICO

XOLOITZCUINTLI

PERU

PERO SIN PELO

DILUTING PRIMITIVE DOGS

As Europeans settled in the Americas, Africa, and Australia, their accompanying European breeds bred with indigenous primitive breeds. For example, in Africa, European settlers crossed the Basutos's Shenzi dogs with their own European dogs, producing the Rhodesian Ridgeback. And putting paid to the "genetically pure" tag of Australia's Dingo, DNA results reveal that over three-quarters of the breed are descendants of hybridization with European dogs.

skeleton of a young girl. Lying around the girl, and facing in four directions, were the remains of four dogs.

THE DOG DEVELOPS ...

At least 12,000 years ago, when our distant ancestors had settled into permanent habitation, the primitive dog came under natural environmental pressures. As a result, its shape began to change. Its smaller body and brain cavity, and more-compacted teeth, for example, provide us with the first extensive fossil evidence of the modern dog. After many generations of selective breeding, a diversity of dog breeds began to evolve. Archaeological evidence tells us that sight hounds, ancestors of the modern Afghan, Saluki, and Greyhound, existed in Mesopotamia

Dogs as hunters
The design of this Greek pottery jug from around 550 BC provides an early illustration of how dogs were used to help man hunt. The obedient dog remains close to its master's side.

6,000–7,000 years ago. Over 5,000 years ago, guarding dogs, ancestors of Rottweilers and Bulldogs, existed in Tibet. More recently, scent hounds, ancestors of the modern Basset Hound and dachshunds, were evident in Italy 1,700 years ago. Water spaniels and retrievers made their appearance in Europe 1,300 years ago, and terriers only 100 years later. Now, as then, the evolution of the dog throughout the world continues unabated.

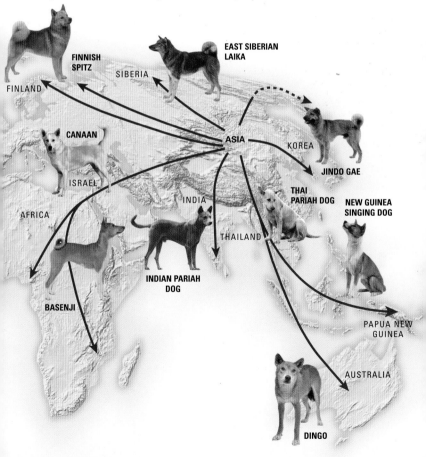

FINNISH SPITZ

FINLAND

SIBERIA

EAST SIBERIAN LAIKA

ASIA

KOREA

JINDO GAE

CANAAN

ISRAEL

INDIA

THAI PARIAH DOG

NEW GUINEA SINGING DOG

AFRICA

THAILAND

BASENJI

INDIAN PARIAH DOG

PAPUA NEW GUINEA

AUSTRALIA

DINGO

The genetic relationship

During the late 1990s, scientists learned that all dogs share their DNA with wolves. Only a few years later, they discovered ways to analyse genetic data to reveal the antiquity of modern breeds and found that many of them are not quite what they seem.

CLUES IN THE GENES

Mitochondria are curious structures within cells, and what biologists love about them is that they contain their own DNA and provide a unique signature to a line of descent. By studying mitochondrial DNA, scientists established that the dog diverged from the wolf between 40,000 and 100,000 years ago. Further evidence, published in 2004, showed that three out of four modern dogs share their mitochondrial DNA with a single female wolf ancestor. In other words, three-quarters of all dogs today descend from one family of wolves. The remaining one out of four modern dogs shares its mitochondrial DNA with three other wolf ancestors.

SCIENTIFIC BREED GROUPINGS

Just as the greatest diversity in human genes exists in Africa, where our ancestors evolved, the greatest diversity in canine genes exists in Asia. In recent genetic research, 85 dog breeds were studied and geneticists observed that all breeds fit into one of four different clusters of related breeds. The most ancient of these, closest to the wolf,

> ### REPRODUCTION WOLVES
>
> Genetic evidence has shown that several dog breeds commonly believed to be of ancient origin, such as the Pharaoh Hound and the Ibizan Hound, have actually been recreated in modern times from combinations of other breeds. Scientists had previously considered that these "ancient" breeds were descended directly from Egyptian dogs drawn on tomb walls 5,000 years ago. The German Shepherd, too, although wolf-like in looks, is a fully modern dog sharing its genetic heritage with breeds such as the Rottweiler and the Boxer.
>
> **GERMAN SHEPHERD**
>
> **PHARAOH HOUND**

include the Chow Chow and Shar Pei from China, and the Japanese Akita and Shiba Inu. More surprisingly, it was found that four Asian companion breeds – the Tibetan Terrier, Lhasa Apso, and Shih Tzu, all from Tibet, and the Pekingese from China – trace their origins to

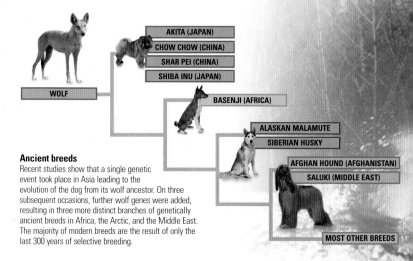

Ancient breeds

Recent studies show that a single genetic event took place in Asia leading to the evolution of the dog from its wolf ancestor. On three subsequent occasions, further wolf genes were added, resulting in three more distinct branches of genetically ancient breeds in Africa, the Arctic, and the Middle East. The majority of modern breeds are the result of only the last 300 years of selective breeding.

AKITA (JAPAN)
CHOW CHOW (CHINA)
SHAR PEI (CHINA)
SHIBA INU (JAPAN)
WOLF
BASENJI (AFRICA)
ALASKAN MALAMUTE
SIBERIAN HUSKY
AFGHAN HOUND (AFGHANISTAN)
SALUKI (MIDDLE EAST)
MOST OTHER BREEDS

antiquity. This makes them more closely related to the wolf than the "wolf-like" German Shepherd and the vast majority of existing dog breeds which, genetically speaking, have relatively recent origins – each emerging within the last 300 years. Within the modern breeds, genetic studies have revealed three distinct subgroups: mastiff-like breeds; herding breeds; and hunting breeds, reflecting the traditional breed groupings based on human activity.

Labrador
The Labrador, together with the Golden Retriever, and all spaniels, pointers, setters, scent hounds, and terriers, are the most recent breeds, developed within the last 300 years to assist in hunting with guns.

Pekingese
It is hard to believe, but the small, flat-faced Pekingese is one of a small group of breeds most closely related to the wolf.

Border Collie
Collies, and a few other herding dogs such as the Belgian Shepherd, trace their origins to the Middle Ages, as do many mastiff-type breeds, such as the Pyrenean Mastiff and the majestic Bernese Mountain Dog.

Husky
Huskies (*below*) and other Nordic breeds, such as the Alaskan Malamute, are truly ancient and are among the wolf's closest relatives.

The wolf within

Significant behavioural differences exist between dog breeds, and some breeds are noticeably more wolflike than others. Through centuries of selective breeding we have enhanced a variety of un-wolflike traits in our canine companions, and the changes are still going on.

A TRUE WOLF IN DISGUISE

All dogs communicate with each other and with us in a variety of defined ways. They use posture, body language, voice, even odour. These combined communication skills have been studied extensively in wolves and in dogs and have been classified as "wolfish" and "doggish". The communication skills of the young have also been studied, and these behaviours have been classified as "puppyish". Using the range of communication skills of the adult wolf as their baseline, a team of biologists observed 10 different breeds of adult dogs. Their results showed that while all the breeds of dog were capable of all aspects of "puppyish" communication, in some breeds communication stalled at that level while in others it developed into full "wolfish" communication.

Only one of these 10 breeds is genetically ancient and that breed, the Siberian Husky, is the only one that has retained its ability to communicate in all 15 different aspects of "wolfish" behaviour. At the other end of the spectrum, the Cavalier King Charles Spaniel retains an ability in only two of the 15 different ways that adult wolves communicate.

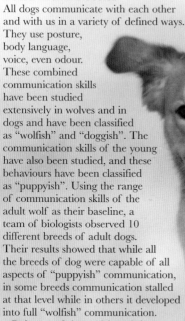

Dog or wolf?
Strikingly different in appearance to its wolf ancestor, studies reveal that the Golden Retriever in fact shares 80 per cent of the wolf's communication skills.

CAN YOU TRUST YOUR DOG'S SIGNALS?

In a subtle experiment carried out in 2004, skilled dog trainers showed that it is possible to train dogs to detect the presence of bladder cancer simply by scenting affected urine samples. However, they observed that some dogs – always the goofy retrievers – were prone to detect "false positives", a positive result from a negative sample. There are some breeds that are just so puppyish, so desperate to please us, that they will guess at an answer to avoid disappointing their owners.

"TANGLE", THE CANCER-DETECTOR DOG

Changing times, changing roles
Today, we demand qualities from our pets that they weren't originally bred for. The Bernese Mountain Dog, for example, is now more likely to be a companion dog than a herder.

The King Charles Spaniel's ability to communicate is arrested in puppyhood. In that sense, it is a perpetual puppy with a limited adult social vocabulary.

A MEMBER OF THE HUMAN FAMILY

During the time I have practised veterinary medicine, the role of the dog has changed faster than perhaps ever before. Some dogs exist for practical reasons, but the majority of those dogs we share our homes with are thought of as hairy but honorary members of the human family. We get profound emotional rewards from living with them and, in many ways, these are similar to the rewards we get from caring for our own young. The difference here is that our own kids grow up and leave home. Not so our dogs. Look at what we want from them – perpetual puppyhood. Today, we breed dogs selectively for their puppy-like behaviour rather than their wolf-like aptitudes. We want full-body wags, a rocking-horse greeting when we meet, kisses, rolling over to be tickled, obedience, *no aggression*. In just a matter of decades the behaviour of whole breeds – the Bernese Mountain Dog and the Pyrenean Mountain Dog, for example – has changed from "wolfish" to "puppyish" simply through selective breeding for these characteristics. This appears to be the future for virtually all breeds of dog as they continue to move from the workplace to the fireside.

TOP 10 – FROM "WOLFISH" TO "PUPPYISH"

Researchers graded 10 dog breeds on a scale of 0–15 to identify the presence of 15 signals that wolves use to convey threat or submission. Nine of them were threat signals and included growling, standing erect, standing over an opponent, and baring teeth. Six submissive signals included muzzle licking, looking away, crouching, passive submission, and a submissive grin. A grade of 15/15 was awarded to the Siberian Husky, the breed sharing the most "wolfish" qualities.

1. SIBERIAN HUSKY 15/15

2. GOLDEN RETRIEVER 12/15

3. GERMAN SHEPHERD 11/15

4. LABRADOR RETRIEVER 8/15

5. MUNSTERLANDER 7/15

6. COCKER SPANIEL 6/15

7. SHETLAND SHEEPDOG 4/15

8. FRENCH BULLDOG 4/15

9. NORFOLK TERRIER 3/15

10. CAVALIER KING CHARLES SPANIEL 2/15

Street dogs

Thousands of years of domestication have effectively created a surplus of dogs. The net result is that for every pet dog in the world there is a street dog. Accounting for half of the canine population, street dogs – also called pariah dogs – survive by scavenging and begging from us.

WHAT IS A PARIAH DOG?

A pariah is an outcast, and throughout the world pariah dogs behave as fully wild animals, living on the fringe of human society. There are millions of pariah dogs roaming free in India, Thailand, Sri Lanka, Indonesia, and elsewhere, some treated with kindness, most simply disregarded, and some killed with malicious barbarity.

Asian street dogs probably descend from the first domesticated dogs that came to India with the Aryan's invasion of the subcontinent. Generally speaking, they are moderate in size, weighing around 16kg (35lb), and brown or brown-white in colour, although other colours exist. Because pet dogs have always been allowed to stray, many if not most Asian street dogs have been influenced by cross-breeding with modern domestic dogs.

RABIES AND STREET DOGS

There are 100 annual human rabies fatalities in Sri Lanka and most are caused by dog bites. The problem is even greater in Mexico. In Mexico City alone, 70 people die each year from rabies and over 100,000 are treated for dog bites. Still more die from rabies in Brazil, where the world's highest number of cases are reported each year. Although 42 million dogs are vaccinated against rabies annually in Latin America, bites from rabid dogs cause countless deaths. Street dogs may seem docile and submissive, but they are potentially lethal.

THE NUMBERS GAME

In Latin America there are nearly 70 million stray dogs, almost as many as there are pet dogs in the neighbouring United States. In Mexico City alone there are one million stray dogs. That's more

Street dogs in Mexico
Mexico has a serious poverty problem, with more than half of the population officially living on or close to the breadline. For the country's street dogs, the knock-on effect of this deprivation is a desperately bleak existence.

strays in one city than the entire canine population of Sweden. Although almost 250,000 dogs are destroyed in Mexico City's municipal pounds each year, this regrettable need to cull doesn't even begin to dent the population.

Street dogs are tremendously resilient creatures. On the resort island of Phuket in Thailand, most street dogs disappeared after the December 2004 tsunami, but in less than a year their numbers returned to pre-tsunami proportions.

FROM PARIAH TO PUREBRED
Some of the "breeds" described in the Breed Diversity section (*see* pp.50–51) are breeds only because people intervened in their natural selection, created breed standards, and gave indigenous street dogs an approved name. These pariahs turned purebreds include the Basenji from Africa, Xoloitzcuintli from Mexico, and the Canaan Dog from Israel. Potential pariahs turned purebreds include the Aso (Philippines), Bali Dog (Bali/Polynesia), Sica (Natal, South Africa), and Telomian (Malaysia).

FROM PUREBRED TO PARIAH
In Eastern Europe, the consequences of political change in the 1990s created a boom in street dog numbers, but these animals look quite different from typical

SOS DOGS ORADEA, ROMANIA
The stray dog population of the town of Oradea in Romania is in decline thanks to SOS Dogs Oradea, a project set up in conjunction with UK dog welfare charity Dogs Trust. A "catch, neuter, and return" project has been introduced, providing a humane way of reducing numbers of street dogs instead of shooting or poisoning them. It is hoped that Oradea's neutering clinic (*below*) will eventually rid the town of strays.

pariah-type dogs. The shaggy-haired, mournful-eyed, limping street dogs of Romania are the descendants of pets – often pure-bred creatures – abandoned for political or financial reasons. So too are the street dogs of the Balkan states, descendants of pure-bred dogs abandoned during the conflicts of the 1990s. In both examples, pariah dogs often endure pitiful lives, and it seems they will remain a social concern until economic standards in the countries where they exist allow for their eventual rehabilitation.

DIFFERENT COUNTRIES, DIFFERENT DOGS
Street dogs reflect both the genetic diversity of a region's dog population and the changing value of dogs to that region's human population. Around the world, the look and behaviour of street dogs is relatively constant. In North America and Britain, however, while street dogs once had terrier characteristics, today they display guarding-dog traits.

Indian Pariah Dog
These usually tan or tan-and-white dogs evolved over millennia to cope with the hot environment they live in. Their light, fine coats reflect heat.

Italian street dog with cat
Short-legged dogs with moderate coats are legion in Italy. It would only take a written standard to make this type of dog a new "breed".

Bucharest street dog
The toll of human conflict and massive political upheaval on the street dogs of some of eastern Europe's emerging nations is evident in their appearance.

THE DOMESTICATED DOG

The dog has been our favourite animal companion for millennia
because it has a plastic ability to adapt to our changing needs.
Until recently, dogs' primary roles were practical and utilitarian.
Today, the core benefits they bring to the human family
are more social and psychological.

OPENING THE DOOR TO DOGS

It's only in the last 100 years or so that
the dog has so cleverly and successfully
moved into our homes and our hearts.
The genetic potential to adapt to a range
of new environments was always within
the dog, but by moving into our homes
that ability to adapt was accelerated.
It is still happening today. Only a few
generations ago, dogs were bred to have
temperaments that were appropriate for
specific jobs, such as working, guarding,
or hunting. Dogs have inherited their
flexible brains from their wolf ancestors.
Wolves, then as now, used the "learning
centres" in their brains to deal with
problems encountered in the wild. Dogs
have turned this learning ability to the
demands of domesticity. Regardless of
their original jobs, dogs have increasingly
been bred for companionship and to
integrate with members of the human
family. And we love them for it.
Who wouldn't rather return home to a
wagging tail than a cold, empty house?

DESTINED FOR DOMESTICATION

So why are we so quick to welcome the
world's most numerous carnivore (other
than us) into our homes? Maybe it's
because we share a great reciprocal
relationship – a mutual understanding.
Dogs have an uncanny ability to read
us; a capacity to interpret from our
gestures what we want them to do.

Making himself at home
Humans originally domesticated dogs for their usefulness,
but changes in lifestyles in the developed world have led
to a comfortable life for many of today's dogs.

This is evident in the results of a simple
experiment carried out by scientists in
which they hid food under one of two
containers, designed so that no odour
could escape. They then let groups of
chimps, wolves, and young and adult dogs
examine which container concealed the
food, giving clues to the animals by gazing
at the "food container", by pointing at it,
or by tapping on it. Dogs and pups quickly
understood. Wolves and chimps didn't.
Somehow, in the evolution of its brain,
the dog has acquired an improved ability
to respond to us, to pick up cues from
humans that wolves or chimpanzees
are not capable of recognizing.

It is this kind of ability that is key in
comprehending why the bond between
human and dog is so strong. The process
of domestication has only served to make
this bond stronger. All it took was for the
dog to understand its position in our
social hierarchy. From that point onwards,
dogs have grown ever closer to us as they
evolve social behaviour that improves
our mutually beneficial partnership.

Best of friends
Our relationship with dogs, the oldest union we have with
any other mammal species, began because we were good
for each other. Domestication cemented this relationship.

Dog design

While the dog's shape and size vary more than those of any other mammal, its design remains constant: that of a beautifully evolved, powerfully muscled meat-eater. Just as in the wolf, every sinew is primed for a life of hunting, capturing, and eating prey.

AN INTEGRATED UNIT

Any anomalies that exist between the genetic design of the dog and that of its wolf ancestor are minimal. For example, all dogs share an identical skeleton with the wolf. However, sight hounds have longer bones, allowing for greater speed, while bassets and dachshunds have shorter bones, enabling the smallest of them to follow prey into their earth dens.

Both dogs and wolves share the same carnivorous scavenger's arrangement of teeth, with 12 small incisors for cutting and biting, 4 large canine teeth for holding and tearing meat, 16 premolars for shearing and holding, and 10 molars to chew and grind meat and other food.

While all wolves, and most dogs, have a double coat of insulating downy hair and longer, protective guard hair, some breeds of dog, such as the Basenji, have adapted to warmer climates and lost their need for a downy undercoat.

The wolf and dog also share identical types of muscles and nerves. Combined with strong ligaments and elastic tendons,

the result is a powerfully built creature, readily adapted for prolonged chases rather than lightning bursts of speed.

The dog's brain and hormone-producing glands are lighter in weight than their wolf equivalents. One benefit of domestication for the dog has been less stress and thus less need for micro-managing responses to external events.

ANAL SACS

The anal sacs, filled with secretion, play a role in territory marking and social recognition. Each time a dog passes a stool, muscles around the anus squeeze the sacs, anointing the just-deposited stool with a few drops of quite smelly liquid. This pheromone-laden substance helps disseminate a dog's personal data.

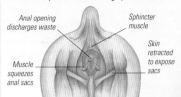

Anal opening discharges waste

Sphincter muscle

Skin retracted to expose sacs

Muscle squeezes anal sacs

Skeleton

The dog's skeleton provides a superb framework for its body. The system is held together by strong, elastic ligaments and tendons. Through selectively breeding giant and miniature dogs, we have both dramatically enhanced and diminished the size of skeletons, as illustrated below.

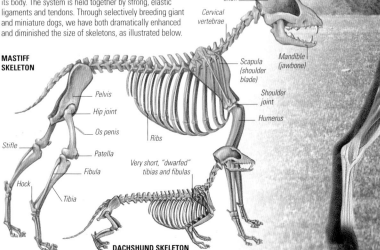

Skull

Cervical vertebrae

Mandible (jawbone)

MASTIFF SKELETON

Scapula (shoulder blade)

Shoulder joint

Humerus

Pelvis

Hip joint

Os penis

Ribs

Stifle

Patella

Fibula

Very short, "dwarfed" tibias and fibulas

Hock

Tibia

DACHSHUND SKELETON

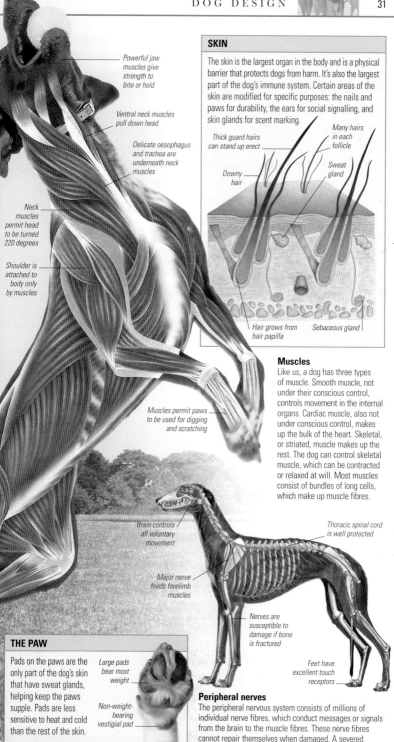

Powerful jaw muscles give strength to bite or hold

Ventral neck muscles pull down head

Delicate oesophagus and trachea are underneath neck muscles

Neck muscles permit head to be turned 220 degrees

Shoulder is attached to body only by muscles

Muscles permit paws to be used for digging and scratching

SKIN

The skin is the largest organ in the body and is a physical barrier that protects dogs from harm. It's also the largest part of the dog's immune system. Certain areas of the skin are modified for specific purposes: the nails and paws for durability, the ears for social signalling, and skin glands for scent marking.

Thick guard hairs can stand up erect

Many hairs in each follicle

Downy hair

Sweat gland

Hair grows from hair papilla

Sebaceous gland

Muscles

Like us, a dog has three types of muscle. Smooth muscle, not under their conscious control, controls movement in the internal organs. Cardiac muscle, also not under conscious control, makes up the bulk of the heart. Skeletal, or striated, muscle makes up the rest. The dog can control skeletal muscle, which can be contracted or relaxed at will. Most muscles consist of bundles of long cells, which make up muscle fibres.

Brain controls all voluntary movement

Thoracic spinal cord is well protected

Major nerve feeds forelimb muscles

Nerves are susceptible to damage if bone is fractured

Feet have excellent touch receptors

THE PAW

Pads on the paws are the only part of the dog's skin that have sweat glands, helping keep the paws supple. Pads are less sensitive to heat and cold than the rest of the skin.

Large pads bear most weight

Non-weight-bearing vestigial pad

Peripheral nerves

The peripheral nervous system consists of millions of individual nerve fibres, which conduct messages or signals from the brain to the muscle fibres. These nerve fibres cannot repair themselves when damaged. A severed nerve results in permanent inactivity of its muscle.

The heart, lungs, and circulation

Just as in humans, a dog's blood carries nourishment and oxygen around the body. New blood is manufactured in the spleen and bone marrow, while the liver processes toxins in blood returning to the heart. When a dog exercises vigorously, the blood supply to the heart increases fourfold and to the skeletal muscles twentyfold. Carbon dioxide in the lungs is replaced with fresh oxygen, while at the same time blood flow to other parts of the body temporarily diminishes.

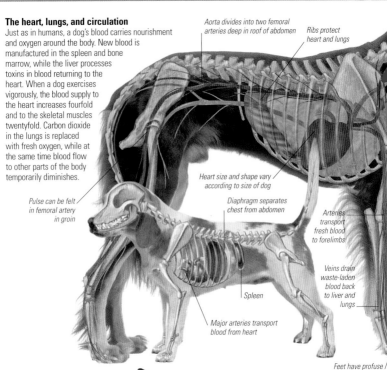

Aorta divides into two femoral arteries deep in roof of abdomen

Ribs protect heart and lungs

Pulse can be felt in femoral artery in groin

Heart size and shape vary according to size of dog

Diaphragm separates chest from abdomen

Arteries transport fresh blood to forelimbs

Veins drain waste-laden blood back to liver and lungs

Spleen

Major arteries transport blood from heart

Feet have profuse supply of blood

THE HEART

The heart is divided into four chambers – two atria and two ventricles. Blood returns from the body to the right atrium, passes to the right ventricle, and is then pumped to the lungs, where waste carbon dioxide is replaced with fresh oxygen. The blood then returns to the left atrium, passes through a valve to the left ventricle, from where it is pumped out to all body parts. The valves quickly snap shut when the ventricles contract, ensuring blood moves only forwards.

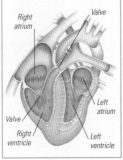

Right atrium

Valve

Valve

Right ventricle

Left atrium

Left ventricle

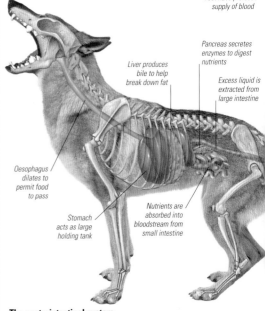

Pancreas secretes enzymes to digest nutrients

Liver produces bile to help break down fat

Excess liquid is extracted from large intestine

Oesophagus dilates to permit food to pass

Stomach acts as large holding tank

Nutrients are absorbed into bloodstream from small intestine

The gastrointestinal system

Dogs have a digestive system built to gorge on animals they've killed. The stomach is large, while the intestines are relatively short. The pancreas, a gland adjacent to the small intestine, secretes digestive enzymes directly into the intestine, as does the liver through the bile duct. Food is digested and absorbed in the small intestine, while water and salts are absorbed in the large intestine.

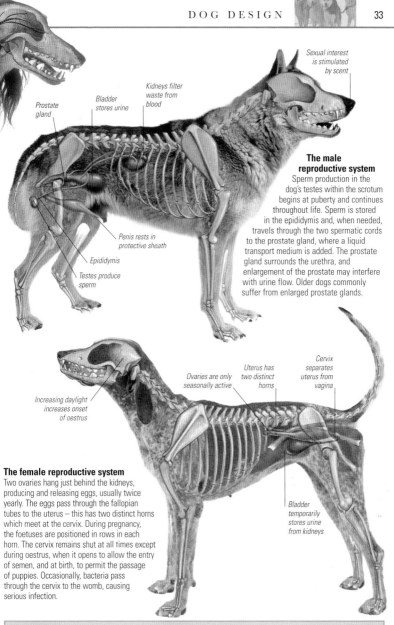

Kidneys filter waste from blood

Sexual interest is stimulated by scent

Prostate gland

Bladder stores urine

Penis rests in protective sheath

Epididymis

Testes produce sperm

The male reproductive system

Sperm production in the dog's testes within the scrotum begins at puberty and continues throughout life. Sperm is stored in the epididymis and, when needed, travels through the two spermatic cords to the prostate gland, where a liquid transport medium is added. The prostate gland surrounds the urethra, and enlargement of the prostate may interfere with urine flow. Older dogs commonly suffer from enlarged prostate glands.

Increasing daylight increases onset of oestrus

Ovaries are only seasonally active

Uterus has two distinct horns

Cervix separates uterus from vagina

Bladder temporarily stores urine from kidneys

The female reproductive system

Two ovaries hang just behind the kidneys, producing and releasing eggs, usually twice yearly. The eggs pass through the fallopian tubes to the uterus – this has two distinct horns which meet at the cervix. During pregnancy, the foetuses are positioned in rows in each horn. The cervix remains shut at all times except during oestrus, when it opens to allow the entry of semen, and at birth, to permit the passage of puppies. Occasionally, bacteria pass through the cervix to the womb, causing serious infection.

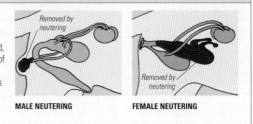

NEUTERING

A male dog is neutered simply by surgically removing the testes, thus diminishing male hormone production. Neutering a female is more complicated, usually involving the removal, not only of the ovaries, but also of the uterus. This eliminates future reproductive problems and oestrus cycles, and diminishes oestrus-related behavioural changes.

Removed by neutering

Removed by neutering

MALE NEUTERING

FEMALE NEUTERING

The senses

With a sense of smell about one million times better than our own, the dog's olfactory ability is its prime asset. Additionally, selective breeding has enabled us to hone the dog's senses, optimizing the desired traits and so producing a whole range of super-sensory canines.

MAKING SENSE OF IT ALL

Dogs and humans share the same senses, but the dog's senses are markedly superior to ours. The reason for this is tied up in the needs of our respective ancestors. Where early man may have coveted the canine's acute survival-oriented senses – for example, the sight hound's long-distance vision or the wolf's sensitive hearing – modern man is much less dependent on his senses, instead being more reliant on verbal communication. The dog, however, retains the exceptional sensory inheritance of its wolf ancestor.

In dogs, sensory information is transmitted from nerve receptors in the organs and tissues, travels through peripheral nerves to the spinal cord, and then to the brain. The brain triggers either a body response – pain, for example – or a hormonal response, from an action such as smelling another dog's scent. Part of the response is pre-determined by the brain's hard-wiring. Sensory information is also interpreted by the cognitive part of the brain, the cerebral cortex, and a dog's response to this data is based on past experience and anticipated consequences.

Smell
Scent is transmitted onto the nasal membranes, which cover the nose's turbinate bones. These bones have convoluted folds, ensuring that the tiniest amount of scent is captured within them. Sensory cells are closely packed along the nasal-membrane lining, and convert scent to chemical messages transmitted to the olfactory bulb region of the cerebral cortex.

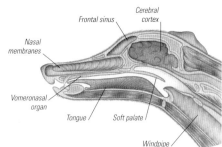

Cerebral cortex
Frontal sinus
Nasal membranes
Vomeronasal organ
Tongue
Soft palate
Windpipe

Taste
Dogs have a relatively poor sense of taste. Once food has been chewed, it is swallowed. The epiglottis keeps food out of the airway before the food passes from the back of the mouth into the oesophagus. From here, it is propelled towards the stomach.

Muscle wall (oesophagus)
Opening to windpipe
Interior of oesophagus
Epiglottis
Body of tongue
Taste buds
Tip curls both ways

Hearing
Independently mobile ears capture and transmit sound to the middle and inner ear, and to the brain. Dogs can locate the source of a sound in six-hundredths of a second, much faster than we can, and can hear sounds at much higher and lower frequencies.

OUTER EAR
Pinna (auricle)
Ear cartilage
Skull bone
INNER EAR
Organs of balance
Ear canal
Cochlea
Ear drum
MIDDLE EAR

Sight
Dogs' eyes are flatter than ours, with better sensitivity to seeing movement. An enhanced reflective membrane behind the retina increases sight in bad light. Large lenses make adjusting focal length difficult, however, so dogs have relatively poor near vision.

Sclera
Lacrimal gland
Uvea
Optic nerve
Cornea
Pupil
Iris
Retina
Posterior chamber
Lens
Third eyelid
Lower eyelid

Touch

Touch is the dog's most primitive sense, and it remains a powerfully important sense throughout life. There are touch receptors throughout the skin, but the most refined are in the paws. Aiding touch receptors are the touch-sensitive long hairs (vibrissae) on the muzzle, chin, and above the eyes.

More than just common sense
Domestication and selective breeding mean that today's pet dog is no longer as dependent on all of its senses as its hunter ancestors were, yet it still retains awesome sensory ability.

FIELD OF VISION

Some breeds of dog, such as the Greyhound (*far right*), have better peripheral vision than us because their eyes point a little sideways. We have bred other dogs, such as the Boston Terrier (*right*), to have closer-set, forward-pointing eyes, similar to ours, and consequently a narrower overall field of vision but a wider binocular field of vision (represented by blue areas in diagram).

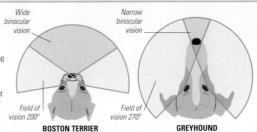

Wide binocular vision

Narrow binocular vision

Field of vision 200°

Field of vision 270°

BOSTON TERRIER

GREYHOUND

Instinctive behaviour

Of all the body systems and senses, the brain is structurally the most complex and difficult to understand. Within the brain rest all of the dog's potential behaviours and abilities. These inherited, hard-wired capabilities form the bedrock of the dog's mental make-up.

INTELLIGENCE OR INSTINCT?

In any breed description I guarantee you will find the word "intelligent" quoted somewhere. My clients repeat it daily. "She's so intelligent. She knows I'm going out even before I put my coat on." Or "This is the most intelligent dog I've ever owned." Just as often I hear the opposite. "She's cute, but she sure is dumb." "Intelligent" is an ambiguous word. In essence, there are three different types of canine mental ability, each underpinned by instinct – behaviour hard-wired into the dog's brain during its evolutionary history. These are an ability to learn, a facility for problem solving, and communication intelligence.

LEARNING AND PROBLEM SOLVING

Dogs have inherited an innate ability to learn – an in-built mental flexibility – from their wild ancestors. Learning from experience is a skill that helps a dog adapt to its environment or alter its environment to make it a better place to live in. Dogs are instinctively cautious and wary of unfamiliar people, but they soon learn who to trust and who to avoid. Problem solving is slightly different. This is the ability to construct mentally a solution to a problem. The faster a dog solves the problem with the fewest false starts, the better its problem-solving capacity. Generally speaking, dogs are not good at mental problem solving, but some are better than others. Sheep-herding breeds, such as the Border Collie, have been selectively bred for their problem-solving capabilities.

Understanding relationships
Dogs instinctively build relationships, both within their packs and between their pack and other packs. There is a hard-wired ability to perceive pack hierarchy, and dogs communicate continuously to reinforce the pecking order.

COMMUNICATION INTELLIGENCE

This is sometimes called obedience or working intelligence, and helps the dog work with us. A dog may have good problem-solving and learning ability, but it also needs efficient communication skills to understand what we want it

What's good to eat
Dogs naturally understand what should and shouldn't be eaten. This dog is grazing on grass, adding roughage to his diet. Some dogs eat grass simply for pleasure, much as we eat salads, while others do so only when they experience gastrointestinal discomfort.

Interpreting body language
Dogs have an instinctive ability to interpret canine body language, such as this play bow, an invitation to play games. They interpret our body language under these terms. Reaching from above, for example, is seen as a dominant gesture, like a paw on the withers.

to do. Dogs instinctively perceive pack hierarchy and communicate with each other largely through body language and scent, but they need a willingness to take directions from people – usually through vocal commands. Gundogs, such as Labradors, have excellent communication intelligence; their longer attention spans and greater persistence make them more capable of concentrating on what they are being asked to do.

Marking territory
Dogs don't need to be taught to patrol, investigate, and mark a territory. This too is an instinctive ability, becoming active during puppyhood.

Mapping a trail
The ability to map mentally large territories exists in all breeds of dog. However, because few are given the opportunity to do so they never learn how to use this facility. This unfulfilled potential results in many dogs lacking a keen sense of direction.

Exercising caution
This dog stops at the doorway in case there is danger if he proceeds. Knowing when to be cautious and what is potentially dangerous is another instinctive capability dogs possess.

Keeping cool
Maggi, a Labrador–Border Collie cross, learned from experience that sunshine makes sand hot, but if you dig down, as she has, the sand underneath is cooler and more comfortable. Dogs with good learning ability need exposure to a situation only several times in order to form stable responses.

Understanding motion
This terrier is retreating from the incoming tide because she can judge motion and forces; she knows that the surf will continue to break further up the beach.

Mating
Instinctively, a dog feels the need to mate, the time to mate, and who to mate with. This form of behaviour, of course, depends on the successful interaction of sex hormones and the brain's wiring.

The first dog jobs

Dogs have a natural ability to learn from experience, solve problems, and work as a member of a team. Even more crucially, dogs are able to understand what we want when we use specific gestures or vocal commands, allowing them to fulfil vital roles in human communities.

GUARDING THE HOME

It is likely that one of the first uses for dogs was as a sentinel within family campsites. Wolfdogs raised from puppies looked upon the people who raised them as their pack. With superior hearing and scenting ability and sharper peripheral vision, they were able to warn the settlements of potential danger from prey animals or from other people. The dog's ability to protect us and our homes remains one of the main reasons that people keep dogs. Consistently, when dog owners are asked why they keep dogs, over 75 per cent include "protection" among their answers. This is reflected in the types of dogs that remain popular today. The world's most numerous dog, the German Shepherd, is a wonderful companion, but its primary role is to guard and protect.

To serve and protect
There is still no better deterrent to potential burglars, reliant on stealth, than a barking dog. This snarling German Shepherd is enough to repel anyone from entering its territory.

GUARDING LIVESTOCK

Just as a dog raised from puppyhood with people will protect its human family, a dog raised from youth with livestock will protect a herd rather than prey upon it. In ancient times, large mastiff dogs were bred to work as livestock guardians. From Tibet through to Spain, especially in mountainous regions where livestock were at risk from wolves and bears, pups were raised with livestock to act not only as sentinels but also as fearless attack dogs, assaulting interlopers, be they other animals or strange people.

HUNTING BY SIGHT

Geneticists have shown that sight hounds, breeds of dog such as Salukis and Afghans, are truly ancient. This is perfectly consistent with what was probably the next job that evolved for dogs: helping on the hunt. In this latest role, dogs that were socialized to people would, of their own inclination, accompany men when they left the campsite or settlement to hunt for meat. With their exceptional senses and their vastly greater speed, dogs helped detect and capture prey. Until the development of the gun, this remained a primary job for dogs. Fast, greyhound-type breeds evolved in China, Tibet, India, Afghanistan, and Russia, and from Arabia through to European countries such as Hungary, Poland, France, Spain, and

Dog in sheep's clothing
This Pyrenean Mountain Dog has been bred to share the same colourings and "woolly" coat as the sheep herd it guards. The result is that the sheep have accepted the dog more easily.

Superior sight and speed
Long, lean, powerfully muscled sight hounds such as this Greyhound can outrun all but the fastest of animals. Greyhounds have been clocked running at speeds over 66km/h (40mph). In greyhound racing, a mechanical hare replaces the original prey they were developed to hunt.

Britain. Their descendants today are the regional greyhound breeds, often used for coursing hares and racing.

HUNTING BY SCENT

Another early dog job was to hunt prey by scent, but it took longer for people to realize how to improve and capitalize on the dog's inherent abilities. It was only when people fully understood how to breed dogs selectively for shortened legs and a superior ability to track prey that the role of the dog as scent hunter truly flourished.

Dwarfing, the reduction of the length of long bones, decreases a dog's running speed, and in regions such as India and Arabia, where men hunted on horseback over vast distances, short-legged dogs were not developed. Instead, these heavier, slower breeds were most useful when deployed in mountainous or wooded regions of Europe where it was only possible to hunt on foot.

THE HUNTER WITHIN

Whereas our ancestors developed dogs to suit a variety of different roles and uses, most dogs are bred today to conform as best they can to written breed standards.

The Yorkshire Terrier, for example, was originally a robust and talented ratter. In the 1950s, Yorkies weighed around 8kg (18lb) and, in the absence of rats, were efficient skunk, porcupine, and muskrat hunters. Breed standards call for a long silky coat, and fashion trends demand ever smaller size. However, underneath the luxurious exterior of today's show-winning Yorkshire Terrier remains an instinctive vermin killer.

One small step for dogkind
Selective breeding to shorten the Basset Hound's legs created an expert tracker of rabbits and hares, whose pace was matched to the human hunting companions on foot. Pendulous, velvety ears help the breed pick up the scent of game.

THE DOG'S ROLE EVOLVES

As well as guarding livestock, early dogs were used to herd animals to new pastures. Such skills were honed over time to the levels demonstrated in the sheepdog trials that evolved as a sport at the beginning of the 20th century and which are still popular today.

New canine skills – setting, to indicate the position of game, and retrieving – were called into play in the hunting world with the invention of guns, and many new breeds were developed specifically for this purpose.

CLASSIFYING BREEDS

As physical traits were bred for in particular dogs to aid them in their work, so distinct "classes" of dog evolved according to their specialized abilities. With the inauguration of kennel clubs around 150 years ago, the chosen breed classifications mirrored the uses of dogs in that era. The first kennel club was set up in the United Kingdom and was simply called "The Kennel Club". It classifies most breeds pragmatically: hounds bred to hunt by scent or sight, pastoral dogs used for herding, gundogs

Retrieving game
This "dual purpose" German Short-haired Pointer finds game then retrieves it after it has been shot by his master.

trained to find or retrieve shot or wounded game, working dogs bred to guard and protect, and terriers bred to hunt vermin. That leaves a lot of dogs unaccounted for, so the Kennel Club has two additional categories: toy dogs, based upon size, not working ability, and utility dogs, a mélange of wonderful breeds, almost all of which were not British in origins, where selectors couldn't agree on where to place them.

The American Kennel Club is equally arbitrary. While it mirrors the UK's Kennel Club, classifying dogs as hounds, herders, sporting, working, terriers, and toys, it classifies the rest – somewhat unsportingly – as non-sporting dogs. The International Federation of Cynological Sports, an association of national kennel clubs that evolved in Europe, has an extended range of classifications that

Moving livestock to market
Livestock must occasionally be moved from one pasture to another and eventually either to market or to transport to market. This Australian Kelpie drives a flock of sheep and prevents any from straying.

A fighting chance
Dogs originally bred for fighting, such as the Dogo Argentino or the American Pit Bull Terrier, exist on all continents. In Japan, this Tosa, in traditional regalia, is a representative fighting dog, although today he wins in conformation rather than in fights. The controversial practice of dog fights remains common worldwide.

indigenous people used dogs to pull loads and, of course, Nordic spitz-type dogs were indispensable, pulling the sleds of people living in Arctic regions. This was a vital dog job until the 1970s, with the advent of the motorized sled. Elsewhere, in mountainous climates where nights were cold, hairless dogs acted as living hot water bottles.

UNFORTUNATE DOG JOBS
Two of the earliest functions of the dog regrettably still exist. In China, Korea, the Philippines, and elsewhere, dogs are regularly eaten. In countries throughout the world, dogs have also been used to attack each other for our amusement (in southern Asia dogs are still used to fight bears), or as fearsome warrior dogs to attack people.

more accurately reflects the practical uses of dogs: sheep-dogs and cattle dogs, Molossoid (mastiff) breeds, along with pinschers, schnauzers, and Swiss mountain and cattle dogs, terriers, dachshunds, spitz and primitive types, scent hounds and related breeds, pointing dogs, retrievers, flushing dogs and water dogs, companion and toy dogs, and sight hounds. While this list is more extensive and reflects the role dogs play as companions, it still doesn't reflect the true variety of dog jobs.

LOST DOG JOBS
Dogs were once used extensively for their muscle power. In Europe, "turnspit" dogs, whose job it was to turn the spit on which meat was roasting, were once common. In parts of North America, some

DOGS FOR CONSUMPTION
It's a sad reality that throughout the world millions of dogs are eaten each year, but the practice isn't a recent innovation. In parts of Mexico, dogs were once raised by indigenous people as home-living livestock, fed cultivated maize, and ultimately consumed. Across the Far East dogs are still eaten for cultural reasons, often, it is supposed, to enhance the eater's sexual prowess. Stalls selling dog meat, such as this one in Vietnam, are a common sight in the Far East. Support for educational charities involved in international animal welfare will help end this abhorrent custom.

A welcome winter warmer
In Mexico, Peru, China, and perhaps even in mountainous regions of Africa, hairless dogs such as this Chinese Crested acted as super-efficient hot water bottles, keeping their mistresses warm at night.

Changing roles

While many dogs continue to fulfil their original, practical roles, most have readily adapted to the ever-evolving demands placed upon them. Today, the dog's most profound role is as a permanent, reliable companion, fulfilling our social and psychological needs.

PET OR PARASITE?

It has been argued that dogs are superb parasites, that they have adapted their behaviours to parasitize our biological need to nurture. In a sense that's true. In an extraordinarily short time, we have moved from relatively small communities of people where three generations lived together to where we are today – a primarily urban species where parents may live great distances both from their own parents and from their children.

Throughout these changes and upheavals, dogs have been available and willing to fill a void in our lives, to provide companionship and community.

THE CANINE AS A CONSTANT

Beyond obvious roles – assisting people with disabilities, for example, or helping search for people who are lost – there are many less overt questions we ask of dogs. We humans are no different from any other species of intelligent animal. We

Friends for life
This Border Collie thrives on playful activity with the member of his family he is most similar to. They differ, however, in that his little buddy will mature into a responsible adult. Dogs never age mentally, remaining ever youthful.

A family affair
This Border Collie is part of the family, fulfilling a deep-seated need we all have for stability, reliability, and honesty in our lives.

Always there
It feels good to return home to the familiar and the routine. This Whippet, contentedly sitting on a sofa, waits to greet its pack leader.

Perfect partners
Whether hiking with your Labrador or out and about in town with your Westie, a dog provides unstinting companionship for all your activities.

enjoy familiarity. We thrive on stability. We worry about change or the unknown. The world is evolving faster than at any time in the history of our species. New dangers emerge. Conflict has become personal. Trust between neighbours in a new, urban society is questioned. And yet, standing tall among all this doubt and uncertainty is the innocent-eyed canine: honest, uncomplicated, stable, a lifelong Peter Pan, interested only in us and doing things with us. This may well be a case of successful parasitism, but it's a parasite we need more than ever before.

REASONS TO BE CHEERFUL

Why do we keep dogs? "They make us smile. They make us laugh," many people reason. We may have dogs "for the children" or "to protect us", but their mirth-making ability – and the Labrador (*below*) personifies this characteristic to perfection – is a profound reason why the canine–human relationship is so successful. Just watching a dog can trigger chemical changes in your brain that lift your mood and put you in a positive frame of mind.

NEW JOBS FOR DOGS

While the dog's original responsibilities evolved over thousands of years, a great variety of new jobs have been developed within the last 75 years. As trainers acknowledged the potent power of reward, rather than punishment, as a training tool, a whole range of new opportunities opened up. Most of these roles, in search and rescue, drug and ordnance detection, and in assisting people with a wide range of disabilities, require careful, specialized training and a strong bond between dog and handler. Training dogs from an early age helps if they are to carry out such complex and responsible jobs.

ASSISTANCE ROLES

The oldest "new" role for dogs is assisting blind people. The first guide dogs were trained in Germany after World War I. The first national scheme developed in Switzerland, and by the 1930s there were training schools around the globe. The largest guide dog or seeing-eye dog associations breed their own dogs; these are often Labrador–Golden Retriever crosses.

A guide dog in action
This Golden Retriever–Labrador cross waits at the kerb until it is sure it is safe for both dog and owner to cross.

Assistance dogs for disabled people, usually Golden Retrievers, are trained to help people who are restricted to wheelchairs. They do so by picking up items from the floor that their owners can't reach, reaching up with a paw to turn on light switches, even taking laundry out of a washing machine.

Hearing dogs act as ears for deaf people, using physical contact to tell the deaf owner that, for example, the baby is crying or someone is knocking at the door. I've been involved with a hearing-dog organization since its inception. When we asked a psychologist to interview recipients, we discovered that these dogs don't just fill a sensory void. After acquiring a hearing dog, deaf people have an ongoing improvement in their feelings of self-confidence, self-esteem, and self-worth. What's more, their fear of vehicles is profoundly diminished, increasing mobility and independence. The support of a dog can reduce a person's sense of vulnerability and greatly improve their quality of life.

A welcome visitor to hospital patients
After having been checked for germs and passing a temperament test, this German Shepherd visits patients in hospital. In some hospitals, in special circumstances, even children receiving chemotherapy may have canine visitors.

A NOSE FOR DETECTION

Following either natural or man-made disasters, dogs are often used in search and rescue. In mountainous regions, search and rescue dogs need good insulation, physical stamina, and superior scenting abilities. While the St Bernard is famous for its role in avalanche rescue, other breeds, the Border Collie in particular, are perfectly adapted for rescue work.

Any individual dog with natural air-scenting ability can be trained in search and rescue. After the Hanshin earthquake in Japan in 1995, dog trainers began training family pets to help track down the missing.

Other uses for dogs include sniffing out land mines, guns, drugs, illicit chemicals, and illegal immigrants. Dogs in Scandinavia have been trained to detect mould in lumber yards, while in Florida, termite-detector dogs can ensure that your house stays standing. Roles for dogs simply continue to evolve as our needs demand.

Detecting banned goods
Sniffer dogs like this Shetland Sheepdog help to enforce import laws and protect our ports and airports.

When disaster strikes…
Almost any dog can be trained in search and rescue. Here, Ma Klea, a locally trained dog, searches in the north of the Thai resort island of Phuket for victims after the December 2004 tsunami. Teams of dogs from Australia, Europe, and North America assisted in searching for survivors.

Dogs in modern cultures

There are as many roles for dogs in the world today as there are varieties of new and evolving lifestyles. For some people, dogs are child substitutes, for others, fashion accessories. A dog may be a politician's image of honesty or a social climber's symbol of his personal aspirations.

OUR DEPENDENCY ON DOGS

The relationship you enjoy with your dog is likely to be one of the most intense, honest, and trusting you'll ever have the pleasure of sharing. Just hold that thought for a minute. In a grasping world, where it is difficult sometimes to trust anyone's motives, one fact is certain: that your dog is interested in you simply because you're you. Call it "love", call it "fidelity", for many people, dogs are reliable and true when it's hard to know whether the same can be said of friends and associates.

You need only open the daily papers or switch on the television to sense the kind of dependency we have on dogs today.

Handbag hound
It might seem frivolous, but dogs such as this Shih Tzu feel perfectly at home in purpose-made dog carriers.

Throughout North America, Europe, Japan, and Australasia we are experiencing a dramatic shift in our cultural values. The cult of fame has set deep roots. People who are in essence no different to you and me suddenly find themselves both immensely wealthy and under intense media scrutiny. Prominent personalities attract people who may or may not be interested in that person's well-being. Is it really any wonder that so many international stars appear in the press with their dogs?

THE DOG AS FASHION ACCESSORY

Look closely and you'll spot one. The Chihuahua tucked surreptitiously under the leading lady's arm at the movie première. The Fox Terrier sitting up at the table to eat in one of the world's most glamorous restaurants. Always in vogue, dogs are the ultimate fashion accessories.

An accessory to modern life

In the park, at the office, in pavement cafés, or peeking out of a handbag … dogs are everywhere. An integral part of our lives, they often act as surrogate children for those not ready or able to have kids of their own.

When I first started working as a veterinary surgeon I met lots of geriatric miniature and toy poodles, the remnants of the poodle's "fifteen minutes of fame" in the 1960s. Bichon Frises followed in the 1970s and then Shar Peis in the 1980s. In the 1990s, the Staffordshire Bull Terrier became the most fashionable breed among my clients, and now, in the 21st century, I'm seeing increasing numbers of Labradoodles, intentional crosses of Labradors and Standard Poodles. Four of these wonderfully droll-looking dogs are exercised in the small park near my home. Among my most fashionable clients, I'm also seeing a resurgent interest in hard-to-find small breeds: Havanese, Coton de Tulear, and Bolognese. And now that the Chihuahua's temperament is more reliable, I'm seeing many more of these, frequently carried in expensive designer-label pooch carriers. Often these dogs wear carefully chosen collars and leads, sometimes costing exorbitant sums. I should know. We were asked so often for distinctive items we ended up stocking fashion accessories at the veterinary clinic.

A SYMBOL OF FAMILY VALUES

While the dog's role has modified because of cultural changes, its role has also been affected by the changing values we place on dog ownership. In Western culture, the dog is a symbol of family values. The nuclear family has 2.3 kids, an SUV parked on the drive, and a family pooch. Many families choose to own a dog because these creatures symbolize youth, playfulness, and a sense of innocence while providing us with companionship and unconditional love. By owning a puppy, children can learn about care and responsibility, love and loyalty, and respect for other living beings. In other words, a dog encompasses the family values we identify with best.

Political parties in the US regard dogs as essential in helping them rise to power. The Republican Party asks its candidates for public office to have pet dogs

included in family portraits, but never cats. Advertisers tell us that cats symbolize sleekness, venality, independence, selfishness, and the feminine, while the dog is an icon of honesty, integrity, reliability, and downright manhood.

THE EXTENDED FAMILY MEMBER

Cultural shifts also influence dog keeping. We live in an era where couples are choosing to have children later on in their lives. Increased work commitments, spiralling house prices, cohabiting, and a general increase in the cost of living often mean that having kids can be put on hold. Women may decide to wait until their late thirties to have their own children and, in the absence of "the

All the president's pooches
A symbol of honesty, reliability, and trust – and that's just his dog. Former US president Ronald Reagan pictured with his Bouvier des Flandres, Lucky. America's leaders are actively encouraged to own dogs, a practice that dates back to the first US president, George Washington.

real thing", the family dog takes on increased significance. It may be treated just like a child; partners in relationships often encourage their dogs to participate in as many aspects of their daily lives as is possible, including jogging, hiking, even dining with them, and thus create a family unit.

The emergence of confident urban gay communities has also created a new sector of dog owners. Almost invariably, couples who don't have children are honest with themselves and with their vets when they acknowledge that dog ownership adds glue to their relationships, a common bond, something that both individuals can embrace and care for.

New families
All over the world, modern nuclear families take many forms these days, and dogs can happily take their place at the heart of them.

of canine ownership trends, mongrels used to belong to the working classes, who couldn't afford a pure-bred dog. Now that owning purebreds isn't so exclusive, middle-class families are visibly showing their ecological and environmental values by acquiring homeless dogs from rescue centres. Owning mutts isn't just the preserve of the middle class, however; they're also kept by members of the British Royal Family and Japan's Imperial Family.

WORLDWIDE ATTITUDES TOWARDS DOGS

The family dog is a broad cultural phenomenon, but the popularity and intensity of this relationship varies from country to country. In excess of 40 per

THE DOG AS STATUS SYMBOL

Some people consciously choose dogs to represent their social order. The Labrador is overwhelmingly the most popular dog, and although nowadays owned by all strata of society, it is still the traditional symbol of people who divide their time between town and country. Owning a Springer or a working Cocker Spaniel broadcasts the same message.

At a different position on the social spectrum is the Staffordshire Bull Terrier, successor to the Dobermanns and Rottweilers that were popular with my working-class clients in the 1980s. A Staffie, especially one wearing a wide designer collar, symbolizes the tough-as-nuts-on-the-outside, soft-as-a-jelly-baby-on-the-inside values of their owners. Among my middle-class clients, a new breed has emerged during the last decade as the most popular: the recycled mutt. In a complete role reversal

cent of households in countries as diverse as Australia, Poland, and the United States keep dogs, while in Canada, France, Holland, and Hungary around one-third of homes have dogs. Roughly one-quarter of households in the United Kingdom, Spain, and Italy have canine occupants, while in Japan, Switzerland, Germany, and Scandinavia that number is lower, with around one-fifth of households being home to dogs.

Tradition is a powerful influence among many dog lovers, and the ancient tradition of docking the tails of a number of breeds remains a contentious issue. Historically, tails were amputated for a variety of reasons, including to prevent injuries during dog fights or while hunting game, to enhance muscular appearance, and even, it was once alleged, to prevent rabies. Today, few dogs "work" as they once did and in some countries, such as Germany, the Netherlands, and Sweden, the practice of docking for cosmetic reasons is banned on humane grounds. In other countries, including the UK, it is frowned upon but a ban is not enforced. The procedure is still common in the US.

The unspoken language of dogs
These Shetland Sheepdogs in Beijing are being exercised, but at the same time they are also broadcasting to others that their owner identifies with Western values and is wealthy enough to license and feed several dogs.

Living in a classless canine society
It wasn't long ago that you could tell how well-off a person was by the breed of dog they owned. Today, whether it be a Golden Retriever, a Corgi, or a mutt on the end of your lead, the boundaries in dog ownership are eroding.

BREED DIVERSITY

Introducing dog breeds

Throughout the world there are hundreds of dog breeds, each with its own written standards describing what it should look like and, in many cases, how it should behave. On the surface, it seems a simple method of classification, but is often confused by disagreement, or even by politics.

HONING THE HOUND

Long before the concept of breed standards was defined or the term "selective breeding" coined, canines faced their own, intra-species battle to be top dog, namely the survival of the fittest. Dogs suited to the conditions they were living in were more likely to stay alive and reproduce than those which were not suited to their surroundings. Possessing a warm, double coat, for example, while battling against the coldest, harshest conditions, often meant the difference between those dogs that lived and those that became extinct.

Another evolutionary trait that enhanced the survival chances of certain types of dogs was their tendency to associate with humans. In time, pressed into the service of man, those dogs were bred to bring out other traits that would help them fulfil certain roles, such as hunting and guarding. It was at this point that the concept of selective breeding was realized, and humans

Unrecognized breeds
Despite breeding true to type, the New Guinea Singing Dog (*pictured left*) remains unrecognized by most breed registries. As the dogs' numbers increase, kennel clubs may well write a breed standard for them.

began to exaggerate both the preferred psychological and physical characteristics we saw as being practical, functional, or utilitarian. It wasn't until the 19th century, however, that kennel clubs were formed, breed classifications created, and breed standards written (*see* pp.40–41).

IN THE EYE OF THE BEHOLDER

By their nature, breed standards are open to interpretation. For example, breeders may interpret the word "brown" to mean any colour from dark tan to almost black. There is no harm in having this range of interpretations, but it certainly was when standards for some breeds called for extremes such as "the back

SIZE MATTERS

While kennel clubs continue to classify breeds on the basis of their now historic mid-19th century functions, most dog owners today keep dogs primarily for companionship. Invariably, the most important consideration for a dog-owner-to-be is size. In the following section, all of the breeds are classified according to four sizes: small, medium-sized, large, and extra-large. Size generally increases as you read through each section, and within each section dogs are also grouped according to their original function or their present form. Remember, size does not equate to the need for activity; small dogs may need more exercise than extra-large ones.

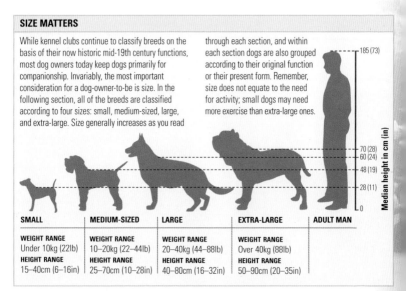

Median height in cm (in)

185 (73)
70 (28)
60 (24)
48 (19)
28 (11)
0

SMALL	MEDIUM-SIZED	LARGE	EXTRA-LARGE	ADULT MAN
WEIGHT RANGE Under 10kg (22lb)	**WEIGHT RANGE** 10–20kg (22–44lb)	**WEIGHT RANGE** 20–40kg (44–88lb)	**WEIGHT RANGE** Over 40kg (88lb)	
HEIGHT RANGE 15–40cm (6–16in)	**HEIGHT RANGE** 25–70cm (10–28in)	**HEIGHT RANGE** 40–80cm (16–32in)	**HEIGHT RANGE** 50–90cm (20–35in)	

as long as possible". Until these standards were rewritten, mostly during the 1980s, breeders bred for grossly exaggerated features. Some still do. An extreme example was the Bulldog, bred with heads so large that mothers could give birth to pups only by Caesarian section.

POLITICAL DOGS

Even when breed standards seem innocuous, there may be a hidden agenda behind their creation and adaptation. A historic example is the Cocker Spaniel. In the US in the 1930s, disagreements over interpretation of breed standards within the Cocker Spaniel Club became so intense they led to the creation of the American Cocker Spaniel (*see* pp.152–153). Political rather than personal conflict can also produce "new" breeds. When the Soviet Union seized most of the Finnish province of Karelia in the mid-20th century, it became home to hundreds of Finnish Karelian Bear Dogs (*see* p.159). Dogs identical to these, but living on the Russian side of the border, were later renamed Russo-European Laikas (*see* p.159). What these examples tell us is that breed classifications and standards are not fixed, instead being liable to change as the canine world evolves.

"NEW" BREEDS

Breeding only from within the closed genetic pool of an individual dog breed increases the risk of inherited diseases, for example cancers or heart disease. During the last 20 years, crossing recognized breeds, for example the Standard Poodle and Labrador, and Cocker Spaniel and Miniature Poodle, has resulted in the Labradoodle and Cockerpoo – breeds that, hopefully, are less genetically inclined to breed-specific illnesses.

LABRADOODLE

COCKERPOO

Pedigree dog shows
Dog shows are the highlight of the breeder's calendar. Below, pure-bred dogs are carefully inspected and the winner is, in the eyes of the judge, the individual whose conformation is closest to breed perfection.

SMALL DOGS
UNDER 10KG (22LB)

It's a curious paradox, but small dogs are perhaps our biggest canine companions. From virtually palm-sized balls of fluff to solid armfuls of robust muscle, these diminutively built, highly portable characters thrive in almost any environment. As we have become increasingly urbanized, numbers of small dogs have multiplied enormously.

VALUED COMPANIONS

Small dogs are an accident of nature that is perpetuated by human intervention. Both dwarfism, where the long limb bones shorten and the joints thicken but all other features are normal, and miniaturization, where all parts of the skeleton are equally reduced in size, can occur spontaneously by a genetic mutation within a single generation. To preserve this happenstance of small size, humans have selectively bred miniature and dwarfed dogs to maintain small-dog lines. The human fascination with oddity was probably the initial spur, but our ancestors were quick to recognize the small dog's potential to give warmth, companionship, and later, to hunt in the confined spaces of burrows.

From the Pekingese, sleeve-dog at the Chinese Royal Courts over 2,000 years ago, to today's pocket Yorkshire Terrier,

Pint-sized pooch
Bright eyed and big eared, the Chihuahua is the ultimate toy lapdog. Although small and fragile, this graceful and alert breed is easily adaptable and perfect for urban living.

small dogs have always been fashionable. But that does not mean that their sheer "doggedness" has been curtailed: not all small dogs are lapdogs. Terriers and dachshunds were diminished in size so that they could more efficiently help us hunt. In Germany, the dachshunds worked rabbit warrens and badger setts, while in Scotland and England, Border, Cairn, Norfolk, Norwich, and Jack Russell terriers carried out similar work. Other breeds of terrier were selectively bred to confront foxes, while the Lancashire Heeler and Shetland Sheepdog evolved as effective livestock herders.

Petite pooches invariably possess big personalities. It is this sense of character, combined with their practicality, which means the trend towards owning small dogs shows no signs of slowing down.

Small but perfectly formed
The world's most popular terrier, to many the Yorkie (*left*) is regarded as a fashion accessory. Behind its soft looks, however, is a dog with an enviable ratting heritage.

Staying true to his roots
Despite being a loyal companion dog and making the transition to household pet quite readily, the Jack Russell Terrier has retained its hunting and fox-bolting instincts.

CHIHUAHUA

SIZE 1–3kg (2–7lb), 15–23cm (6–9in)
GROOMING Minimal/average
TRAINING Average
COLOURS All colours

Instantly recognizable, the Chihuahua is one of the best-known lapdogs in the world. It truly earns this designation, being nowhere so happy as on a human lap; its light build and large, prominent eyes complete the

Lapdog lifestyle
Short-haired Chihuahuas need additional insulation in cold weather. Their small size and seeming helplessness also provide an outlet for our inherent parenting instinct, for our need to nurture.

picture of a devoted and dependent companion. This tiny breed requires little exercise and is ideally suited to urban life. It is, however, vulnerable to the slightest degree of cold, the short-haired variety especially so. Unfortunately, Chihuahuas are also susceptible to epilepsy, a trait they share with other breeds with domed skulls.

In spite of the tiny size of its frame, the breed has the hunting and protective instincts of a much larger dog. Breeding for a more relaxed temperament has been quite successful. Nevertheless, Chihuahuas are still apt to act first, and although their teeth are small they are still very accurate. Often a one-person dog, and with injury-prone legs, the fragile Chihuahua isn't suitable for boisterous families.

Large, prominent dark eyes

Long coat is rarer than short coat

LONG-HAIRED VARIETY

HISTORY OF THE BREED

Surprisingly little is certain about this popular breed's origins. It was exported to the United States in the 1850s from the neighbouring Mexican state from which it takes its name, which means "dry, sandy place", but before this date all is mystery. Miniaturized dogs may have arrived in the Americas with the Spanish in the 16th century, but some speculate that they arrived much earlier from China. There are even legends of these dogs being used as sacrifices by the Aztecs, but these are questionable at best.

PRAZSKY KRYSARIK

SIZE 1–3kg (2–6lb), 16–22cm (6–9in)
GROOMING Average
TRAINING Average
COLOURS Black and tan

A tiny build and a friendly temperament make this recently developed breed an ideal city dog. The short, fine coat needs no special care to keep its shine, but with such a thin coat on a lean body, these dogs need protection in cold climates.

Lean, delicate body is covered with thin skin

Thin-boned legs are injury prone

Very short, thin, glossy hair

MINIATURE PINSCHER

SIZE 3.5–4.5kg (8–10lb), 25–30cm (10–12in)
GROOMING Average
TRAINING Easy
COLOURS Black and tan, red, chocolate

This German breed, called Zwergpinscher in its native land, has been known since the 16th century. It was originally used for ratting, but over time breeders have refined the once-stocky build to create a lighter, more agile dog that has become a popular companion. Despite a resemblance to a tiny Dobermann, the two breeds are not directly related.

Pinscher means "terrier" or "biter", and this breed remains a terrier inside, willing to challenge dogs much larger than itself. The "Min Pin" is energetic, confident, and curious, and, combined with its fearless nature, these qualities make it an effective small guard dog.

Large, erect ears

Short, smooth coat, firm to the touch

Compact feet with well-arched toes

YORKSHIRE TERRIER

SIZE 2.5–3.5kg (6–8lb), 23–24cm (9in)
GROOMING Time-consuming
TRAINING Average
COLOURS Black and tan

Hair can be held up with ribbons

Body hair long and straight

SHOW COAT

The Yorkie is today the world's most popular toy or lapdog. While show individuals sport lustrous coats that are strikingly dramatic, even in the world of the show ring, pet Yorkies are likely to have more manageable hair, although it mats easily and needs routine trimming.

Yorkshire Terriers were not always as compact as they are now. Their ancestors were black-and-tan terriers from the Paisley and Clyde regions of Scotland, brought to Yorkshire when Scottish weavers migrated to the newly opened cotton mills in the West Riding of that northern English county. In the early 1800s, Yorkies acquired their present name and were used both as household vermin catchers and in organized, public rat-catching events.

Until the 1950s their size varied enormously. While large dogs are now uncommon, individuals who grow to 8kg (18lb) are still produced on occasion by their very small mothers. Selective breeding for small size exacerbated three problems: collapsing windpipes, slipping kneecaps, and gum disease. Nervousness has also crept into the breed, a trait that early socializing can diminish.

The Yorkshire Terrier still has the inclination and the will to behave as it evolved to do. Tenacious and stubborn, it is a big personality in a small package. While some Dobermanns and German Shepherds secretly desire (and try) to live on their owner's laps, Yorkies that are given free reign are fearless canine dynamos. Bursting with energy, and seemingly unaware of its small size, the Yorkie makes a good guard and sparky pet.

PUPPY

FASHION TRENDS

Small breeds are more likely to be affected by fashion trends than are larger dogs. As the popularity of both Miniature and Toy Poodles declined in the 1960s, these stylish breeds were replaced as icons of fashion by the feisty Yorkie. Its reign as the fashionista's favourite, however, may now be waning.

Short-haired terrier
Breed standards call for erect ears, but one or both ears may occasionally bend. Yorkshire Terriers do not have downy, insulating undercoats, so the hair can be left shorter and thus easier to manage.

AUSTRALIAN SILKY TERRIER

SIZE 4–5kg (9–11lb), 23cm (9in)
GROOMING Time-consuming
TRAINING Time-consuming
COLOURS Blue and tan

A little dog with big ideas, the Australian Silky Terrier emerged as a companion breed in the 20th century, probably as a result of crossing the Australian Terrier and the Yorkshire Terrier.

Showing all the feistiness and territorial qualities of its forebears, it needs firm obedience training and plenty of handling early in life. The silky coat mats very easily and needs daily attention.

Despite its length, this coat lacks a dense insulating layer, and the Australian Silky Terrier is happiest in warm climates.

Thin ears, V-shaped and erect

Silver-grey hair covers body down to pasterns

AUSTRALIAN TERRIER

SIZE 5–6.5kg (11–14lb), 25cm (10in)
GROOMING Minimal
TRAINING Time-consuming
COLOURS Blue and tan, sandy

Developed as a farm ratter and watchdog in Australia in the 19th century, this tough, pugnacious breed is now found throughout the English-speaking world. It is descended from a range of British breeds brought to Australia by settlers, and its long head and body show a family resemblance to Cairn, Yorkshire, and Skye terriers.

The Australian Terrier will take on all-comers, including snakes, and still makes an effective small watchdog. Given firm training when young, it is a robust and energetic companion. The coat is long but wiry, and so does not mat easily.

Small, dark, vibrant eyes

Long body in relation to height

AMERICAN TOY TERRIER

SIZE 2–3kg (4–7lb), 25cm (10in)
GROOMING Minimal
TRAINING Time-consuming
COLOURS Black and white, tan and white, tricolour

The breeders who developed the American Toy Terrier miniaturized its body, but not its personality. Also called the Toy Fox Terrier or Amertoy, this breed shows the influence of Chihuahuas and English Toy Terriers in its domed head and erect ears, but that of the Smooth Fox Terrier in its nature.

These busy, querulous dogs were bred in the 1930s for their ratting ability. Today, they are family companions suited to both urban and rural life, and with patient training have proved natural and obedient guard dogs and sentinels.

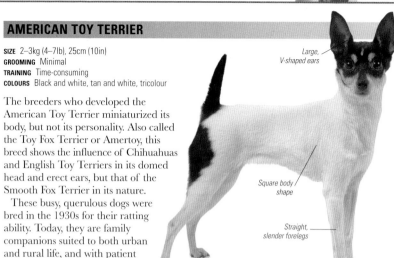

Large, V-shaped ears

Square body shape

Straight, slender forelegs

ENGLISH TOY TERRIER

SIZE 2.5–5.5kg (6–12lb), 25–30cm (10–12in)
GROOMING Average
TRAINING Time-consuming
COLOURS Black and tan

Originally bred for hunting rats and rabbits, the English Toy Terrier appeared a little over a century ago and remains relatively rare. Developed from runt Manchester Terriers, it is also known as the Toy Manchester Terrier or Black-and-tan Toy Terrier in different countries. The American and Canadian versions are slightly heavier. It has a distinctive look with a narrow, wedge-shaped head, and dramatic "candle-flame" ears.

The English Toy Terrier makes a reliable small guard dog and lively companion with plenty of personality. It is well suited to city living, although problems can arise around other dogs.

Slightly curved back

"Candle-flame" ears

Deep, narrow chest

Thick, smooth coat

Dainty, arched feet

RAT KILLING

Most small terriers are natural ratters and helped keep homes free from these disease-carrying vermin. In the 1900s, the role of the ratter evolved into a "sport". Brown rats were intentionally domesticated and then bred as "bait" in rat-killing contests, staged in deep-sided, walled pits. The terrier that killed the most rats in the allotted time was declared the winner.

MALTESE

SIZE 2–3kg (4–7lb), 20–25cm (8–10in)
GROOMING Time-consuming
TRAINING Average
COLOURS White

This easy-going little dog has been a companion breed since its earliest history. Once called the Maltese Terrier, the ancient "Melita" (an archaic name for Malta) breed probably came to Malta 2,000 years ago with the Phoenicians. It is likely that today's Maltese, also known as the Bichon Maltais, was bred from miniature spaniels and the Miniature Poodle.

The Maltese relishes exercise, but will also adapt to a more sedentary life. It behaves well around children and other dogs, and suits city living. The only drawback is the breed's luxurious coat, which mats easily and demands daily grooming.

Large, round, dark eyes protruding very slightly

PUPPY

Long, straight coat should not impede the dog's action

SHOW COAT

BICHON FRISE

SIZE 3–6kg (7–13lb), 23–30cm (9–12in)
GROOMING Time-consuming
TRAINING Average
COLOURS White

The Bichon Frise originated in the Mediterranean region, and by the 14th century it had been taken to Tenerife, hence its other name of Tenerife Dog. By the 15th century it was a favourite at court, but after that it fell into obscurity until its successful resurgence in the 1970s.

Of "powder-puff" appearance, the Bichon makes a good-tempered family dog. It is so amenable to training that it has even proved itself at herding sheep. The coat needs daily grooming, and the teeth and gums require attention. However, unlike many white-haired breeds, the Bichon has fewer allergic skin problems.

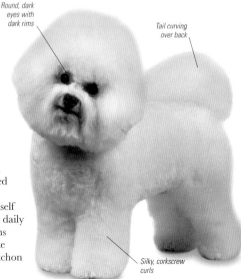

Round, dark eyes with dark rims

Tail curving over back

Silky, corkscrew curls

COTON DE TULEAR

SIZE 5.5–7kg (12–15lb), 25–30cm (10–12in)
GROOMING Time-consuming
TRAINING Average
COLOURS White, yellow and white, black and white

This breed is related to the Italian Bolognese and the French bichon breeds, and like them, it is a loyal and sweet-natured companion, gentle with children, and friendly around other dogs. The long, fluffy white coat sometimes has yellow or black patches. The Coton de Tulear may have arrived on Madagascar with French troops or administrators in the 17th century, and was a favourite breed in the southern town of Tulear for centuries. Unknown in the wider world until about 25 years ago, its popularity has since grown.

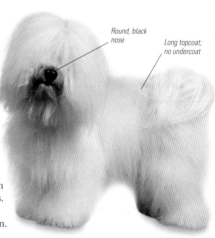

Round, black nose

Long topcoat; no undercoat

BOLOGNESE

SIZE 3–4kg (7–9lb), 25–30cm (10–12in)
GROOMING Time-consuming
TRAINING Average
COLOURS White

Less extrovert and less well known than the Bichon Frise, the Bolognese, or Bichon Bolognese, is a loyal companion and is well-behaved in the company of other dogs and children. The tufted, cottony coat has no undercoat, making this a dog suited to warmer climates. Although its name is taken from the city of Bologna in northern Italy, it is possible that the breed originated from the Bichons of southern Italy. The Bolognese was described as long ago as the 13th century, and was popular in the courts of Renaissance nobility.

HAVANESE

SIZE 3–6kg (7–13lb), 20–28cm (8–11in)
GROOMING Time-consuming
TRAINING Average
COLOURS Silver, cream, gold, blue, black

Also called the Bichon Havanese or Havana Silk Dog, this breed may be descended from Spanish-owned Maltese or from crosses of the Bolognese and poodles. It is a loyal companion, gentle, responsive, and sometimes shy, and very tolerant around children.

The Havanese dates back to the 18th or 19th century, but its popularity suffered in its homeland of Cuba following the revolution, as often happens to the favoured companions of the ousted regime. It has recently become better known in the United States and Great Britain.

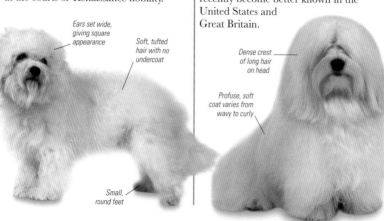

Ears set wide, giving square appearance

Soft, tufted hair with no undercoat

Dense crest of long hair on head

Profuse, soft coat varies from wavy to curly

Small, round feet

AFFENPINSCHER

SIZE 3–3.5kg (7–8lb), 25–30cm (10–12in)
GROOMING Average
TRAINING Time-consuming
COLOURS Usually black or grey, but also silver, red, black and tan, or beige, sometimes with white patches

The comical look of this breed is best summed up by its other name: Monkey Dog. Despite its impish features, this breed was first developed in Germany as an adept ratter, and it will still hunt vermin and track small game. The origins of the Affenpinscher are obscure, but its anatomy suggests that it was developed from crossing small, local pinschers with pug-like dogs from Asia. It is probably the parent of the Belgian griffons.

Distinct moustache

DETAIL SHOWING "APE FACE"

A DEVIL IN DISGUISE

Although Affenpinschers are now more likely to be found in North America than in their country of origin, this breed still exists throughout Europe. Its French name, *Diablotin Moustachu*, "moustachioed little devil", is an accurate description of the Affenpinscher's looks, as well as its deliciously confident personality.

As a companion breed, the Affenpinscher is feisty and stubborn, with a tendency to snap. However, it adapts well to urban living and, unlike most terriers, does not feel the need to challenge other dogs. The bushy, coarse coat doesn't mat easily. While breathing problems in this short-nosed breed are uncommon, gum disease, caused by closely packed teeth, is more frequent.

Tail has short hair and is carried high

Rough, harsh-textured coat

Broad chest covered with dense, dry hair; there is no gloss

Straight, well-boned, medium-length legs

BELGIAN GRIFFON

SIZE 2.5–5.5kg (6–12lb), 18–20cm (7–8in)
GROOMING Easy
TRAINING Average
COLOURS Black, black and tan, red

In their homeland, the Brussels Griffon and Petit Brabançon are regarded as separate breeds from the Belgian Griffon or Griffon Bruxellois, but in other countries the three are treated as one. Bred as ratters, today they make biddable companions, tolerant of children and other dogs.

The Belgian Griffon is a neat, terrier-type dog with short, wiry hair. Its ancestor, the Griffon d'Écurie, or Stable Griffon, was crossed with the English Toy Spaniel in the 19th century, resulting in reduced size, a shortened face, and the loss of the ratting instinct. The longer hair of the Brussels Griffon is a legacy of the international assortment of breeds used in its development, probably including the Dutch Smoushond, the Yorkshire Terrier, the Affenpinscher from Germany, and the Barbet from France.

Broad, deep chest covered by short hair

BELGIAN GRIFFON

Short, smooth coat

PETIT BRABANÇON

Despite the Brussels and Belgian Griffons' long coats, they are not suited to very cold climates. In French, *griffon* means "wire haired", therefore the smooth-coated variety has a different breed name: the Petit Brabançon. The coat and the face show the influence of Pugs in its breeding. Unfortunately, the domed head also indicates an increased risk of epilepsy in this good-natured breed.

Brussels Griffon
The Brussels Griffon has a longer wiry coat than the Belgian. This provides additional weather protection, although snow tends to attach to the beard.

PEKINGESE

SIZE 3–5.5kg (7–12lb), 15–23cm (6–9in)
GROOMING Time-consuming
TRAINING Time-consuming
COLOURS All colours

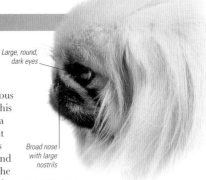

Large, round, dark eyes

Broad nose with large nostrils

FLATTENED FACE

The origins of the Chinese court's famous "sleeve dog" are unknown, as dogs of this type have been described for well over a thousand years. They were first brought to the West in 1860, after British troops entered the Forbidden City in the Second Opium War. By the late 19th century, the breed standard, a list of rules set down by the Dowager Empress Cixi (Tzu-Hsi), stated that the breed should have fastidious eating habits, a ruff to give it an aura of dignity, hairy feet to allow it to walk silently, and a coat of any colour so that there would be a dog to suit every garment in the royal wardrobe. They also stated that the legs should be bowed to discourage wandering, which gives the Peke its bouncy gait.

Strong-willed, the Pekingese is not easily trained. The breed is a rewarding and calm companion for those with the time to look after them, for the luxurious coat requires daily grooming. Surprisingly long-lived, they are prone to benign fatty tumours, called lipomas, that grow to great size under the skin. The long back and short nose can lead to serious back and breathing problems.

PUPPY

Large head with broad skull

Breathing through mouth helps dissipate excess heat

Heavy mane, and ruff of long, coarse hair

CHINESE CRESTED

SIZE 2.5–5.5kg (6–12lb), 23–33cm (9–13in)
GROOMING Minimal
TRAINING Average
COLOURS Variety of colours

This extraordinary-looking breed is a friendly, active dog that settles happily into urban or family life. It comes in two varieties: the hairless and the "powder-puff". Although grooming for the hairless is minimal, its skin needs protection from both sun and cold weather, and it is also prone to teeth and toenail abnormalities. Breeding hairless dogs with the more genetically sound "powder-puff" ensures the continuity of this striking breed.

Erect ears covered with long, sparse hair

HAIRLESS VARIETY

Plain or spotted skin lightens in summer

Ears droop due to weight of hair

Lean, elegant body covered in long hair

"POWDER-PUFF" VARIETY

HISTORY OF THE HAIRLESS

Hairlessness is a genetic accident, but the trait was perpetuated both in China and in central and South America for the same reason: hairless dogs make excellent hot-water bottles. Some canine experts believe that all hairless dogs descend from a common source. It is more likely, however, that the genetic trait of hairlessness occurs randomly and, on occasion, is perpetuated through our intervention.

JAPANESE CHIN

SIZE 2–5kg (4–11lb), 23–25cm (9–10in)
GROOMING Time-consuming
TRAINING Average
COLOURS Black and white, red and white

The pampered pets of Japanese nobility since the Middle Ages, Chins, or Japanese Spaniels, came to the West in the 17th century. They were presented to royalty and favoured by European ladies as loyal companions. Chins were probably crossed with toy spaniels, such as the King Charles Spaniel.

"Chin" means catlike, and the breed has a reputation as a quiet dog, ideal for urban life. The long, straight coat requires daily grooming, and the flat face can lead to breathing and heart problems.

Large, dark eyes set wide apart

Short, wide, well-cushioned muzzle

Long, profuse, straight coat, free from curl

SMALL POODLES

SIZE Toy: 2.5–4kg (6–9lb), 25–28cm (10–11in)
Miniature: 4.5–8kg (10–18lb), 28–38cm (11–15in)
GROOMING Time-consuming
TRAINING Easy
COLOURS Ranging from white through cream, silver, brown, black, blue, red, apricot

Small versions of the tall, elegant Standard Poodle (*see* p.207) have existed since the 1700s, but it wasn't until well into the 20th century that the Miniature Poodle, and then 20 years later the Toy Poodle, were recognized by kennel clubs. The Toy and Miniature sizes are recognized in most English-speaking countries. In most European countries, a poodle about the size of the Miniature is called the Dwarf, which is curious because it does not have dwarfed legs (*see* p.55), and "Miniature" is used to describe a medium-sized Poodle ranging up to Standard Poodle size. Very small individuals, weighing under 2kg (4.5lb) are often marketed as "Teacups", but this is not a recognized size.

Small Poodles suffer from bad press. It is true that the temperament of the breed deteriorated through breeding for quantity rather than quality, but that was 50 years ago. Nervousness and unpredictability around children today can be attributed more to poor socializing rather than to an inherently inferior temperament.

Poodles don't shed their dense, woolly coats and need to be clipped around eight times yearly. A uniform clip, producing the appearance of a new-born lamb, is

FROM PUP TO PENSIONER

Your poodle puppy may be small and cute, but it is a long-term commitment. Pet insurance actuarial statistics show that of all breeds of dogs, Miniature Poodles have the longest median life expectancy of 14.8 years. Toy Poodles can expect to live almost as long, reaching an average of 14.4 years.

the generally preferred style. While only solid colours are recognized by breed registries, parti-coloured poodles can look stunning. An excellent advantage of owning a poodle is that they seldom have a doggy odour, although they are very prone to gum disease and associated halitosis. Some lines are predisposed to inherited blindness caused by cataracts or progressive retinal atrophy (PRA). Breeding animals should always be examined for these conditions. Because thick hair grows down their ear canals, poodles are also prone to ear infection, making routine ear hair removal essential.

Long, wide ears covered with wavy hair

Hair trimmed, but never shaved

Woolly, springy hair

English Saddle trim
This Miniature Poodle's coat has been clipped into one of the most common show trims, also known as a Lion trim.

Puppy trim
This Toy Poodle has an American Puppy trim, an early cut where hair is clipped from face, feet, and tail.

Standard Lamb trim
This Miniature Poodle has a practical pet trim, in which the hair is clipped all over. It is never used for showing.

In good shape
The origins of today's large variety of show trims were in the practical cuts of working dogs. Pet trims, like this Lamb trim, help keep the hair manageable.

POMERANIAN

SIZE 2–2.5kg (4–6lb), 22–28cm (9–11in)
GROOMING Time-consuming
TRAINING Easy
COLOURS Orange, white, cream, sable, grey, blue, red-orange, brown, black

Bred in Germany, and popularized elsewhere by Queen Victoria, the Pomeranian, or Dwarf Spitz, is a miniaturized version of the German Spitz. In its mind, it is still that larger breed, so it will challenge other dogs, even large ones, and makes a noisy watchdog.

Also called the Loulou, the Pomeranian is an active and vibrant companion, good for family and city life. The long, straight coat with ruff and plumed tail is the breed's most distinctive characteristic. Originally, the coat colour most often seen was white, but by reducing size, breeders also brought out the brown-toned coat colours that are now most popular. Poms are surprisingly amenable to early obedience training.

Ruff typical of spitz breeds

Fine-boned legs

SHOW TIME

By the 1870s the Pomeranian was routinely shown in Britain, and 30 years later was recognized in the United States. This calm individual, being sprayed to maintain its "powder-puff" looks, is about to enter the ring at a championship dog show in London in 1925. The breed's luxurious coat takes three years to reach maturity.

ORANGE COAT

VOLPINO

SIZE 4–5kg (9–11lb), 27–30cm (11–12in)
GROOMING Time-consuming
TRAINING Easy
COLOURS White, fawn, black

Similar to the Pomeranian in its foxy appearance, the Volpino, or Cane de Quirinale, developed separately in Italy in the 17th century, and remains much less well known than its northern counterpart. Volpinos were favoured by Renaissance ladies, who would adorn them with ivory bracelets, and they still make affectionate and active companions. They are good watchdogs, and some have even been successfully trained to act as gundogs. The Volpino's coat is usually white, with a moderate ruff and a dense undercoat.

Tail curls over body

Small, erect ears typical of spitz breeds

Finely boned forelegs with two coats of hair

PHALÈNE

SIZE 4–4.5kg (9–10lb), 20–28cm (8–11in)
GROOMING Time-consuming
TRAINING Easy
COLOURS All colours with white

This breed, also called the Squirrel Dog, differs from the Papillon only in the positioning of its ears, which are dropped, giving a more spaniel-like appearance. In all other respects the two are the same, and in Britain and the United States they are treated as one breed. Both originated in the 17th century, descended perhaps from the Spanish Dwarf Spaniel, but showing the influence of spitz-type dogs in the shape and coat. They are exceptionally clean in their habits, and, like most toy breeds, both can suffer from slipped kneecaps.

Pendant ears covered with long hair

Coat mostly white with no undercoat

PAPILLON

SIZE 4–4.5kg (9–10lb), 20–28cm (8–11in)
GROOMING Time-consuming
TRAINING Easy
COLOURS All colours with white

Papillon is French for butterfly, and it is easy to see where this breed gets its name (it is also called the Continental Toy Spaniel). The slanted ears with cascading hair have an undeniably wing-like appearance. The fine, silky coat has no dense undercoat, and the plumed tail is carried over the back. The favourite dogs of Marie Antoinette, the luxurious coat gives the impression of a pampered lapdog. Such an image is misleading: the Papillon is an obedient, energetic, and outgoing companion.

White, narrow blaze

Obliquely carried ears abundantly fringed

SCHIPPERKE

SIZE 3–8kg (7–18lb), 22–33cm (9–13in)
GROOMING Average
TRAINING Average
COLOURS Black

This compact, spitz-type breed originated in Belgium in the early 1500s and is probably related to the Pomeranian and German Spitz. The name is said to mean "little captain", from the breed's past as guard dogs and ratters on Flanders and Brabant canal barges. These are energetic companions, and although they respond well to training they can be aggressive around other dogs. The Schipperke's build is muscular, with a deep chest and straight legs. The hard coat has a dense undercoat and a ruff around the neck, framing the typically fox-like face and pointed muzzle.

FOX-LIKE FACE

LÖWCHEN

SIZE 4–8kg (9–18lb), 25–33cm (10–13in)
GROOMING Time-consuming
TRAINING Time-consuming
COLOURS All colours

The Löwchen, or Little Lion Dog, lives up to its name. It is a resilient and active breed, quite prepared to challenge larger dogs, and too strong-willed and arrogant to take easily to obedience training. Although dogs of this kind have been known since the 16th century, the

Plume of hair on curled tail

Long, wavy coat providing little insulation

UNTRIMMED COAT

LION-CUT COAT

Löwchen became rare by the 20th century and is still uncommon. It is a French bichon breed, and probably shares its ancestry with other bichons of southern Europe, but is the only one still to sport the lion-cut of the coat, found in paintings by artists such as Goya. Its hair is fine, so this dog is comfortable in warm climates and needs some protection in the cold.

TIBETAN SPANIEL

SIZE 4–7kg (9–15lb), 25cm (10in)
GROOMING Average
TRAINING Time-consuming
COLOURS All colours

This breed may not be Tibetan, and it is not truly a spaniel. Dogs of this type have been found in the area that is now Korea since at least the 8th century, and may have arrived there from either Tibet or China. Unlike true spaniels, they were also never used for hunting, but were associated with monasteries, where they were kept as companions and, probably, as watchdogs. Today they remain outgoing, entertaining companions, although they have a strong independent streak and need plenty of exercise.

The Tibetan Spaniel may be the ancestor of the Japanese Chin, and it also has similarities with the Pekingese, particularly in the slightly bowed front legs. Due to their longer faces and legs, however, Tibetan Spaniels do not suffer the same level of breathing and back problems as the Pekingese.

Slightly domed skull

Snout tipped by black nose

Coat not as profuse as that of the Pekingese

JAPANESE SPITZ

SIZE 5–6kg (11–13lb), 30–36cm (12–14in)
GROOMING Time-consuming
TRAINING Average
COLOURS White

In everything but size, the Japanese Spitz resembles a Samoyed, from which it was probably derived in the early 20th century. It is a robust little dog with a well-muscled form and the classic spitz-type face and curled tail. Japanese Spitzes make reliable family companions and alert watchdogs, amenable to training and living with other dogs. Selective breeding has to some extent reduced the chances of persistent barking. The breed's numbers in Japan have declined from a peak in the 1950s, but they are increasingly popular in Europe and North America.

LHASA APSO

SIZE 6–7kg (13–15lb), 25–28cm (10–11in)
GROOMING Time-consuming
TRAINING Time-consuming
COLOURS Gold, honey, sand, grizzle, slate and smoke grey, parti-colour, black

Named after the capital city of Tibet and a favourite gift of earlier Dalai Lamas, this somewhat reserved breed was probably developed by Buddhist monks in Tibet

Long parting from back of head

Heavy, straight coat

Superb insulation
Under this dense, heavy coat of hair is a rugged little dog, surprisingly well muscled. The legs and feet are covered by hair, natural insulation and protection against snow.

and neighbouring Bhutan, to act as both a companion and a noisy guardian. Its Tibetan name, Apso Seng Kyi, roughly translates as "bark lion sentinel dog". When Lhasas first arrived in the West, they were classified together with Shih Tzus and Tibetan Terriers as a single breed. Even today it can be difficult to differentiate between a large Shih Tzu and a small Lhasa Apso. Lhasas have profusely dense, long coats, ideal insulation for breeds of dog living at an elevation of 5,000 metres in Tibet, but demanding to keep well groomed and clean. They generally bond closely to one particular individual.

Distinguished face
The Lhasa Apso's heavy hair on the ears and head merges with equally dense whiskers and beard, giving a proud, almost noble appearance.

SHIH TZU

SIZE 5–7kg (11–15lb), 25–27cm (10–11in)
GROOMING Time-consuming
TRAINING Average
COLOURS Any colour

More dynamic in spirit than its close associate the Lhasa Apso, this popular breed comes from Tibet via China, where it was a favourite of the Chinese imperial court. What we see today is probably the result of selective breeding in the Dowager Empress Cixi (Tzu-Hsi) kennels in Peking in the late 19th century, almost undoubtedly of Tibetan dogs similar to the Lhasa Apso, with smaller Pekingese-type dogs.

Shih Tzus have dense, thick coats like their Lhasa Apso relatives. It's best to tie up the hair in a topknot to enhance vision or simply keep facial hair clipped short. Like the Pekingese, Shih Tzus seem to be unaware when their prominent eyes brush against vegetation or other objects and as a result they are prone to sometimes serious eye injuries. Shih Tzus are more extrovert than Lhasas. Their small size and willingness to spend considerable amounts of time ensconced on sofas make them ideal companions for people who live in small dwellings. Their median life expectancy, 13.4 years, is almost identical to that of the Pekingese. As with most small dogs, they are prone to gum disease.

Large, dropping ears appear to blend into neck

Length of body exceeds height

Short, muscular legs covered with abundant hair

Hair tied in topknot

A distinctive moustache surrounds the black nose

Long, dense topcoat

Heavily plumed tail held high

Luxurious coats
While the Shih Tzu's long, outer coat is robust, the insulating, downy undercoat can be very fine and is prone to matting. These dogs are commonly clipped, particularly in hot climates.

JACK RUSSELL TERRIER

SIZE 4–7kg (9–15lb), 25–30cm (10–12in)
GROOMING Minimal/average
TRAINING Time-consuming
COLOURS Black and white, brown and white, tricolour

Long, pointed muzzle

Strong, straight legs

SMOOTH-COATED VARIETY

Rough stuff
This Jack Russell's rough coat provides protection from skin damage. Smooth coats afford dogs greater water-repellent qualities.

ROUGH-COATED VARIETY

Immensely popular in Britain, this breed was developed as a ratter in 19th-century Devon, England, by the Reverend John Russell, the "Sporting Parson". It retains all of its terrier instincts, and is feisty and outgoing, generally exuberant and affectionate, but needing competent discipline to curb its more aggressive tendencies. Explorer Sir Ranulph Fiennes walked his Jack Russell to both the North and South Poles, testament to how much exercise these rugged little dogs crave.

The waterproof double coat may be smooth- or wire-haired, the build is short-legged and muscular, and the long head has generally folded ears. As working dogs, Jack Russells originally had their tails cut short, a habit that persists in some breed registries. Until recently, the name "Jack Russell" was also used to describe the type now called the Parson Russell Terrier.

PARSON RUSSELL TERRIER

SIZE 5–8kg (11–18lb), 28–38cm (11–15in)
GROOMING Minimal/average
TRAINING Time-consuming
COLOURS Black and white, brown and white, tricolour

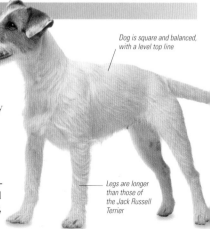

Dog is square and balanced, with a level top line

Legs are longer than those of the Jack Russell Terrier

Less common than the Jack Russell, this is the Reverend John Russell's other legacy to breed registries: a longer-legged terrier, able to keep up with horses on a hunt but still compact enough to dig after foxes. Originally classified with the Jack Russell, it has the same ebullience and energy as its near-namesake, and also comes in wire- and smooth-haired coats. The wire-haired type was preferred by the breed's originator, but both types are equally popular today.

JAPANESE TERRIER

SIZE 4.5–6kg (10–13lb), 33cm (13in)
GROOMING Minimal
TRAINING Time-consuming
COLOURS Black and white

The Japanese Terrier is a streamlined, elegant dog with a distinctive colour scheme. It is probably descended from Smooth Fox terriers taken to Japan by the Dutch in the early 18th century. The body is white and flecked with black, while the head is solid black.

Although they make very competent retrievers on land and in water, historically these dogs have been most popular as companions. Also called the Nippon or Nihon Terrier, the breed is virtually unknown outside its native land, and rare even there. Inbreeding is an ever-present problem, and is not helped by a tendency to breed for miniaturization.

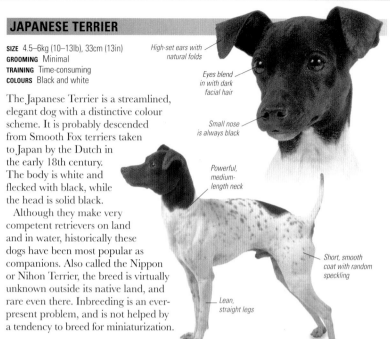

High-set ears with natural folds

Eyes blend in with dark facial hair

Small nose is always black

Powerful, medium-length neck

Short, smooth coat with random speckling

Lean, straight legs

MANCHESTER TERRIER

SIZE 7.5–8kg (17–18lb), 38–41cm (15–16in)
GROOMING Minimal
TRAINING Time-consuming
COLOURS Black and tan

Black-and-tan terriers have been known in Britain since since the Middle Ages. In the 19th century, a Manchester breeder named John Hulme crossed them with Whippets to produce this athletic breed, which became immensely popular as the "English Gentleman's Terrier". It was then exported to Europe and North America. Prized as a ratter, its numbers waned with the decline of rat-baiting, and it is now rare. This terrier's independent streak, combined with a tendency to snap first and ask questions later, make it a challenging choice.

CROPPED OUT

This Manchester Terrier from the 1940s is pictured with cropped ears, the fashion accessory of fighting dogs of that era. Ironically, the breed was only ever used as a ratter, and a ban on ear cropping in the United Kingdom may partly explain why the terriers' numbers plummeted.

Thick, sleek coat

Forelegs set well under dog

Jack Russell Terrier
Spirited, tenacious, and resolute, the Jack Russell is the classic terrier, a physically sound breed with an unlimited joy of outdoor activity.

PORTUGUESE PODENGO – SMALL AND MEDIUM

SIZE   Small: 4–6kg (9–13lb), 20–31cm (8–12in)
        Medium: 10–18kg (22–40lb), 34–56cm (13–22in)
GROOMING   Minimal/average
TRAINING   Average
COLOURS   Yellow, tan, black, and all parti-colours

Today, the small Podengo (Podengo Pequeño) is most commonly found in the high Alentejo region of Portugal and along the Tejo River in the heart of the country. The medium Podengo (Podengo Medio) is found further north, in the Douro River region. The water-repellent, fast-drying, smooth coat is more common in the wet north, while the wire-haired coats are seen more frequently in drier regions. Neither has an undercoat. The large podengo (Podengo Grande – *see* p.140) is very rare.

Well-muscled shoulders

Powerful forelegs

SMALL SMOOTH-HAIRED

THE PROLIFERATION OF THE PODENGO

Dogs similar to the Portuguese Podengos also exist in the north of Africa, as these dogs, pictured in Egypt's Dakhla Oasis, illustrate. They are probable descendants of dogs brought to this region of the Mediterranean by Phoenician merchants over 2,500 years ago.

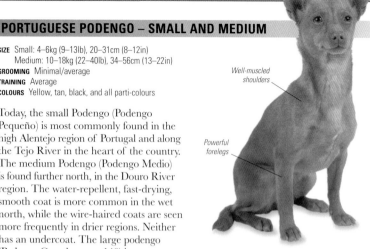

Paintings from the 16th century show Podengo Medio and Pequeño sailing on Portuguese caravels, where they no doubt carried out ratting responsibilities. Both sizes are still kept as house dogs in Portugal. They are excellent rodent controllers still. The small Podengo in particular has true terrier aptitudes, following rabbits, badgers, and foxes into their burrows.

Back line only has slight arch

Dark nose is oblique at tip

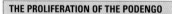

Hard, strong pads

Long legs, moderately feathered with hair

MEDIUM WIRE-HAIRED

LUNDEHUND

SIZE 5.5–6.5kg (12–14lb), 31–39cm (12–15in)
GROOMING Minimal
TRAINING Average
COLOURS Grey, black, brown and white, black and white

This agile little breed's name translates as "Puffin Dog" – historically it was used in Norway to hunt puffins from their nests on cliff faces. Its physical adaptations include paws with exceptionally large pads, double dewclaws, and extra toes, which helped give excellent grip as it hunted. Its erect ears have a soft fold across the cartilage that allows them to fold down for protection. When puffins became a protected species, the Lundehund, which was only recognized in 1943, almost died out, and it remains rare. Individuals can suffer from serious digestive disorders.

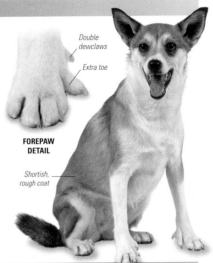

Double dewclaws

Extra toe

FOREPAW DETAIL

Shortish, rough coat

ITALIAN GREYHOUND

SIZE 3–3.5kg (7–8lb), 33–38cm (13–15in)
GROOMING Minimal
TRAINING Easy
COLOURS Cream, fawn, blue, black

A perfect miniature of the standard Greyhound, the Italian Greyhound, or Piccolo Levrieri Italiani, has been a companion of nobility since the days of Egypt's pharoahs and the Roman Empire. Today, its elegant, refined appearance, and the absence of shedding or odour from its sleek coat, ensure its continuing popularity. This breed is a good-natured, affable, and active companion, easy-going and affectionate with those it knows, if a little shy with strangers. The fine-boned build is not as delicate as it looks, but Italian Greyhounds are not well suited to households with boisterous children or larger dogs. Boasting a relaxed temperament, it is not demanding; however, it does enjoy the comforts of life.

Flat and narrow skull

Small, high-set ears with dropped tips

Elegant, arched back

Thin, satin-like coat

Deep, narrow chest

BORDER TERRIER

SIZE 5–7kg (11–15lb), 25–28cm (10–11in)
GROOMING Average
TRAINING Average
COLOURS Wheaten, tan, red, blue and tan,
grizzle (grey)

Little is known about the origins
of this breed, except that by the
late 18th century it seems to
have been found along the
border between England
and Scotland. Its form has
changed little since then,
partly because it has never
become very popular and
so has not been subject to
changing fashions. It remains
long-legged enough to keep
up a good pace, yet compact
enough to chase foxes right
into their holes. Its body is
robust, and its hard coat
is dense and weatherproof.
With a more relaxed
temper than many other
terriers, it makes an
excellent family dog.

Manual dexterity
The Border Terrier's long limbs permit fast
running, deep digging, and the ability to clasp
objects, such as this dog chew.

*Small, V-
shaped ears*

*Hind legs with
sturdy loins*

NORFOLK AND NORWICH TERRIERS

SIZE 5–5.5kg (11–12lb), 24–25cm (9–10in)
GROOMING Average
TRAINING Average
COLOURS Wheaten, red, black and tan, grizzle (grey)

**NORFOLK
TERRIER**

The sole feature that differentiates these two
breeds is their ears: those of the Norwich Terrier
are erect, those of the Norfolk, dropped. From
the earliest days, the Norwich Terrier showed
both ear types, and the
Norfolk was named
as a separate breed
in 1965 to clarify
showing standards.

These two breeds
are typical terriers,
sturdy and feisty, and
with a strong instinct to
hunt vermin. They are
more open to obedience
training than most
terriers, and are superb
for families with older
children. Although lively,
these small dogs don't make
great demands for exercise.

*Permanently
erect ears*

*Thickly muscled
hindquarters give
good propulsion*

**NORWICH
TERRIER**

CAIRN TERRIER

SIZE 6–7kg (13–15lb), 25–30cm (10–12in)
GROOMING Average
TRAINING Easy
COLOURS Variety of colours, ranging from cream and grey through wheaten and red to almost black

The bold yet still amenable, low-maintenance Cairn Terrier, once called the Short-haired Skye Terrier, originated in the west of Scotland. Its present name comes from its original function, flushing out vermin and game hidden in piles of rocks, which are called "cairns" in Scotland.

This is a happy, bossy, and mischievous breed. With its sturdy, squared body, shaggy, double-density harsh coat, and rustic, tousled features, it makes an ideal choice for active families. Cairns are equally at home in the town or country, with single owners or in boisterous young families.

Strong, level jaw

Front feet larger than back feet

BLACK COAT

As pups grow, their coat colour can lighten considerably. Despite an urge to watchdog bark, this typically fearless terrier is quite amenable to obedience training. Cairns, males in particular, should be monitored when meeting children for the first time.

Moderately long forelegs

WHEATEN COAT

TOTO

The most famous Cairn of all time was Toto, Dorothy's companion in the famous 1939 film *The Wizard of Oz*. Toto was in fact a female and her real name was Terry. She featured in all of L. Frank Baum's "Oz" books, although Baum never specified Toto's breed – Warner Bros. studio chose a Cairn Terrier.

Small, erect, pointed ears

Profuse topcoat with furry undercoat

BRINDLE COAT

CREAM COAT

CESKY TERRIER

SIZE 5.5–8kg (12–18lb), 25–36cm (10–14in)
GROOMING Time-consuming
TRAINING Time-consuming
COLOURS Blue-grey or tawny shades

The Cesky was developed by Czech geneticist Dr Frantisek Horak in the 1940s to be a compact dog for burrowing. He used the Sealyham Terrier for its dropped ears, which would not get earth in them underground, and the Scottish Terrier for its dark coat, which makes it less visible. Also called the Czech Terrier or Bohemian Terrier, the Cesky is a strong-willed, fearless little dog with a typical terrier tendency to snap, and makes a good watchdog. The coat is usually kept short on the body, but the longer areas require daily attention.

Prominent eyebrows

Profuse beard is left unclipped

Silky coat is clipped on body

SEALYHAM TERRIER

SIZE 8–9kg (18–20lb), 25–30cm (10–12in)
GROOMING Time-consuming
TRAINING Time-consuming
COLOURS White

The Sealyham was developed in Britain from a range of terriers. The aim was to produce a small, powerfully built dog that would take on otters and badgers above ground, below ground, and in water. It excelled in this role, and was an immensely popular dog in the early 20th century. Today, redundant from the job it was originally

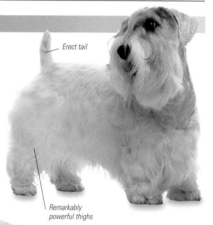

Erect tail

Remarkably powerful thighs

bred for, the Sealyham is seldom seen, and has made the transition to the show ring with only partial success. Although their spirited personalities are attractive and they make good watchdogs, these dogs tend to be territorial and often aggressive towards other dogs. Males in particular can be a challenge to train. The dog's wiry coat is kept at its best by stripping, which may need to be done professionally.

Medium-sized ears with rounded tips

Square appearance lent by long hair on face

Long, wiry coat, requiring expert preparation for show ring

TOY MEXICAN HAIRLESS

SIZE 4–8kg (9–18lb), 28–30cm (11–12in)
GROOMING Average
TRAINING Time-consuming
COLOURS Slate, liver or bronze, charcoal

The smallest version of the Mexican Hairless was created in the 1950s. Along with other sizes of Mexican Hairless, it shares the alternative names of Xoloitzcuintli and Tepeizeuintli. Despite the rather naked-sounding breed name, all of these dogs produce offspring of which one in three is a coated or "powder-

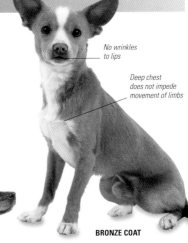

No wrinkles to lips

Deep chest does not impede movement of limbs

BRONZE COAT

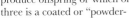

Coated variety (hairless variety also exists)

Thin, bat-like ears

Rather short legs

CHARCOAL COAT

puff" pup. These cannot be shown, but breeding with them is necessary to minimize genetic problems. Hairless individuals are very vulnerable to cold in winter, needing warm coats, and to sunburn in summer, needing to be kept out of direct sunlight. Peaceable, loving companions, they make good guard dogs, barking only when necessary. This is an affectionate, quiet breed, and is good with children.

MINIATURE MEXICAN HAIRLESS

SIZE 6–10kg (13–22lb), 30–38cm (12–15in)
GROOMING Average
TRAINING Time-consuming
COLOURS Slate, liver or bronze, charcoal

Hairlessness is a genetic rarity in dogs, but can occur in other animals. It is not known for certain whether this breed was miniaturized within Mexico or arrived already this size. Exactly when hairless dogs came to Mexico is also a mystery, although they are known to have been there by the early 16th century. This breed, which is more popular than the Standard Mexican Hairless, requires regular cleaning and moisturizing to keep its skin supple. A coat in cold weather and sun-screen in summer are essential for this breed.

Skin feels hot to the touch

Wide-set ears

Low-set tail tapering to a tip

Small, hare-like feet with retracted toes

CAVALIER KING CHARLES SPANIEL

SIZE 5–8kg (11–18lb), 31–33cm (12–13in)
GROOMING Average
TRAINING Easy
COLOURS Blenheim, tricolour, black and tan, solid red (ruby)

One of the world's most popular small breeds, Cavaliers are easy to train, affable, and energetic dogs. It's a shame that there is a high incidence of inherited heart disease within the breed, restricting their median life expectancy to 10.7 years, which is short for such a small dog.

The idea of breeding King Charles Spaniels with long noses was a 19th-century concept. It wasn't until the 1920s, however, when an American by the name of Roswell Eldridge offered prize money at Cruft's Dog Show in London, that this kind of selective breeding intensified. By the 1940s, these dogs were classified as a unique breed and given the prefix "Cavalier", to differentiate them from their forebears.

This is an ideal urban dog, reliable with children and friendly with strangers, although males can be surprisingly bold with other male dogs. They also have a great tendency to urine-mark their territories. Swedish vets have observed that the onset of heart disease, likely to occur in the majority of individuals, can be postponed until later in life through selective breeding. When choosing one of these dogs, it is extremely important to check the medical history of several previous generations. Throat problems, causing intense snoring, are very common. In spite of their serious potential health concerns, however, this is a breed perfect for families unfamiliar with dogs.

Cavalier in more ways than one
Beneath this Cavalier pup's innocent, cartoon-like good looks lies a juvenile, devil-may-care attitude. However, young pups of this breed are among the easiest to obedience train, quickly understanding simple commands.

**TRICOLOUR
COAT**

*Substantial face,
well filled out
beneath eyes*

*Silky feathering
along forelegs*

KING CHARLES SPANIEL

SIZE 4–6kg (9–13lb), 25–27cm (10–11in)
GROOMING Average
TRAINING Easy
COLOURS Blenheim, tricolour, black and tan, solid red (ruby)

Once called the Toy Spaniel, or in North America, the English Toy Spaniel, this affectionate breed formed the basis for the Cavalier King Charles Spaniel, but is now relatively uncommon. It is often quoted as fact, but is sadly only myth, that English law from the time of King Charles II gives these dogs "freedom of the realm" – the right to go wherever they pleased. The king's dogs were larger, with longer noses, than today's breed, but with the demands of fashion, both dog and nose shrank to present-day proportions. Their colour variations also once had royal connotations; tricolour was called Prince Charles, black and tan, King Charles, and chestnut and white was Blenheim. Today, only the Blenheim name remains in use.

PICTURE PERFECT

The round-faced, soft-brown-eyed Cavalier is the result of selective breeding of King Charles Spaniels to restore the original type of longer nose they had at the time that artists such as Van Dyck and Hogarth painted them. Portraits by the French artist LL Boilly, below, show that this type of dog endured into the 18th century.

**TRICOLOUR
COAT**

*Short muzzle with
turned-up nose*

*Long ears
have plenty
of feathering*

*Long, silky, wavy coat;
can also be straight*

*Straight legs
with compact,
well-fringed feet*

BLENHEIM COAT

PUG

SIZE 6–8kg (13–18lb), 25–28cm (10–11in)
GROOMING Easy
TRAINING Time-consuming
COLOURS Black, silver, and fawn with black mask and markings

It's hard to believe that this muscular, compact, exuberant breed is genetically closer to the wolf than, for example, the German Shepherd. Pugs are truly ancient and, as with all ancient breeds, they can be challenging to obedience train fully.

Originally from China, they were brought to Holland nearly 500 years ago. Their Dutch name, *Mopshond*, roughly translating as "grumbling dog", refers to the breed's snorting and snuffling rather than to its temperament. Pugs are opinionated and individualistic. With their enormously endearing flat faces, tightly curled tails, and thick, wrinkly skin they are absolutely distinctive in the world of dogs.

Pugs are susceptible to infection in the nasal fold of the skin and are particularly prone to damaging their prominent eyes, which seem insensitive to potential danger. The breed requires regular exercise to keep the threat of obesity at bay. It's best to avoid taking Pugs to hot climates, as the combination of breathing difficulties, excess weight, and heat can be lethal. Likewise, Pugs should not be left outside in very cold weather.

Tightly curled tail

Fine, smooth, soft coat

Strong, straight, muscular legs

Childlike qualities
The Pug's flat face, large eyes, and "pug nose" all make for a charming sight, but these features also increase health risks, such as eye injuries and breathing problems.

BOSTON TERRIER

SIZE 4.5–11.5kg (10–25lb), 28–43cm (11–17in)
GROOMING Minimal
TRAINING Time-consuming
COLOURS Black and white, brindle and white,
brindle and red

One of the few breeds developed in the
United States, the Boston Terrier is the
state dog of Massachusetts. It originated
in Boston, of course, in the mid-1800s as
a fighting pit dog. By the early 1900s
breeders were paying attention to reduced
size, and by the 1950s small dogs under 7kg
(15lb) were the norm, although larger dogs
were and still are both bred and shown.

Bostons are easy-to-
care-for couch potatoes
if given the chance,

A NATIVE AMERICAN

The Boston Terrier can be traced back to crosses
involving bulldogs and terriers in the city of Boston
some time in the 1800s. This late-19th century souvenir
photograph shows a couple posing with a Boston
at Salisbury Beach, a stretch of Massachusetts
coastline that remains dog-friendly today.

but can also make lively family playmates.
Their tails are naturally short, never cut.
In the US, some individuals still have their
dog's ears amputated or "cropped" – for
the owner's or breeder's vanity, not for the
well-being of the dog. This practice is
illegal in most European countries and
Australia. As with Pugs, Caesarian births
are common because of the relatively
large size of pups' heads, although breeders
have been successful at producing a more
natural head size in recent times. Like
other brachycephalic breeds (those with
short, flattened heads), problems with this
terrier's snoring and breathing can require
veterinary intervention.

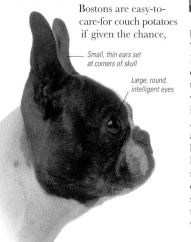

Small, thin ears set
at corners of skull

Large, round,
intelligent eyes

Smooth, bright,
fine-textured coat

Small, round feet with
well-arched toes

**BRINDLE-AND-
WHITE COAT**

MINIATURE SCHNAUZER

SIZE 6–8kg (13–18lb), 30–36cm (12–14in)
GROOMING Time-consuming
TRAINING Easy
COLOURS Salt and pepper, black, silver and black

Sensible haircut
This individual has a pragmatic haircut. The body and ears are clipped short, as is the hair over the eyes, while the hair on the cheeks and jowls has been left long.

With a terrier-like temperament but a greater willingness to respond to obedience training, the Miniature Schnauzer is the smallest, most recent, and overwhelmingly most popular of the various sizes of Schnauzers (*see* p.126).

Developed from wire-haired Pinschers from the Bavarian region of Germany, the family of heavily whiskered dogs now called Schnauzers acquired their name from *Schnauze*, the German word for "snout". The Standard Schnauzer, from which the Miniature descends, was a herding dog and this is perhaps why all Schnauzers are so amenable to training. Until early in the 20th century, bitches produced pups that grew to both Standard and Miniature size. It's possible that both Affenpinscher and Miniature Pinscher bloodlines were used to ensure the smaller size of what is now the Miniature breed.

Like Poodles, Miniature Schnauzers don't moult. Their hair grows prolifically and needs regular trimming, usually about every six to eight weeks. Neither as feisty nor as opinionated as some terriers of equal size, they are amongst the most popular dogs in North America.

Originally bred for ratting, today the breed has an equable temperament and is an excellent companion in active families. Unfortunately, increased popularity has encouraged indiscriminate breeding, resulting in some lines having a nervous disposition. However, this is a robust breed and a hearty barker, but not snappy or intolerant. It settles into family routines and is usually good with other dogs.

CROPPED EARS

In many parts of the world cropped ears are the unique and defining feature of the Miniature Schnauzer. This look is so ubiquitous that some people mistakenly assume that this breed has naturally erect ears. Cropping the ears is a surgical procedure, however, a cosmetic alteration with no medical benefit to the dog.

V-shaped ears hang forwards

Strong, straight back

Dense, profusely bushy beard

Hard, coarse topcoat; soft undercoat

Good angles to hind legs allow for powerful bursts of speed

SALT-AND-PEPPER COAT

SHETLAND SHEEPDOG

SIZE 6–7kg (13–15lb), 35–37cm (14–15in)
GROOMING Time-consuming
TRAINING Easy
COLOURS Tricolour, diverse bicolours, and blue merle

The Shetland Sheepdog is a highly trainable, affectionate dog that thrives on, and is superb at, agility, obedience, Flyball, or just showing off in competition. Its ancestral home is on the remote Shetland Islands in the North Sea. Traders, visitors, and settlers to these islands brought with them a variety of dogs including Scottish Rough Collies, the Sheltie's main ancestors, and spaniel and spitz-type breeds.

Shelties are, in essence, perfectly miniaturized Rough Collies and retain the working abilities of their ancestors. While they can be both timid and wary of strangers if not socialized

Top dog
In its size group, the Shetland Sheepdog dominates dog agility competitions. The sport satisfies the Shelties' need for both mental and physical stimulation.

properly as pups, Shelties are natural watchdogs and, when given the opportunity, equally natural sheep herders.

Miniaturization has brought with it an increased risk of leg-bone fractures. Two hereditary conditions, collie eye anomaly (CEA) and progressive retinal atrophy (PRA), are potential problems. Its dense, rough coat needs routine brushing, but like the Cavalier King Charles Spaniel (*see* pp.84–85), the Sheltie is an ideal dog for both young families and older, more sedentary households.

Distinctive mane

TRICOLOUR COAT

BLUE MERLE COAT

LANCASHIRE HEELER

SIZE 3–6kg (7–13lb), 25–31cm (10–12in)
GROOMING Average
TRAINING Time-consuming
COLOURS Black and tan

Heelers drove livestock by nipping their heels, but they became nearly extinct in the 20th century. This sturdy recreation was developed in the 1960s from mainly Welsh Corgi and Manchester Terrier crosses. While it looks like a heeler, it does not behave like one, which is an advantage in a companion breed. Instead, its terrier origins make it an alert ratter.

Wide-set, relatively large ears

Short legs in relation to body size

WIRE FOX TERRIER

SIZE 7–8kg (15–18lb), 39–40cm (15–16in)
GROOMING Average
TRAINING Time-consuming
COLOURS White, white and tan, black and tan

Appearing in the 1870s, some 20 years after its Smooth cousin (*see below left*), this dog is sometimes confused with its relative, and is in most respects the same dog in a different finish. It has generally proved the more popular of the two. A strong-willed breed, it is not inclined to yield to humans or other dogs, and is happiest when allowed to do its favourite activity – digging.

Dense facial whiskers

Wiry, strong coat

SMOOTH FOX TERRIER

SIZE 7–8kg (15–18lb), 39–40cm (15–16in)
GROOMING Minimal
TRAINING Time-consuming
COLOURS White, white and tan, black and tan

A fox terrier originally meant any dog that went to earth chasing foxes, but controlled breeding in the 1850s resulted in the breed of today. It is a muscular bundle of energy, playful and impulsive at best, but snappish and wilful if not firmly controlled. Ideal for country living.

High-set tail, held upright

Abundant, straight coat

LAKELAND TERRIER

SIZE 7–7.5kg (15–17lb), 33–38cm (13–15in)
GROOMING Average
TRAINING Time-consuming
COLOURS Wheaten, red, blue, black, blue and tan, black and tan

Originally bred in the north of England to protect livestock, this robustly built dog has a fearless temperament. Single-minded, it has a tendency to aggression around other dogs, but with patient training it makes a good guard dog. The hard, wavy coat gives excellent winter protection and can be plucked in summer.

WEST HIGHLAND WHITE TERRIER

SIZE 7–10kg (15–22lb), 25–28cm (10–11in)
GROOMING Average/time-consuming
TRAINING Average
COLOURS White

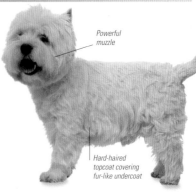

Powerful muzzle

Hard-haired topcoat covering fur-like undercoat

The origins of this most popular of robust terriers is both dramatic and tragic. In the late 1800s, a Scottish landowner, Colonel E.D. Malcolm, out rabbit hunting with his favourite Cairn Terrier, mistook his dog for a rabbit and accidentally shot it. Wheaten-coloured Cairns occasionally produced white pups, and so the Colonel chose to selectively breed his Cairns for white coats to improve the visibility of his hunting terriers. By the early 20th century, these dogs, now called West Highland White Terriers, as they originated near Poltalloch in Argyllshire in the west of Scotland, were appearing at dog shows in England and the United States.

Westies are among the most popular of terriers in many countries. In Japan, their white colour signifies good luck as well as good looks. To keep coats pristine, and skin free from irritation, routine body maintenance involves daily brushing and occasionally clipping the hair on the ears to keep it short. Some Westies have a grey or golden look because of chronic skin irritation, the breed having extremely high incidence of allergic skin disease. Sadly, allergy can also affect the lungs, causing connective tissue changes leading to a chronic cough later in life. Westies are zesty, natural diggers and clowns, happiest when there's lots to do.

Whiter than white
While some lines of Westies have almost bleached white coats, like this handsome dog, others have a distinct wheaten-yellow tint, a throwback to their Cairn origins.

SCOTTISH TERRIER

SIZE 8.5–10.5kg (19–23lb), 25–28cm (10–11in)
GROOMING Time-consuming
TRAINING Time-consuming
COLOURS Wheaten, black, red-brindle, black-brindle

Distinctive eyebrows

Powerful hindquarters

The distinctive Scottish Terrier is a sturdy powerhouse of a dog with a thick, insulating double coat, bred to work outdoors and pursue small game underground. The breed developed in Aberdeen in the 19th century, probably from dogs from the Scottish Western Isles, and was also called the Aberdeen Terrier. Scotties have always been most popular in North America.

The Scottish Terrier makes a quiet, reserved, slightly stubborn companion and a superb guard dog. Its gentlemanly image was perpetuated by its role in the 1955 Walt Disney film, *Lady and the Tramp*. While its classic image is as the black companion to the white Westie, Scottish Terriers come in a variety of colours.

Tail thick and tapering and carried up

Erect, pointed ears

PRESIDENT ROOSEVELT

While many people are familiar with president George W. Bush's two Scotties, Barney and Miss Beazley, the 32nd US president, Franklin D. Roosevelt, also chose a Scottie, Fala, as his White House companion. Fala survived Roosevelt by seven years and was buried alongside him. A statue of the pair is featured in the Franklin Delano Roosevelt Memorial in Washington, DC.

Mother and son
This pup has had its first facial clip, which trims the hair on the ears and head to create this dog's famous bushy eyebrows.

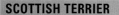

SKYE TERRIER

SIZE 8.5–10.5kg (19–23lb), 23–25cm (9–10in)
GROOMING Time-consuming
TRAINING Time-consuming
COLOURS Cream, grey, fawn, black

Bred on the Inner Hebridean Isle of Skye in the 17th century to hunt otters, weasels, and badgers, these terriers were a favoured companion of Scottish and English royalty. Their popularity, however, declined in the 20th century. Graceful in appearance, with a relatively light build and long, silky coat, the Skye Terrier can be intensely loyal. However, they are not ideal for children, and can be short on patience and liable to snap if provoked.

Long, silky topcoat

LOYAL TO THE LAST

Skye Terriers make highly devoted pets. Legend has it that Greyfriars Bobby, the Scottish dog famed for keeping a 14-year vigil at his master's grave in the mid-1880s, was one such faithful servant.

DANDIE DINMONT TERRIER

SIZE 8–11kg (18–24lb), 20–28cm (8–11in)
GROOMING Average
TRAINING Average
COLOURS Pepper, mustard

An oddity in more than one way, this dog is quite unlike other terriers. It is a peaceable, intensely loyal little character, relaxed around children and other dogs, although it has a surprisingly powerful bark and will fight if pushed. The breed's one drawback is a tendency to spinal problems due to its long back and short legs. That it is named after a fictional character in Sir Walter Scott's 1815 novel, *Guy Mannering*, (although it appeared in paintings of the aristocracy centuries before this) indicates how little is known of its origins. One theory is that the Dandie Dinmont Terrier may be descended from the gypsies' dogs of southern Scotland.

Large skull with domed forehead

Strongly developed jaws

Long, low body

Wiry hair on top of tail with softer coat underneath

GERMAN HUNTING TERRIER

SIZE 9–10kg (20–22lb), 40cm (16in)
GROOMING Minimal
TRAINING Time-consuming
COLOURS Red, brown and tan, black and tan

This robust breed very much lives up to its native name, *Deutscher Jagdterrier* (German Hunting Terrier), and is at its best tracking and retrieving small game above and below ground or in water. It was created in Bavaria in the early years of the 20th century as an all-purpose hunting dog by crossing the Welsh Terrier, Old English Black-and-tan Terrier, and English fox terriers. Needing plenty of physical and mental stimulation, it settles happily into a life outdoors and makes a fine watchdog. A strong-willed,

snappy nature makes this breed demanding as an urban or companion animal, and it is kept mostly by gamekeepers and hunters for the purpose for which it was bred.

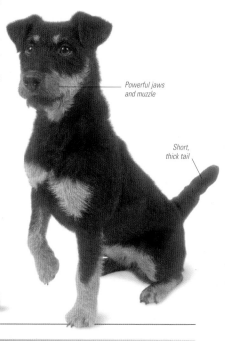

Powerful jaws and muzzle

Short, thick tail

Moderately long, strong, straight back

Coat generally rough, but can be smooth

Long, muscular hind legs with low hocks

BRAZILIAN TERRIER

SIZE 7–9kg (15–20lb), 35–40cm (14–16in)
GROOMING Minimal
TRAINING Average
COLOURS Tricolour

This exuberant South American breed shows its Jack Russell parentage in both character and looks. Miniature Pinschers and possibly large Chihuahuas were also used in its development. A lively and irascible breed, an excellent rat catcher, and a noisy guard dog, the Brazilian Terrier makes a wonderful rural working dog that thrives on physical activity. In its native country, it is used, either alone or in packs, for hunting vermin and game that inhabit rural ranches. The Brazilian Terrier is also a good family companion

(it is happy in the company of children), as long as its feisty temperament and high energy levels can be catered for. The short, close coat requires little grooming.

Flat, triangular skull

Short, easy-to-maintain coat

Narrow chest

Well-balanced body

WELSH TERRIER

SIZE 9–10kg (20–22lb), 35–39cm (14–15in)
GROOMING Average
TRAINING Average
COLOURS Black and tan

Small, dark, alert eyes

This breed dates back to the 1760s and originated in North Wales as a ratter. Today, it is more often seen in North America and is kept as a companion, although it still makes a good vermin hunter and guard dog. Probably descended from the now-extinct Old English Broken (or Coarse-haired) Black-and-tan Terrier, it is a strong, healthy breed, and needs plenty of activity. Coming from a working background, the Welsh Terrier isn't particularly difficult to train, but it doesn't back down from dog fights. The coat is fairly easy to care for except for the beard, which can become messy and needs regular attention.

BASENJI

SIZE 9.5–11kg (21–24lb), 41–43cm (16–17in)
GROOMING Minimal
TRAINING Time-consuming
COLOURS Black and white, tan and white, black, brindle

Dogs similar to the Basenji are depicted in Egyptian tomb reliefs dating from the Fourth Dynasty over 4,000 years ago. However, today's Basenji descends from dogs that came from Zaire in the 1930s. The breed shows many traits of a dog that evolved in a warm climate, notably a short coat, especially on the ears, a light build, and white patches, all of which help with heat loss. It also bears similarities to its genetically close wolf ancestors in its quietness, its tendency to communicate with howls rather than barks, and the fact that the female comes into season only once a year. A distinctive breed with a permanently surprised expression, although not easy to train, the Basenji makes a docile, undemanding pet.

Tail curled in a tight ring

Highly visible and mobile ears

Very fine, short, sleek coat

Legs long compared with body length

SHIBA INU

SIZE 8–10kg (18–22lb), 35–40cm (14–16in)
GROOMING Average
TRAINING Time-consuming
COLOURS Variety of colours

This typically spitz-type dog is the smallest and the most popular of Japan's indigenous breeds. Dogs have existed in Japan for over 2,500 years, and the strong, graceful Shiba Inu has been used for hunting in the Sanin region, at the western tip of Honshu island, for centuries. The breed almost became extinct during the latter phase of World War II, but today numbers are stable in Japan

Short, level back

Deep chest, with well-rounded ribs

Straight forelegs, with elbows held close to body

Small, triangular eyes

Pointed muzzle, with dark nose

Harsh, double coat

and becoming more widespread in Europe, Australia, and North America. While they are relaxed with children and other dogs, these are independent, agile, and robust individuals, best suited to an experienced owner. They seldom bark, preferring to shriek in an extraordinary manner, but they make good guard dogs.

BEDLINGTON TERRIER

SIZE 8–10kg (18–22lb), 38–43cm (15–17in)
GROOMING Time-consuming
TRAINING Average
COLOURS Sandy, liver, blue, or any of these with tan markings

A dog in lamb's clothing, the Bedlington has an equally benign disposition behind its mild expression and fuzzy coat, although it can prove destructive without sufficient exercise. First shown in 1870, it is probably descended from functional, athletic terriers bred by gypsies around Rothbury in Northumberland, known as the Rothbury Terriers. These dogs were used to hunt hares and rabbits above ground rather than digging them out. They have one of the longest life expectancies of all dogs – a median of 14 years.

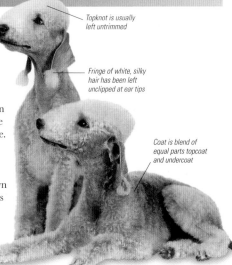

Topknot is usually left untrimmed

Fringe of white, silky hair has been left unclipped at ear tips

Coat is blend of equal parts topcoat and undercoat

DACHSHUNDS

SIZE (UK and US)
    Miniature: 4.5–5kg (10–11lb), 20cm (8in)
    Standard: 7–14.5kg (15–32lb), 26–28cm (10–11in)
GROOMING Easy for Smooth- and Wire-haired Dachshunds;
Average for Long-haired Dachshunds
TRAINING Time-consuming
COLOURS Variety of colours

Dachshunds are true dwarfs. Their bone
structure is normal with the exception of
their long bones, which are dramatically
shortened. Dachshund-like dogs are
portrayed in an ancient Egyptian sculpture
of a pharaoh seated with three dogs, but
today's opinionated individuals probably
originated in the Middle Ages in what
is now Germany. The American
humorist E.B. White said his
dachshunds were so insolent,
they paused to have a smoke
before deigning to follow
him inside the house.

The Smooth-haired
Dachshund is the oldest
variety. The Long-haired
was probably developed
by crossing Smooth-
haired dogs with local
short-legged spaniels,
creating a very
affectionate breed. The
Wire-haired was developed
by crossing Smooth-haired
dogs with rough-coated local
pinschers and then crossing these
individuals with the somewhat
goofy, avuncular, Scottish Dandie
Dinmont. This is probably why
the Wire-haired Dachshund has
a slightly larger head size and a
greatly diminished bloodlust.

Show-standard dogs have
short legs and deep chests that
almost touch the ground.
Working dogs have longer
legs with considerable

ground clearance for chests built to
manoeuvre in rabbit burrows or badger
setts. In Germany, where most dachshunds
are bred to working-dog standards, they
are classified according to chest size as
Kaninchenteckel (Miniature), Zwergteckel
(Dwarf), and Normalschlag (Standard).

They are long-lived (*see box*), although
their long backs and short legs predispose
them to slipped discs, a condition that
can cause complete posterior paralysis.
Probably the most easily recognized of
all breeds, and a favourite of advertisers,
dachshunds remain consistently popular.

Natural hunter
While short legs can lead to reduced
mobility in snowy conditions, this
young Wire-haired Dachshund thrives
on outdoor activity as it stares intently
at its object of interest in the distance.

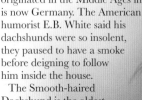

Broad,
mobile ears

Short, dense,
lustrous coat

Full, prominent
forechest

STANDARD SMOOTH-HAIRED

Eyebrows are
strong and
prominent

Ears set above eyes
and covered with
long, silky hair

Distinctive beard
differentiates
appearance from
other dachshunds

MINIATURE WIRE-HAIRED

STANDARD LONG-HAIRED

SHORT LIMBS, LONG LIFESPANS

Despite all varieties of dachshunds being prone to serious back problems, Miniature Dachshunds have the second longest median life expectancy of all breeds: 14.4 years. Only the Miniature Poodle beats it. Standard Dachshunds have a median life expectancy of 12.2 years. It is not uncommon, however, to see dachshunds in their late teens or early twenties.

MEDIUM-SIZED DOGS
10–20kg (22–44lb)

Practical, both in their size and in the services they once performed, this group of dogs evolved mostly on the farm and as gundogs. It was the role of sight and scent hounds to accompany hunters in search of food or in pursuit of sport. Well loved in their native countries, many of these dogs are yet to make their mark worldwide.

BRED FOR ABILITY

Throughout Europe, medium-sized breeds evolved to accompany local men hunting on foot. From the Drevers and Dunkers of Scandinavia to the Cocker and Springer Spaniels of England and Wales to the French bassets, breeds were developed for specific roles, whether they be tracking, pointing, setting, flushing, or retrieving. Meanwhile, medium-sized water dogs were bred to assist hunters who stalked game with bows and arrows or, latterly, the gun. Breeds such as the Portugese and Spanish Water Dogs, French Barbet, and Hungarian Puli are among the oldest water-loving breeds.

While one group of dogs worked closely with hunters on foot, sight hounds – dogs that hunt more by sight than by scent – were bred for the speed to chase down prey. Originating in ancient Arabia, medium-sized sight hounds exist throughout Europe. Found primarily around the Mediterranean, these breeds include the Podenco Canario, Cirneco dell'Etna, and the most numerous, the Whippet.

French fancy
Despite its name, the Petit Bleu de Gascogne is a relatively large breed of hound. It was bred from its closest relative, the Grand Bleu de Gascogne.

Medium-sized dogs are also ideal for working livestock. The Border Collie is perhaps the best-known of these herding and driving breeds. Truly adaptable, this popular breed has proved equally successful in new activities such as field trials, agility trials, and competitive sports including Flyball. Other working farm dogs, such as the Welsh corgis, are now bred primarily as family companions. A size that suits many households, and an eager enjoyment of human interaction, ensures the popularity of this group of dogs.

Pole position
Border Collies are highly intelligent herding dogs, but their skills are not limited to livestock work. They excel at dog agility sports, as this slaloming contestant demonstrates.

A spring in his step
One of the best examples of medium-sized dogs, the English Springer Spaniel is a tireless worker, a splendid companion, and a successful show dog.

FINNISH SPITZ

SIZE 14–16kg (31–35lb), 38–50cm (15–20in)
GROOMING Average
TRAINING Time-consuming
COLOURS Golden red

This lively, independent breed has long been used for hunting in eastern Finland and the Karelian region of Russia. The national dog of Finland, it is still a popular gundog in its homeland. The breed remains close to its origins both physically – with a thick insulating coat that makes it almost impervious to cold – and in character. It is used to follow game that takes refuge in trees, keeping up a continuous loud barking until the hunter arrives. This noisy trait makes it a good choice for a guard dog.

This breed is known as the Finsk Spets, or Suomenpystykorva, in its native land. After the Russian Revolution, those living in Karelia were called Karelo-Finnish Laikas. Distinctly foxlike in appearance, this dog thrives on activity and is not the most biddable of breeds, so may not be the best choice for a family pet.

Dark, vivacious eyes

Tail curls from root

Small, pointed ears

Deep chest

Belly slightly drawn up

Strong forelegs descending from straight shoulders

NORDIC SPITZ

SIZE 12–15kg (26–33lb), 40–47cm (16–19in)
GROOMING Average
TRAINING Time-consuming
COLOURS Brown and white, red and white

Similar in form and function to the slightly larger Finnish Spitz, the Nordic Spitz, or Norbottenspets, hails from Sweden. It was first used to hunt squirrels when their furs were still traded, and then later used for game birds such as black grouse. Today, it is still used as a gundog and makes a good guard dog, though most are now kept as companions. The breed's popularity waned in the first half of the 20th century, when it became almost extinct. It was rescued by Swedish breeders, but this active, strong-willed dog remains rare outside its homeland.

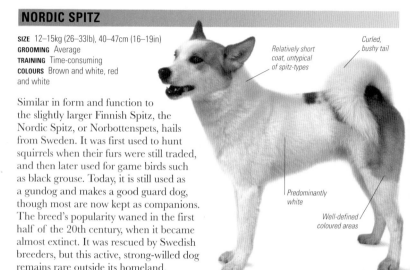

Relatively short coat, untypical of spitz-types

Curled, bushy tail

Predominantly white

Well-defined coloured areas

GERMAN SPITZES

SIZE Giant (Gross): 17.5–18.5kg (39–41lb), 40cm (16in)
Standard (Mittel): 10.5–11.5kg (23–25lb), 29–36cm (11–14in)
Toy (Klein): 8–10kg (18–22lb), 23–28cm (9–11in)
GROOMING Time-consuming
TRAINING Time-consuming
COLOURS White, brown, or black for Giant; range
of colours for other sizes

Dense, long, harsh hair covering chest

GIANT GERMAN SPITZ

Small feet with insulating hair between toes

Spitz-type dogs arrived in central Europe with the Vikings and are mentioned in German literature as early as 1450. The Standard German Spitz was a herding dog, while the Giant and Toy versions were developed as companion breeds. Today they are known widely across Europe, but numbers have been in decline for many years in Germany.

The characteristic long, dense coat needs a good deal of care, and without early learning

STANDARD GERMAN SPITZ

these dogs often resent grooming. Alert and outgoing, they can be stubborn pets. Males may challenge other dogs or strangers; this territorial quality can make them good guard dogs, although not as trainable as some breeds.

TOY STORY

The three squarely built German Spitz breeds can be distinguished primarily by their size, being almost perfect replicas of each other. The Toy German Spitz (*right*) is the ancestor of the Pomeranian; today it is eclipsed in popularity by its "Pom" relative.

JINDO

SIZE 16–18kg (35–40lb), 41–58cm (16–23in)
GROOMING Average
TRAINING Time-consuming
COLOURS Yellow, red, tan, black, and any
of these with white, solid white, brindle

Declared a National Treasure in its Korean homeland, this breed developed on the island of Jindo as a hunting and guarding dog. Like the Akita in Japan, the Jindo descends from the first wolf dogs that arrived centuries ago in what is now Korea. It was virtually unknown outside the country until it spread to North America late in the 20th century. Still true to its purpose, it is intensely loyal

and protective towards a strong owner, but is aloof with strangers and challenging to other dogs. The Jindo needs plenty of exercise, during which it will show a keen desire to hunt anything small and furred, from wild animals to pets.

Almond-shaped eyes in triangular settings

Dense, soft topcoat

Curled tail

Cat-like feet on straight legs

TAN COAT

SALUKI

SIZE 14–25kg (31–55lb), 58–70cm (23–28in)
GROOMING Average
TRAINING Average
COLOURS Range of colours

Capable of amazing turns of speed, this ancient breed deserves its alternative name of Gazelle Hound. Other aliases include Arabian Hound, Persian Greyhound, Persian Sighthound, and Tanji. Salukis closely resemble the hounds depicted in ancient Egyptian art, and may have been deliberately bred for longer than most other dogs. They make gentle, loyal companions, reliable with children but not suitable for a boisterous household. Plenty of exercise is an absolute must, and they have an incorrigible urge to hunt any small animal they encounter.

Long, mobile ears hanging close to sides of head

Powerful leg muscles

Long, muscular, supple neck

Deep chest built for stamina

Lean, straight legs with feathering on the backs

Long, narrow head

SMOOTH-HAIRED VARIETY

FEATHERED VARIETY

WHIPPET

SIZE 12.5–13.5kg (28–30lb), 43–50cm (17–20in)
GROOMING Minimal
TRAINING Average
COLOURS All colours

Very mobile, rose-shaped ears

Alert eyes with quiet, retiring look

Elegant, even delicate, in appearance, the Whippet is in fact a robust, fearless hunter, bred for coursing and racing. While they are active and impressively speedy outdoors and can still be used for hunting, Whippets are calm and docile when indoors, relaxed around children, and make affectionate companions. Plenty of daily exercise is needed when the weather is warm, but in colder seasons this thin-skinned dog needs a coat.

Long, lean head tapering to nose

Second nature
The Whippet's long limbs and powerful muscles combine with an innate love of physical activity to produce a natural athlete.

CIRNECO DELL'ETNA

SIZE 8–12kg (18–26lb), 42–50cm (17–20in)
GROOMING Minimal
TRAINING Time-consuming
COLOURS Tan, white, tan with white

Virtually unknown outside Italy, this venerable breed was preserved in isolation on Sicily for some 2,000 years. It is also called the Sicilian Greyhound, but was only recognized as a breed in 1939. Like many ancient hounds, the Cirneco dell'Etna has a temperament that can prove difficult in an urban environment. It needs plenty of exercise, and is not an easy breed to train, but it is capable of great devotion to one person.

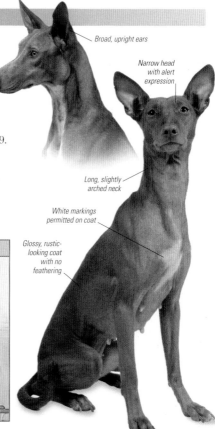

Broad, upright ears

Narrow head with alert expression

Long, slightly arched neck

White markings permitted on coat

Glossy, rustic-looking coat with no feathering

THE EGYPTIAN CONNECTION

The Cirneco dell'Etna is a classic representation of the Egyptian prick-eared running dogs. The breed bears a striking resemblance to Anubis (*below*), the Egyptian god of the dead, who is represented as a jackal in this wall painting from the Valley of the Queens in Thebes, Egypt. The painting dates back to around 2500 BC.

PODENCO CANARIO

SIZE 16–22kg (35–49lb), 53–64cm (21–25in)
GROOMING Minimal
TRAINING Time-consuming
COLOURS All colours

The ancestors of this breed were brought to the Canary Islands from the Iberian mainland some 400 years ago, and were themselves descended from Mediterranean hounds. The Podenco Canario, or Canary Islands Hound, is probably related to the Ibizan Hound, and hunts by hearing and scent as well as sight. In the demanding environment of these volcanic islands, the breed developed into an adaptable hunting dog that will both point and retrieve, and it is still used in packs for hunting rabbits. Podenco Canarios do not suit a sedate or city life: they need exercise and are not very easy to train.

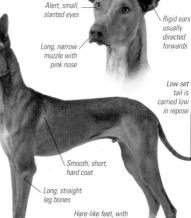

Alert, small, slanted eyes

Rigid ears usually directed forwards

Long, narrow muzzle with pink nose

Low-set tail is carried low in repose

Smooth, short, hard coat

Long, straight leg bones

Hare-like feet, with well-spaced toes

BASSET ARTÉSIEN NORMAND

SIZE 14.5–15.5kg (32–34lb), 32–36cm (13–14in)
GROOMING Minimal
TRAINING Average
COLOURS Tricolour, tan and white

This most common of all French Bassets originated, as its name says, in Artois and Normandy. The English Basset Hound has its origins in this ancient French breed. As with its other short-legged brethren, the wars of the 20th century drastically reduced its numbers, but it was saved from extinction by dedicated breeders.

A version of this breed known as the Basset d'Artois is shorter at the withers and lighter in weight. Both dogs happily work alone or in a pack. Their long backs and short legs mean that all bassets are more susceptible than average to slipped discs.

Ears set below level of eyes

Wide, black nose

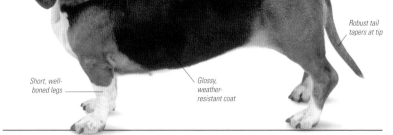

FRENCH BASSETS

A "basset" is simply a short-legged version of a taller hunting dog. It is, in essence, a dwarf. Bassets are ideal hunters in dense bush, forest, or in mountainous regions when hunting on horseback is difficult or impossible. Dwarfed hunting dogs existed in France for centuries, but it was only after the French Revolution, when hunting became the right of ordinary citizens and not just the privileged aristocracy, that the present wide variety of French bassets flourished.

Robust tail tapers at tip

Short, well-boned legs

Glossy, weather-resistant coat

BASSET BLEU DE GASCOGNE

SIZE 16–18kg (35–40lb), 34–42cm (13–17in)
GROOMING Minimal
TRAINING Easy
COLOURS Black, tan and "blue", a mix of black and white hairs

Today's companionable Basset Bleu is a re-creation by the French breeder, Alain Bourbon, of the original breed. With an excellent voice and a superb nose, it could still be a prime hunting companion, but the majority are kept as companions. This fine dog is now seen outside France, especially in the UK and US.

Symmetrical markings on face

Relatively short coat

Strong, oval feet with hard, black nails

Dwarfed bones, resulting in slow running speed

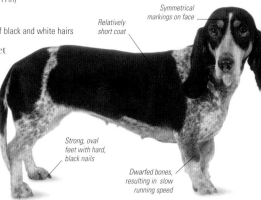

GRAND BASSET GRIFFON VENDÉEN

SIZE 18–20kg (40–44lb), 38–42cm (15–17in)
GROOMING Average
TRAINING Average
COLOURS Tricolour, tan and white, black and white, grey, white

Taller and more elegant than other bassets, this handsome dog is also more independent, perhaps even obstinate, but is not naturally aggressive. This affectionate breed's dense, insulating coat needs frequent attention to avoid excessive odour.

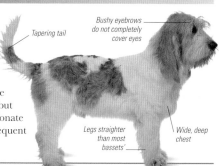

Bushy eyebrows do not completely cover eyes

Tapering tail

Legs straighter than most bassets'

Wide, deep chest

PETIT BASSET GRIFFON VENDÉEN

SIZE 14–18kg (31–40lb), 34–38cm (13–15in)
GROOMING Average
TRAINING Easy
COLOURS Tricolour, orange and white, white

Alert and a natural optimist, this smaller basset from the Vendée region of France has recently successfully colonized North America and the UK, making it the most popular of all French Bassets outside their native land. It has a sonorous voice and will willingly join in the conversation with its human family.

Large, dark eyes with engaging expression

Long hair over eyes

Large black nose

White, often the predominant colour in bi- and tricolour coats

Long ears; when dog is scenting, the ears hang to tip of nose

Deep chest; as deep as a Grand Basset's

BASSET FAUVE DE BRETAGNE

SIZE 16–18kg (35–40lb), 32–38cm (13–15in)
GROOMING Average
TRAINING Average
COLOURS Red, fawn

This cross between the Griffon Fauve de Bretagne (*see* p.172) with the Petit Basset Griffon Vendéen (*see above*) is an opinionated and robust breed that thrives on physical activity. It is rarely seen outside France, although British breeders have taken a keen interest in it. Today, it hunts singly or with a partner rather than in a pack of four, which was its traditional role.

Thick ears set below eye level

Coarse, hard coat

PETIT BLEU DE GASCOGNE

SIZE 18–22kg (40–49lb), 50–60cm (20–24in)
GROOMING Easy
TRAINING Easy
COLOURS Black, tan, and "blue", the roan mix of black and white hairs

The Petit Bleu was created by selectively breeding the Grand Bleu de Gascogne for smaller size, resulting in a breed that can be half the size of its parents but equal in determined resourcefulness. Rarer than the Grand Bleu and still restricted primarily to the southwest Gascony region of France, this dog has an excellent nose for rabbits. Petit Bleus are also bred in North America, the UK, and Germany.

Tapering tail finishing in a point

Powerfully muscled thighs

Deep chest housing large lungs

PETIT GRIFFON DE GASCOGNE

SIZE 18–19kg (40–42lb), 43–52cm (17–21in)
GROOMING Average
TRAINING Average
COLOURS Tricolour; black, tan, and "blue", the roan mix of black and white hairs

Sporting a coarse, bushy, wire-haired coat, probably acquired by breeding Petit Bleus with Wire-haired Pointing Griffons, this good-natured, uncomplaining, resourceful, and diligent hunter remains surprisingly uncommon even in its native Gascony. The coat colour is, in essence, the "national" colour of the wonderful array of hunting dogs – short- and long-limbed, small and large, smooth- and wire-coated – that were all developed in this region of western Europe, reflecting its beautiful, rustic countryside.

Well-muscled, slanting shoulders

Slightly wavy coat, never woolly

HUNTING BY SCENT

Oval feet with firm toes

ANGLO-FRANÇAIS DE PETIT VÉNERIE

SIZE 16–20kg (35–44lb), 48–56cm (19–22in)
GROOMING Easy
TRAINING Easy
COLOURS Tricolour, orange and white, red and white

This most recently developed of all modern French hounds was created at the beginning of the 20th century, by crossing the Beagle or Beagle Harrier with medium-sized, short-haired Poitevins and Porcelaines. Its first standard was written less than 30 years ago. It was once called the Petit Anglo-Français, but as it is not related to the large Anglo-Français or Français hounds (*see* p.174), its name was changed to explain that it is a scent hound that works on the "little chase".

Pointed muzzle with black nose

Medium-length, pendulous ears

Compact, well-muscled neck

Broad chest

Short, smooth coat

Straight forelegs

TRICOLOUR COAT

CHIEN D'ARTOIS

SIZE 18–24kg (40–53lb), 52–58cm (20–23in)
GROOMING Easy
TRAINING Average/time-consuming
COLOURS Tricolour

One of the oldest of French scent hounds, this breed is also known as the Briquet, perhaps a modification of *braquet*, meaning a small braque or small hound. The breed's relatively modest size (and thus smaller appetite) may be one reason it survived the turmoil following the French Revolution. Crossbreeding with British gundogs in the 18th century endangered the type, but it has since been patiently re-established.

HUNTING HOUND

Dogs similar to the Chien d'Artois are mentioned in descriptions of hunting scenes of French kings from the 1400s. In this illustration of hunting dogs bringing down a leopard, from a French 14th century hunting book by Gaston Phébus de Foix, the dog shown bottom-left shares marked similarities with the Chien d'Artois.

Long, broad, flat ears set level with eyes

Strong, lean feet with long toes

BEAGLE

SIZE 8–14kg (18–31lb), 33–40cm (13–16in)
GROOMING Minimal
TRAINING Average
COLOURS Lemon and white, orange and white, red and white, tricolour

This popular breed varies in appearance from country to country, with smaller dogs having a separate class in North America, while the English Beagle tends to be larger. The temperament, however, remains the same everywhere, and a Beagle makes an outgoing, steady, and affectionate addition to any family.

For centuries, Beagles have been hunters' companions, with small dogs sometimes carried in saddlebags, and they still fulfil this hunting role. Probably descended from the much larger Harrier (*see* p.177) and ancient English breeds of hounds, centuries of selection for following rabbits and birds, working alone or in packs, has left them with a thirst for activity, a tolerance of other dogs, and an urge to chase small animals. They also use their curiously harmonious voice readily.

BUSY BEAGLES

The Beagle's non-intimidating appearance is much valued by authorities such as the Australian Quarantine and Inspection Service and the US Department of Agriculture (*below*), both of which use them at airports for detecting illegal imports. Sadly, they have also long been medical investigators' favoured laboratory canine.

Fine-textured ears hanging in graceful folds

Smooth coat, can also be wiry

Straight forelegs

Beagle mission
When allowed to investigate the natural world, Beagle pups thrive. Most individuals will sensibly limit their exercise to minutes at a time, however.

PERUVIAN HAIRLESS

SIZE Small: 4–8kg (9–18lb), 25–40cm (10–16in)
Medium: 8–12kg (18–26lb), 40–50cm (16–20in)
Large: 12–25kg (26–55lb), 50–70cm (20–28in)
GROOMING Easy
TRAINING Average
COLOURS Range of solid colours

This gentle, inquisitive, and agile dog
is bred in three sizes, but is rarely seen
in Peru or elsewhere. The two hairless
breeds from Peru, the Peruvian or
Inca Hairless and the Peruvian Inca
Orchid, can be confused because both
may be called Perro sin pelo del Perú.
Both breeds suffer from missing
premolar teeth, and their skin needs
protection from sun and cold.

Chest of broad width

CHARCOAL COAT

TAWNY COAT

PERUVIAN INCA ORCHID

SIZE 12–23kg (27–51lb), 50–65cm (20–26in)
GROOMING Easy
TRAINING Average
COLOURS Spotted skin

Hair on top of head

Delicate white or pink skin

Wrinkled lips

Hairlessness is a genetic accident,
perpetuated through careful breeding.
Dogs similar to the Peruvian Inca Orchid,
living in the homes of Inca nobility, were
described by the first Spanish explorers
to enter the Inca empire in the 1500s.
Almost extinct by the early
20th century, the breed was rescued
from oblivion by US breeders.

STANDARD MEXICAN HAIRLESS

SIZE 9–13.5kg (20–30lb), 41–57cm (16–22in)
GROOMING Easy
TRAINING Average
COLOURS Range of colours from black to golden,
usually solid

Hairless dogs were known in Mexico
before the Spanish Conquest, and valued
for the warmth they provided; it was even
claimed that contact with them would
produce healing effects. The Mexican
Hairless, also called the Xoloitzcuintli
or Tepeizeuintli, is bred in three sizes,
the Standard and the smaller Miniature
and Toy versions (*see* p.85). The Standard
resembles a classic sight hound in build,
with a long neck and limbs. An alert dog,
it has an affectionate personality, but can be
stubborn, with a tendency to be suspicious

of strangers. As with all
hairless breeds, the skin needs
moisturizing and protection
against cold and sun.

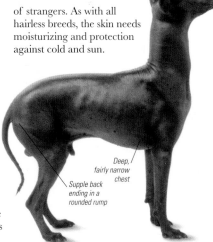

Deep, fairly narrow chest

Supple back ending in a rounded rump

DREVER

SIZE 14.5–15.5kg (32–34lb), 30–38cm (12–15in)
GROOMING Easy
TRAINING Easy
COLOURS Fawn and white, black and white, tricolour

This hunting dog, bred from the now-rare Westphalian Dachsbracke and local Swedish hounds, is also called the Swedish Dachsbracke. The name Drever means "driver", and that is just what this superb tracker does. The Drever's size, shorter than the Beagle but larger than a Dachshund, makes it particularly suited to hunting big game, moving slowly but with great tenacity to drive a specific quarry towards the hunters. Headstrong and tenacious, the breed's immense persistence and apparent imperviousness to cold means these dogs will often want to hunt for far longer than their human partners. Drevers are popular hunting dogs in Sweden, but out of the hunting season they make relaxed companions.

Alert eyes have thin, close-fitting eyelids

Tight upper lip fitting firmly over lower jaw

Tail carried with a downward curve

Thick, close-fitting coat lying flat over body

Short forelegs are vertical and parallel

DUNKER

SIZE 16–22.5kg (35–50lb), 47–57cm (19–22in)
GROOMING Easy
TRAINING Average
COLOURS Black or blue marbled with fawn, with white markings

In Norway this is the most popular of the indigenous hounds, although it is little-known elsewhere. Also called the Norwegian Hound, it was created for hunting hares by the breeder Wilhelm Dunker in the mid-19th century, by crossing the Russian Harlequin Hound with reliable Norwegian scent hounds. It is a muscular dog with a dense, insulating coat, built for endurance rather than speed.

A friendly, relaxed personality completes a breed that makes an engaging companion for anyone who can provide sufficient activity. Occasional cases of hip dysplasia are a potential problem.

Round-tipped, silky ears

Marbled saddle marking on coat

Moderately long muzzle

Sloping, well-muscled shoulders

SCHILLERSTÖVARE

SIZE 18–24kg (40–53lb),
49–61cm (19–24in)
GROOMING Easy
TRAINING Easy
COLOURS Black and tan

This breed, also called the
Schiller Hound, was created
in the 19th century by
Swedish farmer Per Schiller,
who crossed local hounds with
imported German hounds to
produce a fleet-footed tracker
of hares and foxes. Like the
Smålandsstövare, it is a typical
Swedish hunting dog, which
will track but not attack, instead
baying until the hunter arrives.
Scandinavian hunters often call
off their dogs at this point; the
hunt is more important than
the kill. A biddable and engaging
breed, all the Schillerstövare asks
of its owner is endless activity.

Characteristic black saddle

Muscular thighs covered by smooth topcoat

Practical partner
Most Schillerstövares are dual-purpose
dogs in their homeland, acting as both
family companions and hunting dogs.

SMÅLANDSSTÖVARE

SIZE 15–18kg (33–40lb), 46–54cm (18–21in)
GROOMING Easy
TRAINING Easy
COLOURS Black and tan

The Smålandsstövare, or Småland
Hound, is most often found as a hunter's
companion in this southern province of
Sweden, tracking hares and foxes through
the dense forests. The
historical evidence
suggests that the

breed has fulfilled this role since the
Middle Ages, but concerted selective
breeding was not carried out until the
19th century, and breed recognition came
only in 1921. It is likely that the naturally
short tail was fixed as a trait by an early
breeder, Baron von Essen. Although this
breed is an amenable character and makes
a steady companion, it is rarely seen
outside its home country.

High-set ears, with rounded tips, hanging flat

Muzzle, neither heavy nor pointed

Unusually short tail

Smooth, thick, heavy, glossy topcoat

Muscular, thickly boned legs

Schillerstövare
These handsome, muscular Schillerstövaren are perfect examples of the refined hunting hounds developed in Scandinavia in the 1800s.

ISTRIAN SMOOTH-COATED HOUND

SIZE 14–20kg (31–44lb), 44–56cm (17–22in)
GROOMING Easy
TRAINING Average
COLOURS White and orange

Long muzzle with dark nose

Broad ears hanging flat at side of head

Glossy coat with fine texture

The Istrian peninsula of Slovenia, across the Adriatic from neighbouring Italy, is the home of two white-and-orange breeds with markings that are similar to the Italian Spinone (*see* p.235). The Istrian Smooth-coated Hound is still used, singly and in pairs, to hunt foxes, hares, and especially wild boar. Its peaceful nature makes it a fine companion.

ISTRIAN ROUGH-COATED HOUND

SIZE 16–24kg (35–53lb), 46–58cm (18–23in)
GROOMING Average
TRAINING Average
COLOURS White and orange

Ears broadened at middle and hanging without folds

Hindquarters are not very prominent

Broad nose with large nostrils

Rounded forepart of lower jaw

This breed's denser coat, which provides more insulation in cold-weather hunting, was developed by crossing the Istrian Smooth-coated Hound with the Basset Griffon Vendéen (*see* p.109). Its attractive, striking appearance has made it a hit with Slovenian families and it is more often seen as an affectionate companion than as a tireless scent trailer.

SERBIAN HOUND

SIZE 19.5–25kg (43–55lb), 43–53cm (17–21in)
GROOMING Easy
TRAINING Average
COLOURS Tan and black

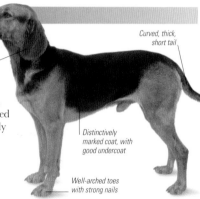

Curved, thick, short tail

Round, pendulous ears

Distinctively marked coat, with good undercoat

Well-arched toes with strong nails

One of the oldest and most common of the hounds from Serbia and Montenegro, until 1996 the Serbian Hound was recognized as the Balkan Hound. Remaining relatively unchanged for at least 250 years, it is a strong scent tracker given to using its high-pitched voice when out working. While its build is rugged and muscular, it has a calm dignity.

SERBIAN TRICOLOURED HOUND

SIZE 19.5–25kg (43–55lb), 46–56cm (18–22in)
GROOMING Easy
TRAINING Average
COLOURS Tricolour

Formerly the Yugoslavian Tricoloured Hound, this classic scent follower is seldom seen outside southern Serbia, where it originates. With a self-cleaning, water-repellent coat, a benign, tranquil disposition at home, and the instincts of a worker, this hound faces an uncertain future unless numbers increase soon.

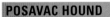

White hair on solid, straight limbs

SERBIAN MOUNTAIN HOUND

SIZE 19.5–25kg (43–55lb), 46–56cm (18–22in)
GROOMING Easy
TRAINING Average
COLOURS Black and tan

From southern Serbia's Planina region, this breed was known as the Yugoslavian Mountain Hound until 1996. Also called the Montenegrin Mountain Hound, this tireless hunter remains rare even in its homeland. Its gentle and affectionate personality makes this breed very similar to its slightly smaller Greek cousin, the Hellenic Hound (*see* p.120).

Thick top coat with insulating undercoat

Long, tapering tail

Strong, fairly short legs

POSAVAC HOUND

SIZE 16–20kg (35–44lb), 43–59cm (17–23in)
GROOMING Easy
TRAINING Average
COLOURS Red, fawn, yellow and white

This breed is most frequently seen on the plains above the Sava River on the Croatia–Bosnia border. A tenacious scent follower, it is used primarily to track small game such as hares. It is typical of all Balkan hounds in being both a tireless worker and a relaxed and gentle household companion. Rarely seen outside its own locality, it took part in Croatia's first canine Search and Rescue training camp held in 2005.

Round-tipped ears hanging flat

White markings mostly confined to underparts

Tough, short, dense coat

Narrow, compact feet

Muscular forelegs

BOSNIAN ROUGH-COATED HOUND

SIZE 16–24kg (35–53lb), 46–55cm (18–22in)
GROOMING Average
TRAINING Average
COLOURS Variety of colours

The harsh climate of mountainous Bosnia called for a hunting dog with a heavily insulated coat. This breed's wiry, rough hair offers both insulation and added protection from hostile elements. Like all Balkan hounds, the Bosnian is an excellent family dog, relaxed with children and family and a keen participator in family activities. In addition, it makes an excellent watchdog.

Long, hard, wiry topcoat

Cat-like feet with hard pads

HELLENIC HOUND

SIZE 17–20kg (37–44lb), 45–55cm (18–22in)
GROOMING Easy
TRAINING Average
COLOURS Black and tan

Coarse-textured, short, dense coat

High-set ears of medium length

The first Greek breed ever recognized outside its homeland (in 1996), the Hellenic Hound is a swift and powerful scent-trailing hunter, ideally suited for working in rocky terrain. Rarely seen outside Greece or Skopje Macedonia, these good-natured, independent dogs willingly use their resonant, harmonious voice when working, but equally will speak up when idle.

Round, compact feet with large, tough pads

SLOVAKIAN HOUND

SIZE 15–20kg (33–44lb), 40–50cm (16–20cm)
GROOMING Easy
TRAINING Average
COLOURS Black and tan

This typical scent hound is locally called the Slovensky Kopov, but is also referred to as the Black Forest Hound. Affectionate but sometimes strong-willed, this breed was developed by Czech and Slovak breeders after World War II from local black-and-tan hounds that had survived the conflict. It is increasingly popular as a companion dog in Slovakia.

Round, medium-long ears

Short, well-muscled neck

Short, dense, glossy coat

Oval paws with well-arched toes

Straight, lean forelegs, with well-muscled shoulders

ALPINE DACHSBRACKE

SIZE 15–18kg (33–40lb), 34–42cm (13–17in)
GROOMING Easy
TRAINING Average
COLOURS Tricolour

Just as the French developed bassets as slower dwarfed hounds, the Austrians and Germans created dachsbrackes, in this instance by crossing local Austrian hounds with Smooth-haired Standard Dachshunds. The Alpine's primary responsibility is to follow the cold-trail of injured animals, as local hunting tradition demands that wounded deer are tracked and killed. The breed is rarely kept as a companion.

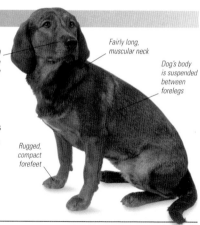

Muzzle and nose are large for head size

Fairly long, muscular neck

Dog's body is suspended between forelegs

Rugged, compact forefeet

STYRIAN ROUGH-HAIRED MOUNTAIN HOUND

SIZE 15–18kg (33–40lb), 44–58cm (17–23in)
GROOMING Easy
TRAINING Average
COLOURS Red, wheaten

Created by crossing local Austrian hounds with Istrian Rough-coated Hounds from neighbouring Slovenia, this well-insulated scent trailer is used primarily for wild-boar hunting in the southern regions of Austria. While some are kept as companions, the vast majority of these robust dogs are kept for their superb silent or vocal trailing abilities.

Ears set below eyes

Dense whiskers covering lips

Powerful thigh muscles

Small feet with arched toes

DEUTSCHE BRACKE

SIZE 15–23kg (33–51lb), 41–53cm (16–21in)
GROOMING Easy
TRAINING Average
COLOURS Tricolour or red with white markings

The only indigenous scent hound officially recognized in Germany. This melodious-voiced tracker, expert at both hot- and cold-trailing, is an ancient breed and the probable progenitor of the nimble, shorter-legged Westphalian Dachsbracke. An all-round hunter, the Deutsche Bracke is popular with hunters and gamekeepers in Sauerland or Westphalia, but is otherwise rare.

SCHWYZER NIEDERLAUFHUND

SIZE 9–14.5kg (20–32lb), 30–38cm (12–15in)
GROOMING Easy
TRAINING Average
COLOURS Orange and white, yellow and white

This dog displays particularly pleasing colours, with excellent proportions for a dwarfed breed. The ears are dramatic and, as with all basset-type dogs, tend to drag through food bowls indoors and muddy trails outdoors.

THE LAUFHUND AND NIEDERLAUFHUND

Laufhunds are Swiss walking dogs which historically accompanied hunters on foot. Short-legged Niederlaufhunds are even slower dogs, created through breeding the four indigenous laufhunds with either imported dachsbrackes or with dwarf laufhund puppies. The Berner, Schwyzer, and Luzerner Laufhunds all have recognized, short-legged relatives. Now extremely rare, niederlaufhunds are seldom seen outside their native country.

Tail carried hanging down

Friendly, alert facial expression

Forelimbs sometimes only moderately shorter than a laufhund's

BERNER NIEDERLAUFHUND

SIZE 9–14.5kg (20–32lb), 30–38cm (12–15in)
GROOMING Easy/average
TRAINING Average
COLOURS Tricolour

While the smooth-coated variety of Berner Niederlaufhund is more common, this dog also occurs in a rough or wiry coat. It is an excellent tracker of small game, and is not shy in using its surprisingly melodic voice, either when working or when bored and alone.

Pendulous ears, similar to a Bloodhound's

Long bones of forelegs are thickened and shortened

ROUGH-COATED VARIETY

LUZERNER NIEDERLAUFHUND

SIZE 9–14.5kg (20–32lb), 30–38cm (12–15in)
GROOMING Easy
TRAINING Average
COLOURS Tricolour, roan

Like its closest relatives, the Luzerner Niederlaufhund's existence is a credit to the dedicated breeders who developed standards recognized by the Swiss Kennel Club over 70 years ago. Given the chance, most individuals will demonstrate their natural small-game hunting abilities.

Muzzle same length as domed skull

Legs much longer than those of other niederlaufhunds

Compact, cat-like feet

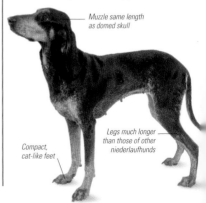

BERNER LAUFHUND

SIZE 15–20kg (33–44lb), 46–58cm (18–23in)
GROOMING Easy
TRAINING Average
COLOURS Tricolour

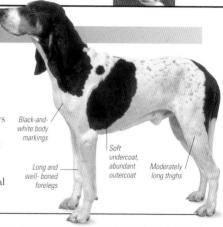

A good working dog, ancestors of this breed have existed in the mountain valleys around Berne for at least 900 years. This dog is benign within the family yet robust when tracking roe deer or smaller game. Closely resembling the Ariège Pointer, its dense undercoat provides excellent thermal protection for cold weather conditions.

Black-and-white body markings

Long and well-boned forelegs

Soft undercoat, abundant outercoat

Moderately long thighs

LUZERNER LAUFHUND

SIZE 15–20kg (33–44lb), 46–58cm (18–23in)
GROOMING Easy
TRAINING Average
COLOURS Tricolour, roan

unknown. The laufhund's relatively small size reduces the risk of heat loss when working in such a challenging climate.

The Luzerner's coat is in part similar to the hunting dogs from distant Gascony in southwest France. However, the exact origins of this dog from Switzerland's Lucerne region are

Heavy ticking in coat, offset against black and tan areas

Tapering tail never held erect

Round feet, with hard, tough pads

SCHWYZER LAUFHUND

SIZE 15–20kg (33–44lb), 46–58cm (18–23in)
GROOMING Easy
TRAINING Average
COLOURS Orange and white, yellow and white

Developed near the Swiss-French border, the Schwyzer shares its coat colour with the now-extinct Français Blanc et Orange. Primarily a hunting companion and not easy to train, it does, however, get on well with children and other dogs.

Head almost flat in profile

Rib cage only moderately sprung

JURA LAUFHUND

SIZE 15–20kg (33–44lb), 46–58cm (18–23in)
GROOMING Easy
TRAINING Average
COLOURS Fawn with a black "blanket"

From the Jura mountains of Switzerland, along with the Jura Niederlaufhund this is the rarest of all laufhunds. Breeders are attempting to increase numbers, but the equable and robust Jura remains unknown outside Switzerland and neighbouring France.

Broad, round skull

Round feet with hard pads

BORDER COLLIE

SIZE 14–22kg (31–49lb), 46–54cm (18–21in),
also larger and smaller for working dogs
GROOMING Average/time-consuming
TRAINING Easy
COLOURS Black and white, tricolour, sable, blue merle,
black, brown, red

Wide-set eyes

Well-developed nostrils

Heavy mane

This breed is consistently top dog in the "canine intelligence" stakes. In only three decades the hyper-alert and ever-vigilant Border Collie has evolved from being the eager, single-minded assistant of Welsh, Scottish, and English shepherds to the world's most successful ever agility and obedience champion. It excels in these activities so greatly that there are some events in which Border Collies compete only with each other while all other breeds compete together at a lower standard.

This is a supremely trainable working dog, bred for ability, not size or colour, and it forms a very close bond with its owner. However, this is not a breed for the novice owner. Their quick minds, deep-seated herding instinct, and need to release their high levels of energy make many of them uncomfortable in family environments, where they are highly prone to behaviour problems and obsessive or compulsive activities. Show lines are bred for show ring conformation and reduced energy levels.

TRICOLOURED

Excess weight is rarely a problem, but a range of inherited eye disorders afflict certain lines. Hip dysplasia can also be a concern. Border Collies are often reserved, even wary with strangers. In the absence of sheep, they will chase cars, bicyclists, joggers, even shadows. Those with rough coats need daily grooming, and even smooth-coated individuals shed profusely.

Fairly broad skull

Slightly blunt, tapering muzzle

Dense, harsh, but shiny topcoat

White coloration should never predominate

LONG-HAIRED BLACK-AND-WHITE

STAR PERFORMERS

Border Collies are among the most adept and trainable search and rescue dogs in the world. In mountainous areas or tricky terrain, trained dogs such as this short-haired Border Collie save lives every year, working with their handlers to locate missing people. When they're not working, it's a pleasure to watch these dogs participating in Flyball, excelling at obedience, or winning agility trials.

Farmer's friend
This dog is taking part in sheepdog trials. In many regions of countryside, sheep farming is impossible to undertake without the practical support of trained Border Collies.

SCHNAUZER

SIZE 14.5–15.5kg (32–34lb), 45–50cm (18–20in)
GROOMING Time-consuming
TRAINING Average
COLOURS Salt and pepper , black

Boasting a moustache to rival the most hirsute of walruses, it is the long facial hair that makes this breed so instantly recognizable. Schnauzers developed in the Middle Ages in southern Germany and across the borders in France and Switzerland. Possibly a cross between spitz-type breeds and guarding dogs, canines of this conformation are found in works by Albrecht Dürer from the early 16th century. Today,

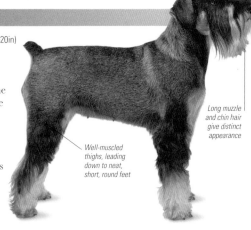

Long muzzle and chin hair give distinct appearance

Well-muscled thighs, leading down to neat, short, round feet

we recognize the Miniature (*see* pp.90–91) and the Giant (*see* p.190), but this is the original size. Once called the Wire-haired Pinscher, it is now also known as the Standard Schnauzer or Mittelschnauzer.

At this size, the breed makes an efficient guard and ratter, and it is often classed as a terrier. Its willingness to learn means it can also be trained to retrieve and makes a superb livestock dog. Like many terrier breeds, it can be aggressive towards other dogs, and like many working dogs it needs a good deal of activity; if you can cope with these traits, they make alert and reliable companions. The coat needs routine clipping every six to eight weeks.

Ears partly erect

Long, powerful head, gradually narrowing from ears to tip of nose

Broad brisket, reaching below elbows

SALT-AND-PEPPER COAT

SALT-AND-PEPPER COAT

CARDIGAN WELSH CORGI

SIZE 11–17kg (24–37lb), 27–32cm (11–13in)
GROOMING Minimal
TRAINING Time-consuming
COLOURS All colours

The Corgi has been in Wales for at least a millenium, and possibly for as long as 3,000 years. Until the 1850s, the Cardigan Welsh Corgi was the only dog known to be kept in some Welsh communities. Records dating from 1574 suggest the breed gets its name from the word *cur*, meaning to watch over, and in old Welsh, *gi* means dog.

Erect, round ears

Long body in relation to height

BLUE MERLE COAT

Eyes set wide apart

BRINDLE-AND-WHITE COAT

Smooth topcoat, harsh to the touch

This breed was originally a robust livestock guard on farms, as well as an instinctive "heeler", driving cattle by nipping at its heels; it was built low enough to the ground to avoid flailing hooves. Corgis are still given to this behaviour today, being self-willed and sometimes snappy. They make exuberant, alert, but opinionated companions for owners with a firm hand.

PEMBROKE WELSH CORGI

SIZE 11–17kg (24–37lb), 27–32cm (11–13in)
GROOMING Minimal
TRAINING Time-consuming
COLOURS All colours

This sturdy breed resembles the Swedish Vallhund (*see* p.133), and the two may be related. Whether the Vikings took breeding stock home with them or brought the lines to Britain is a matter of speculation. What is certain, however, is that these little dogs have been herding cattle, ratting, and guarding farmyards in Wales since at least AD 920.

Although this efficient yet stubborn breed is still worked today, most Pembrokes are kept solely as companions. Breeders have been fairly successful in reducing the inclination of this breed to nip.

RED-AND-WHITE COAT

Trim, compact muzzle

Lack of tail an inherited trait

Body shorter than that of a Cardigan

AUSTRALIAN KELPIE

Weather-resistant double coat

Deep, broad chest has space for lung expansion

SIZE 11–20.5kg (25–45lb), 43–51cm (17–20in)
GROOMING Minimal
TRAINING Average
COLOURS Blue, fawn, red, brown, black, black and tan

Known since 1870, this is Australia's most popular working breed – over 100,000 of these livestock dogs exist there. The breed was created after collies from the north of England were taken to Australia in the 19th century. Mating then took place with a black-and-tan bitch, Kelpie, the name of the benign water spirit in Robert Louis Stevenson's *Kidnapped*.

In spite of very good records of the breed's origins, legends persist that it carries Dingo blood, perhaps because of its ability to work in the sun from dawn to dusk. Often called a "workaholic", this is a breed of seemingly inexhaustible energy and enthusiasm that disregards extremes of both heat and cold, and is not at all suited to a quiet life. Working Kelpies are slightly smaller than their show or "bench" relatives, who are bred more for colour and size than for gathering mobs of sheep. All Kelpies delight in herding everything from cattle to farmyard poultry; if deprived of these, they may round up humans and pets to stave off boredom. Unique among herders, Kelpies will run over the backs of sheep to reach the head of the flock.

Outback management
Kelpies are driven herders. Even though the sheep are contained, this dog's desire to control remains unabated as it marshals the flock.

AUSTRALIAN CATTLE DOG

SIZE 16–20.5kg (35–45lb), 43–51cm (17–20in)
GROOMING Minimal
TRAINING Average
COLOURS Red, blue, blue and tan, blue and black

Australia's climate places strong demands on a working dog, and many of the dogs taken from Britain in the 19th century simply could not endure the heat. Pioneer Thomas Smith Hall from Queensland set out to create a new breed, also called the Australian Heeler, Queensland Heeler, Blue Heeler, or simply Hall's Heeler. The Blue Merle Smooth Highland Collie,

THE ANCIENT AUSSIE

This is a long-lived breed. For trivia collectors, the oldest dog ever, Bluey, who reached 29 years and 5 months of age, was a working Australian Cattle Dog who lived in Victoria, Australia. Bluey retired from active work when he reached 20. This is an extraordinary achievement. Most Australian Cattle Dogs work until approximately 10 years and live until between 11 and 14 years of age.

Life in the old dog
As tough and durable as the land that formed it, many acclaim the Australian Cattle Dog as the ultimate worker.

White hair on puppies, due to Dalmatian blood in ancestry

PUPPIES

Dalmatian, and possibly Bull Terrier were the British breeds used, and the indigenous Dingo was added to these. The result is an alert dog with tremendous stamina for driving stock long distances in harsh, hot conditions. Kelpies and Border Collies have now taken over these responsibilities. Most Australian Cattle Dogs are exclusively companions, and good breeders select for temperament, breeding out the natural tendency to bite. These dogs have a huge reserve of energy demanding copious exercise, and a natural wariness of strangers, including children.

Broad, erect ears

Harsh, dense outercoat

Strong, thick-set neck

Deep, muscular chest

BLUE AND TAN

MUDI

SIZE 8–13kg (18–29lb), 36–51cm (14–20in)
GROOMING Average
TRAINING Average
COLOURS All colours

Coat length about 5cm (2in) on body

Hair on legs shorter than on body

Small, round feet

This is perhaps the least known of the Hungarian breeds, overshadowed by the Puli and Komondor. It does not seem to be the result of planned breeding, and was only recognized as separate from the Puli and the Pumi in the 1930s. The Mudi has been used as a herder, farm guard dog, and hunting companion, and is an inquisitive, adaptable breed. It makes the transition to family life far better than many working breeds, proving to be a tractable and playful, if sometimes vocal, companion. Given these qualities, its rarity is a mystery to the dedicated breeders who have saved it, but this may be due to nothing more than its hazy origins and rustic looks. It is effectively the same breed as the neighbouring Croatian Sheepdog.

PUMI

SIZE 10–15kg (22–33lb), 33–48cm (13–19in)
GROOMING Average
TRAINING Average
COLOURS Black, shades of grey, brown, white

This distinctive breed is one of Hungary's many livestock dogs, known since at least 1815 although not officially recognized until the 1920s. Seldom seen outside its homeland, it was created by crossing the Puli, which has a corded coat, with softer-coated German spitzes. The resulting medium-length coat is curly, but does not mat easily. In personality,

High, wide-set, erect ears curl down at tips

Long, tapering muzzle

WHITE COAT

Slightly oblique, dark eyes have close-fitting lids

Deep chest with somewhat flat ribs

Compact hind feet, set back from body

BLACK COAT

this is a typically lively and persistent herding breed, which needs plenty of activity to keep it occupied. As a working dog it serves many functions, such as exterminating vermin, herding cattle, and guarding the farm. Never afraid to use its voice, the Pumi makes a fine watchdog. It has become popular as a companion dog.

CROATIAN SHEEPDOG

SIZE 13–16kg (29–35lb), 40–50cm (16–20in)
GROOMING Average
TRAINING Time-consuming
COLOURS Black, with or without white markings

Lean muzzle on relatively long head

Muscular, broad rump slopes slightly

Small, elongated feet with close-set toes

Records suggest that dogs of this type, with a black, curly coat, have been in Croatia since as early as 1374. They are believed to be descended from dogs brought to the region from elsewhere in the Balkans, or from Greece or Turkey, sometime in the 7th century. No planned breeding appears to have taken place until the 1930s.

Also called the Hrvatski Ovcar, this breed is slightly larger, and more common in the Croatian countryside, than the almost identical Hungarian Mudi. An instinctive herder, unless socialized early it may have trouble adapting to any lifestyle other than that of a working dog. This "no-nonsense" breed tends to be wary of strangers, and can be troublesome with other dogs around.

ICELANDIC SHEEPDOG

SIZE 9–14kg (20–31lb), 31–41cm (12–16in)
GROOMING Average
TRAINING Easy
COLOURS Cream, fawn, chestnut, black; all with white

Spitz-type dogs were brought to Iceland by Viking settlers at the end of the 9th century, and from those dogs evolved this tough, agile, enthusiastic, and expert herder, also known as the Icelandic Dog, Islandsk Farehond, and Friaar Dog.

Its history is troubled. In the late 19th century, canine distemper reduced numbers drastically. Then, before effective tapeworm treatments were developed, the breed was banned from Iceland's capital city of Reykjavik following the spread of the *Echinococcus* parasite in humans – the result of dogs consuming contaminated sheep carcasses. The ban still survives today. No longer on the brink of extinction, the Icelandic Sheepdog makes a fine guard dog and companion. It exists mainly in Scandinavia and northern Europe.

Alert guardians
The legacy of the Icelandic Sheepdog as herd protector is evident today in its role as watchdog. These dogs won't hesitate to bark an alarm when their territory is approached.

POLISH LOWLAND SHEEPDOG

SIZE 14–16kg (31–35lb), 41–51cm (16–20in)
GROOMING Time-consuming
TRAINING Average
COLOURS All colours

This muscular, high maintenance, water-loving sheepdog, also called the Polski Owczarek Nizinny, has been known in Poland since the Middle Ages. It is probably a descendant of sheepdogs with corded coats from the Hungarian plains and small, long-coated mountain herders. Legend has it that in the 16th century it provided the foundation stock for the Bearded Collie in Scotland.

Despite its long history, the breed was almost extinct by the end of World War II. It is now popular in Poland and beyond, especially where Poles have migrated and settled. A curious feature is that some are virtually tailless while others have abundant tails. This sheepdog makes not only an excellent herding dog but also a lively companion for people who can provide enough activity to keep it mentally and physically occupied.

LONG LINEAGE

Because of the Polish Lowland Sheepdog's long heritage, it is seen by some as being an important link between shaggy herding dogs, such as the Bearded Collie, and the ancient corded breeds that were brought into Europe from Asia over 1,000 years ago.

BEARDED COLLIE

— Medium-size head

Long, dense, shaggy coat covering body

Legs covered with harsh hair

GREY-AND-WHITE COAT

Copious hair on forehead, cheeks, and chin

Deep chest

PUPPY

DANISH/SWEDISH FARM DOG

SIZE 11.5–13.5kg (25–30lb), 30–40cm (12–16in)
GROOMING Minimal
TRAINING Average
COLOURS Shades of red or brown with white, black with white, tricolour

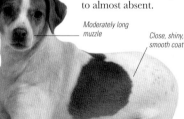

Lopped ears set to sides of head

Moderately long muzzle

Close, shiny, smooth coat

This charming breed makes a playful family dog with a thirst for activity. It is a remnant of the many all-purpose farm dogs once found herding and ratting all over Europe. Also known as the Dansk/Svensk Gaardhund and Danish Chicken Dog, it accompanied the Danes when they occupied southern Sweden, hence its dual nationality. The breed was almost forgotten until it was revived by breeders in the late 20th century, and is still rarely seen. Curiously, its tail varies naturally from full-length to almost absent.

SWEDISH VALLHUND

SIZE 14–16kg (31–35lb), 41–51cm (16–20in)
GROOMING Average
TRAINING Average
COLOURS All colours

Muzzle separated from skull by distinct stop

Long neck with muscular nape

Vallhund means "herding dog", and this determined, energetic breed resembles the Welsh Corgis (*see* p.127) in more than just its looks. It has the tenacity, toughness, and courage of all heeler breeds, and also the potential to nip at the ankles of anything that passes. The Vallhund, Vastgötaspets, or Swedish Cattle Dog is classed as an indigenous breed in Sweden. It is possible that it is descended from the Corgis, arriving in Scandinavia with Vikings returning from Pembrokeshire settlements, and ultimately, the ancestors of both breeds are probably the short-legged bassets of central Europe. The breed was close to extinction after World War II, but was saved by the efforts of two breeders, Björn von Rosen and Karl-Gustaf Zettersten. It is a breed that remains fairly rare, but its popularity is growing steadily.

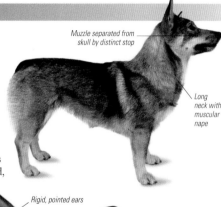

Rigid, pointed ears

Hard, medium-length coat with dense, soft undercoat

Powerful legs

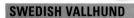

Short, oval feet with round pads

SHAR PEI

SIZE 16–20kg (35–44lb), 46–51cm (18–20in)
GROOMING Time-consuming
TRAINING Time-consuming
COLOURS All colours

Round tail set high on back

Strong, short neck with loose skin

Over-sized, prickly coat; hair stands on end

MATURE COAT

With a Chinese breed standard that calls for a melon-shaped head with a grandmotherly face, clam-shell ears, and a butterfly nose, supported on a water-buffalo neck and a body with horses' buttocks on dragons' legs, it is no surprise that the Shar Pei, or "sand skin", looks unique. In spite of a frowning appearance, they are fairly amenable, although they tend to be aggressive towards other dogs, traits reflecting a mixed past as herding, hunting, and fighting dogs. Skin and eye problems persist, and the harsh coat, needing routine shampoos, can provoke allergic reactions in humans.

Large head in relation to body size

Deep, broad chest

Compact feet

JUVENILE COAT

Ear tips point towards eyes

Abundant folds of loose skin

Strong, muscular hindquarters

PUPPY

EXTRAORDINARY FACIAL FOLDS

In the 1980s, at the height of the Shar Pei's meteoric rise to canine popularity, the wrinkliest dogs were the most coveted. Exaggerated facial folds were the result of selective breeding. Although they added character, these folds acted like sandpaper, damaging the eyes in particular – a condition known as entropion. Selective breeding, again, has since reduced the extremity of this look.

CANAAN DOG

SIZE 16–25kg (35–55lb), 48–61cm (19–24in)
GROOMING Minimal
TRAINING Time-consuming
COLOURS White, sandy, brown, black, brown or black with white

Carvings and burials show that dogs have been in ancient Canaan, a region which today encompasses Israel, for 2,000 years. Developed from local dogs in the 1930s by Dr Rudolphina

Menzel, a dog trainer and breeder from Austria, these are steady, confident dogs, loyal to their family, and aloof with others. The Canaan Dog is used for herding and tracking, but is primarily a companion. It requires patience to train fully.

Straight, harsh coat

Bushy tail curls over back when dog is alert

AUSTRIAN PINSCHER

SIZE 12–18kg (26–40lb), 36–51cm (14–20in)
GROOMING Minimal
TRAINING Time-consuming
COLOURS Variety of colours

Short but very powerful muzzle

Tail curls over back

Like other Pinschers or "biters", this is an old farm breed, used for vermin control and guard duties. It has existed in countries of the old Austrian Empire since the late 18th century, but now is rarely seen outside Austria, where it is called the Österreichischer Kurzhaariger Pinscher. It is a good guard dog, with a willingness to bark, but a tendency to bite and to be aggressive towards other dogs make the transition to the role of companion difficult.

Short, hard topcoat with equally short, dense undercoat

Compact feet with well-arched toes

KROMFOHRLÄNDER

SIZE 9–16kg (20–35lb), 38–46cm (15–18in)
GROOMING Minimal
TRAINING Easy
COLOURS Shades of brown, always with white

Long, smooth, straight coat

Wedge-shaped head

Deep chest

SMOOTH-HAIRED VARIETY

Medium-sized, dark nose

Short, rough, wiry coat, with dense undercoat

Strong hind legs

WIRE-HAIRED VARIETY

This engaging breed owes its existence to a stray in the district of krumme Furche, or krom Fohr, in northwestern Germany, given to Ilse Schliefenbaum in 1945 by passing American soldiers. Crosses with a Wire-haired Fox Terrier bitch produced robust, distinctive puppies, and the breed was recognized in 1955. They are devoted and biddable companions, easy-going with children and other dogs, and with no strong urge to chase wildlife. Despite these traits they remain rare, with small breeding populations in Germany and Finland.

IRISH TERRIER

SIZE 11.5–12kg (25–26lb), 46–48cm (18–19in)
GROOMING Average/time-consuming
TRAINING Average
COLOURS Yellow, wheaten, red, sometimes with small white markings

Also called Irish Red Terriers, but aptly nicknamed "Daredevils" by their fans, Irish Terriers are reckless, animated dogs that both work hard and play hard. Bred around Cork in the far south of Ireland as a superb vermin hunter and water dog, they have an elegant, racy build and a striding gait that covers plenty of ground. They make entertaining and loyal family companions, but are inclined to take the mere presence of another dog as a challenge. Thorough training is vital, as exercising on a lead can be the best way to tire them out.

Small, neat beard requires clipping

Deep, muscular chest

Straight legs with plenty of bone and muscle

Ears have high folds and drop to cheeks

Wiry topcoat with soft undercoat

Dense, crisp hair on legs

KERRY BLUE TERRIER

SIZE 15–17kg (33–37lb), 46–48cm (18–19in)
GROOMING Time-consuming
TRAINING Average
COLOURS Blue

The national dog of Ireland, the Kerry Blue, or Irish Blue, has been used for ratting and hunting in the far southwest of Ireland since the 18th century; it was recognized in 1922. Today it is still used in hunting, and makes a fine guard dog, but is more often found as an energetic household companion. Exercise and grooming demands of this breed are high. The non-shedding,

Long, lean head on a strong neck

Profuse beard covering powerful jaws

curly coat mats, especially the luxuriant beard, and also needs regular clipping. Born black, their coat lightens at between nine months and two years.

Well groomed
The Kerry Blue's body hair is trimmed shorter than hair on the legs, while the beard is left long.

SOFT-COATED WHEATEN TERRIER

SIZE 16–20.5kg (35–45lb), 46–48cm (18–19in)
GROOMING Time-consuming
TRAINING Average
COLOURS Wheaten

A law of 1698 stated that in Ireland only the landed gentry could own a "hound, beagle, greyhound, or land spaniel". The terrier or all-purpose working dog was the peasant's lot, and into this category fell the versatile Wheaten, used for guarding, herding, droving, and hunting since at least the 18th century. It is among the most easy-going and obedient of the terrier breeds, less aggressive towards other dogs than most, although still with an inclination to chase small pets. Mildly prone to hip dysplasia, the breed is popular as a guard dog and companion today, particularly in North America. Bitches often produce litters of up to ten pups.

Small, compact feet

Distinctively coloured coat does not shed

GLEN OF IMAAL TERRIER

SIZE 15.5–22kg (34–49lb), 36cm (14in)
GROOMING Average
TRAINING Average
COLOURS Wheaten, blue, red brindle, black brindle

The looks of this rare Irish breed reflect its origins as a tough, powerful country dog, designed to hunt down and kill foxes and badgers and triumph in fights. The bone and muscle of the broad body make the Glen extraordinarily heavy for its size, and it gives the impression that it will go over or through anything that gets in its way (which largely it can). Selective breeding has modified the breed's temperament, and it now makes a friendly companion that is relaxed around people. With other dogs it is now less inclined to start fights, but it will still finish them. Think of this breed as a big dog: firm training is essential, and can produce a good guard dog. The rough topcoat should be plucked out in summer.

Rose-shaped ears hang back when relaxed

Powerful head with a tapered muzzle

BLACK BRINDLE COAT

Rough topcoat covering fine, insulating undercoat

WHEATEN COAT

STAFFORDSHIRE BULL TERRIER

SIZE 11–17kg (24–37lb), 36–41cm (14–16in)
GROOMING Easy
TRAINING Average
COLOURS All colours except liver, with or without white

Short, smooth coat

Straight, well-boned forelegs, set wide apart

To own a Staffie is to have two dogs for the price of one. Most of the time you will enjoy the company of a genial, affectionate, playful character who is the most loyal and devoted family member imaginable. Should another dog appear, however, you may be faced with a ferocious throwback to pit-fighting days, determined to destroy its opponent at any cost. As bull-baiting declined in the 17th century, breeders crossed terriers with bull-baiters, whose faces were too short for fighting other dogs. This created a range of bull terriers that would fight each other, until this "sport" too was outlawed in Britain and other countries in 1835. Breeders worked to save their favourites, and the Staffordshire Bull Terrier was recognized and shown as a distinct breed in 1935. Their fighting history still shows in their dual personality and also in their powerful, muscular build. Caesarian births are often needed and sunburn is a hazard in sunny climates. Skin allergies are not uncommon.

Be Staffie savvy
Powerful and possessing tremendous stamina, Staffordshire Bull Terriers should be let off the lead in public only when response to command is guaranteed.

EARLY LEARNING

Although Staffies – sometimes called kegs-on-legs – are excellent with children, it can take a strong adult to control an ill-disciplined dog on a lead. Consistent, early training is vital to ensure both the safety of others and of this curious and fearless dog. Staffie puppies love to use those muscular jaws to chew, so provide plenty of sturdy toys.

AMERICAN STAFFORDSHIRE TERRIER

SIZE 18–22.5kg (40–50lb), 43–48cm (17–19in)
GROOMING Minimal
TRAINING Time-consuming
COLOURS All colours, with or without white

This breed was created from English Staffordshire Bull Terriers that crossed the Atlantic in the 19th century. The American breeders preferred a heftier dog, and bred for greater height and a bulkier build, resulting in this separate breed being recognized in 1936. Its ears are often cropped in the United States, a practice that is illegal throughout Europe and elsewhere. American Staffordshires were used for dog fighting until this was banned in the United States in 1900. Like the British Staffie, this is a gentle, loyal, and affectionate breed, good with children, but it needs early socialization to curb its instinct to attack other dogs.

AMERICAN PIT BULL TERRIER

SIZE 14–36kg (31–79lb), 46–56cm (18–22in)
GROOMING Minimal
TRAINING Time-consuming
COLOURS All colours

The black sheep of the bull terrier family, the American Pit Bull is subject to more laws than perhaps any other breed. In the 19th century, some bull terrier lines in the United States were developed into the American Staffordshire, others into the American Pit Bull. Even today, it is possible for individuals listed as one breed with one registry to be listed as the other with another registry.

Pit Bulls are victims of their reputation: famed as fighting dogs, they have too often been bought by those eager to project a macho image, who give little or no time to the dog's care and socialization. With proper discipline from puppyhood, most members of this breed are people-oriented companions, with the usual caveat that they will attack other dogs without apparent provocation. The American Temperament Test Society (www.atts.org) finds few differences between temperament scores of American Pit Bulls and Staffordshires.

Massive cheek muscles clearly visible

Thick, short, silky coat

Thin tail in comparison to rest of body

Strong, muscular forelegs

PORTUGUESE PODENGO – LARGE

SIZE Over 19kg (42lb), 55–70cm (22–28in)
GROOMING Easy
TRAINING Time-consuming
COLOURS Yellow, tan, black, and any parti-colour

The large Podengo (Podengo Grande) was at one time a popular pack dog, bred to assist in the hunt for game such as wild boar. However, unlike its small and medium-sized relatives (*see* pp.80–81), the large Podengo faded into obscurity after Portugal's agricultural and forestry policies changed following the country's admission to the European Union in the 1980s.

The large Podengo has been rescued from probable extinction through the work of breeders in the high Alentejo region of Portugal, where numbers have steadily increased. It remains very rare outside Portugal, although similar dogs exist in Brazil, central Africa, and India, descendants of large Podengos taken to these regions by Portuguese settlers.

Tail erect when dog alert

SMOOTH-COATED VARIETY

Back line has slight arch

Medium-length, shaggy coat

ROUGH-COATED VARIETY

MINIATURE BULL TERRIER

SIZE 11–15kg (24–33lb), 25–35cm (10–14in)
GROOMING Easy
TRAINING Time-consuming
COLOURS Black, brindle, red, fawn (solid or with white), tricolour, white

Not a true miniature, this breed was developed in the 1930s – going against type in a period when breeding consistently larger Bull Terriers was the norm. It was initially defined by a lower weight, but is now defined by its height, which allows the dog to keep the same sturdy build characteristic as the Bull Terrier. The Miniature Bull Terrier shows more typical terrier temperament than the larger version, being aggressive towards other dogs and inclined to snap if teased. It settles into urban life well and will make an effective watchdog and humorous companion.

Ears point straight up when held stiffly erect

Muscular thighs join stifles, which descend to hocks

Chest extremely broad when viewed from front

FRENCH BULLDOG

SIZE 10–12.5kg (22–28lb), 30–31cm (12in)
GROOMING Minimal
TRAINING Average
COLOURS Fawn, pied, red brindle, black brindle

The Bulldog in 19th century Britain came in one size only, and small individuals were marginalized. They found more favour in France, where they were developed into this feisty and enthusiastic little companion. The French Bulldog became something of a fashion accessory,

PIED

as well as the favoured companion of Parisian butchers and coachmen. Curiously, the breed was first officially recognized in the United States, where it continues to be popular. The breathing and eye problems associated with short faces make this a potentially expensive breed, and it is not as numerous at it once was. French Bulldogs are susceptible to overheating, meaning it is advisable to carry a water bottle to quench their thirst when walking in warm weather.

CHANGING ROLES

The French Bulldog was at its most popular in France over 100 years ago (Degas and Toulouse-Lautrec painted them; Colette wrote about hers). Unlike the bull-baiting origins of its larger English relative, the French Bulldog was originally developed for ratting. Like other bulldogs, little of the breed's hereditary aggression remains, and the French Bulldog makes an affectionate, playful, and reliable pet.

Batlike ears

Muscular, solid, compact thighs

Broad skull

Broad, short, snub nose

Very short, thick, glossy, soft coat

Forelegs slightly shorter than hind legs

French Bulldog
Originally bred for the utilitarian purpose of ratting, the French Bulldog now leads a more sedentary life as a companion dog.

PORTUGUESE WATER DOG

SIZE 16–25kg (35–55lb), 43–57cm (17–22in)
GROOMING Time-consuming
TRAINING Time-consuming
COLOURS Black, brown, white, black and white, brown and white

Now seen increasingly at dog shows, this somewhat opinionated and circumspect breed was used as a successful rabbit hunter on land. But it was in the water that it shone, used at sea by Portuguese fishermen to pull nets and to carry messages between boats. Its ancestors probably arrived in Portugal with Visigoth invaders from central Europe.

WATER DOGS

All dogs can dog paddle, but some are born to swim. Water is their second home. Throughout Europe and later in America, medium-sized breeds were developed to work in water. Some had surprising uses, such as collecting shot arrows that had fallen on water, but the majority were bred selectively to retrieve and return game that had landed in water. The curious show cuts of some modern breeds have their origins in clipping hair to reduce drag in water, while leaving dense hair over the joints to help keep them warm. The Portuguese Water Dog pictured below benefits from this practice, emerging from the sea to reveal a suitably functional cut for a hard-working fisherman's friend.

Plume of hair helps tail to float

Short, straight, muscular neck

Eyes set wide apart

Long, wavy hair

Large, domed head with long muzzle

Single coat grows profusely

Powerful forelegs

LAGOTTO ROMAGNOLO

SIZE 11–16kg (24–35lb), 41–48cm (16–19in)
GROOMING Time-consuming
TRAINING Time-consuming
COLOURS Brown, orange, brown roan, white with brown or orange spots, dirty white

This water-loving duck hunter is from the northern Italian region of Romagna, by the Swiss border. It may look like a toy but it's a sharp-voiced, boisterous and ardent worker, most content when active, for example when truffle hunting or retrieving. Breeders in the UK and Scandinavia have selected it for companionship as well as workability. The darker coats lighten considerably with age. Because it doesn't shed its hair and is not prone to inflammatory skin conditions, the Lagotto is, as long as it is routinely washed and clipped, a good selection for dog-loving allergy sufferers.

Broad head with rounded skull

Well-covered ears hanging flat

Water-resistant, short, woolly coat

BARBET

SIZE 15–25kg (33–55lb), 46–56cm (18–22in)
GROOMING Time-consuming
TRAINING Average
COLOURS Black, chestnut, fawn, grey, white

Face fully covered with hair

Good covering of water-resistant hair

An ancient breed, possibly a forerunner to the Poodle and a probable relative of the Puli and Iberian water dogs, the Barbet was originally used to retrieve fallen arrows and game from the water. Once Europe's most common water dog, today it is rare even in France, where it is still used as a retriever. As with all water dogs, the coat can develop a distinctly doggy aroma.

SPANISH WATER DOG

SIZE 12–20kg (26–44lb), 38–50cm (15–20in)
GROOMING Time-consuming
TRAINING Time-consuming
COLOURS Black, chestnut, white, chestnut and white

Heavy topknot covering eyes

Rarely seen outside Spain, this multi-tasking dog assists with hunting and herding, as well as fishing. Hunters use it to retrieve shot ducks. These dogs are most numerous on the south coast of Spain, where they herd goats, but are also seen in coastal regions or in northern Galicia. Show people have not yet paid much attention to this breed, and, as a consequence, there is a considerable variation in body size and colour.

Well-muscled hind legs for endurance in swimming

Coat forms heavy cords of hair

HUNGARIAN PULI

SIZE 10–15kg (22–33lb), 37–44cm (15–17in)
GROOMING Time-consuming
TRAINING Time-consuming
COLOURS Black, apricot, white

Coat often has a slightly rusty colour

BLACK COAT

Some cords grow to floor length

Probably brought to Hungary by invading Magyars from the east, the somewhat aloof and virtually waterproof Puli ("leader" in Hungarian) served as both a herding dog and a retriever. Saved from extinction after World War II by Hungarians living abroad, it remains a unique-looking companion, admired for its dreadlocks.

Coat consideration
Caring for a Puli's profuse corded coat, such as this white-haired individual's, requires each of the cords to be groomed separately.

WETTERHOUN

SIZE 15–20kg (33–44lb), 53–58cm (21–23in)
GROOMING Average
TRAINING Average
COLOURS Black, liver, black and white, liver and white

Developed in the Dutch province of Friesland hundreds of years ago, this natural guard was once used to kill otters, the fisherman's perceived enemy, as well as retrieve wild fowl that had fallen into the water. It is a rugged and capable retriever and responds well to obedience training. Wetterhouns (Frisian for "water dogs") are rarely seen outside the Netherlands and northern Germany.

Spatula-shaped ears

Prominent eyes

Thick-set, powerful neck

A dog to rely on
Built like a military tank and insulated by dense, protective hair, this Wetterhoun thrives as a hunting companion even in inclement weather.

AMERICAN WATER SPANIEL

SIZE 11–20kg (24–44lb), 36–46cm (14–18in)
GROOMING Average
TRAINING Easy
COLOURS Dark chocolate, liver

Wisconsin's State Dog was probably developed by crossing a variety of water dogs, including the Irish Water Spaniel (*see* p.209), which has given this breed its benign and obedient disposition. After flushing game, it retrieves it from the water with a typically soft mouth. This breed remains a popular hunter's companion in the American midwest.

Tightly curled, dense coat

Straight, strong forelegs, feathered with waterproof hair

ÉPAGNEUL PONT-AUDEMER

SIZE 18–24kg (40–53lb), 51–58cm (20–23in)
GROOMING Average
TRAINING Easy
COLOURS Liver, liver and white

Related to the Barbet, this gentle and biddable dog from northern France was revived after World War II through the introduction of Irish Water Spaniel lines. The coat is not as oily, and therefore not as smelly, as that of other water dogs. Although rare, even in France, it thrives on work, which transforms it into a whirlwind of exuberance.

Short hair on face

Weather-resistant, wavy coat

Low-set ears with long feathering

BRITTANY

SIZE 13–15kg (29–33lb), 47–50cm (19–20in)
GROOMING Average
TRAINING Easy
COLOURS Black and white, orange and white, liver and white, tricolour

This breed, brought back from the brink of extinction in the 1900s by local breeder Arthur Enaud, is still the most popular gundog in its native France. It is also a favourite with hunters in North America. Despite its other names of Brittany Spaniel or Épagneul Breton, the reliable Brittany is primarily a pointer or setter in its behaviour, although it will also flush and retrieve from water.

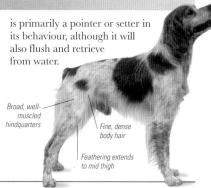

Broad, well-muscled hindquarters

Fine, dense body hair

Feathering extends to mid thigh

KOOIKERHONDJE

Ears with distinctive black markings

Wavy topcoat over downy undercoat

SIZE 9–11kg (20–24lb), 35–41cm (14–16in)
GROOMING Average
TRAINING Easy
COLOURS Tan and white, sometimes with black, especially on ears

This breed is also known as the Kooiker Dog or Dutch Decoy Spaniel. For centuries, it used its bushy tail and silent antics to lure ducks into a large tunnel of woven reed matting, in which they were trapped alive to be taken to market. Some Kooikerhondjes are still used in this way, trapping birds for banding and study. They also make friendly companions.

NOVA SCOTIA DUCK TOLLING RETRIEVER

SIZE 17–23kg (37–51lb), 43–53cm (17–21in)
GROOMING Average
TRAINING Easy
COLOURS Any shade of red

Also called the Little River Duck Dog and the Yarmouth Toller, the breed's odd name comes from its equally peculiar role in the hunt. A hunter concealed in a hide throws a stick along the bank, which the dog chases and retrieves silently but animatedly until this lures or "tolls" curious ducks or geese within range of the guns. The obedient Toller also acts as an efficient retriever.

High-set, triangular ears

Deep chest, well-insulated for cold-water swimming

Dense, water-repellent coat

Compact, well-muscled body on sturdy legs

WELSH SPRINGER SPANIEL

SIZE 16–20.5kg (35–45lb), 46–48cm (18–19in)
GROOMING Average
TRAINING Easy
COLOURS Red and white

Equally popular as a working gundog and a companion, the Welsh Springer is a good-natured and tractable breed with stamina to spare. Its original function was to flush or "spring" game birds for hunters, but it has also proved capable at herding cattle and sheep. It makes a cheerful and energetic companion, although it can be somewhat reserved with strangers. The Welsh Springer is reliable around children and naturally inclined to obedience training. It revels in physical exercise, especially any activities involving water.

Red-and-white dogs of this type can be traced back to the 18th century in Wales and further back in England. The breed was only officially recognized in 1902, however, and was previously called the Welsh Cocker. It is popular, but somewhat overshadowed by the English Springer Spaniel (*see* p.219): despite sharing a name, the two breeds are not in fact closely linked.

Thick, silky topcoat; it is never curly

Ears smaller than an English Springer's

Long, muscular neck

Feathering on legs

Anticipating action

This well-camouflaged Welsh Springer lies obediently in the grass, awaiting the command to leap into action. While some dogs retrieve game, the majority are content retrieving thrown toys.

SUSSEX SPANIEL

SIZE 18–22.5kg (40–50lb), 38–41cm (15–16in)
GROOMING Average
TRAINING Easy
COLOURS Rich golden-liver

Massive and low, with a distinctive rolling gait, the Sussex Spaniel is the result of breeding for a dog that could flush game from dense undergrowth. Unlike most other spaniels it bays when at work, and an experienced hunter can tell what is being trailed from the tone of the dog's voice. The dog as it is known today has been bred as much for companionship as for working, and makes a steady,

calm addition to a household. Eye and ear problems are not uncommon. Developed in the 19th century, today it is rare even in its home county, although it is also found in North America, where the show standard calls for a smaller and lighter dog than is bred in Britain.

Broad skull and wrinkled brows

Large, hazel eyes with soft expression

Long, lean, muscular back

Strong legs with thick pads on feet

FIELD SPANIEL

SIZE 16–23kg (35–50lb), 45cm (18in)
GROOMING Average
TRAINING Easy
COLOURS Black, liver, roan, or any of these with tan or white markings

The Field Spaniel is descended from the English Cocker Spaniel (*see* pp.150–151), only recognized as a separate breed in 1892. Breeding for show led to a great change in the way it was bred, with an emphasis on

long backs and short legs. The dog lost its working abilities and was almost extinct by the end of World War II. In the 1960s, this affectionate breed was rejuvenated using English Cocker and Springer Spaniel crosses.

Low-set ears hanging in folds

Weather-resistant, silky, glossy coat; it is never curled

Very long rib cage

Round feet with short, soft hair between toes

ENGLISH COCKER SPANIEL

SIZE 13–15kg (29–33lb), 38–41cm (15–16in)
GROOMING Average
TRAINING Easy
COLOURS All colours

Well-developed nose, giving good scenting ability

Strong, compact body

Muscular neck merging into shoulders

Well-bent stifles

ORANGE-AND-WHITE COAT

Dog owners love their spaniels and their spaniels love them. These have always been affectionate dogs from the time they emerged from Spain almost a thousand years ago. In the 1300s, Chaucer, writing about the Wife of Bath, said of her, "for as a spaniel she would on him leap". "Spaniel" was once a generic word, referring to dogs that flushed birds from thicket or marsh and then retrieved them for their masters. By 1800, small spaniels used for hunting woodcock in southwest England and Wales were called "cocker spaniels": the origin of the modern English Cocker Spaniel.

The doe-eyed Cocker Spaniel has long been a family favourite throughout the world. Its domed head, floppy ears, and big eyes epitomize companionship. Some Cockers do still have working roles, but the majority are household companions, selected for their looks and luxurious coats, which come in over 30 colour combinations. While dogs bred to show-ring standards retain their potential to work in the field, the so-called Working Cocker Spaniel is often bred from completely different lines of dogs. These individuals have shorter bodies, less pendulous ears, and a more frenetic desire to work that is reminiscent of the English Springer Spaniel. These lines of Cockers are the most successful of all breeds as hearing dogs for deaf people.

BLACK COAT

GOLDEN COAT

TRICOLOURED PUPPY

Well-defined, square muzzle

Pendulous ears covered with long, silky hair

BROWN COAT

Slightly wavy coat, well-feathered, with dense, protective undercoat

Popularity has its drawbacks, however, and unprincipled breeding of Cocker Spaniels has led to an increased occurrence of eye disorders and skin complaints. There is also a higher incidence of hypothyroidism (a condition in which the thyroid gland stops producing sufficient hormone) in Cockers than in any other breed. Cases of cancer and heart disease remain low, but behavioural problems can occur, particularly in solid-coloured dogs. The vast majority of Cockers live blissfully free of these disorders, however.

Water lovers

Whether bred for work or companionship, Cocker Spaniels thrive on two activities: retrieving and swimming. Given the opportunity, there is nothing more satisfying than combining both pleasures, as this dog demonstrates.

LITERARY LEANINGS

A Cocker Spaniel whose fame spread further than most was Flush, the dog belonging to 19th-century poet, Elizabeth Barrett Browning. Inspired by references to the dog in love letters between Elizabeth Barrett and her future husband, Robert Browning, author Virginia Woolf (*right*) wrote the dog's biography, giving his perspective on the love affair. *Flush*, when it appeared in 1933, was an instant best-seller.

AMERICAN COCKER SPANIEL

SIZE 11–13kg (24–29lb), 34–39cm (13–15in)
GROOMING Time-consuming
TRAINING Easy
COLOURS Variety of colours

In the 1930s, a conflict arose among Cocker Spaniel breeders in America. Some wanted to breed for working ability, while others wanted to breed for the show ring, emphasizing the drama of the coat and muzzle. Those who favoured working ability broke away to form a new club, leaving the original Cocker Spaniel Club, founded in 1881, to continue breeding selectively for the new, slightly smaller "Americanized" variety: shorter at the withers, with a smaller head and muzzle, longer, denser, silkier hair, and a more dramatic down-slope of the top line. In the United States, the name "Cocker Spaniel" refers to this new American Cocker Spaniel, while the older style is called the English Cocker Spaniel (*see* pp.150–151). In Britain, the older variety is the Cocker Spaniel and the newer, the American Cocker Spaniel.

Cocker Spaniels appear almost invariably in every country's top ten most popular dog breeds. All Cockers retain their hunting instincts, but the popularity of the

Ears set level with eyes

Long hair covering ears

Shorter and more down-sloping back than the English Cocker's

Dense feathering on forelegs

BROWN-AND-TAN COAT

LADY AND THE TRAMP

The most popular breed with American dog owners from the late 1930s and for the next 50 years, the American Cocker Spaniel was the obvious choice of dog to portray the refined and gentle Lady in Walt Disney's 1955 film, *Lady and the Tramp*. With her flowing ears, the pampered pooch personified the innocent abroad, taken under the wing of the scruffy, streetwise Tramp. Romance blossoms over spaghetti, and the rest is history.

American Cocker, particularly in North, Central, and South America, as well as Japan, is based squarely on its charm, striking looks, and gentle companionship. This is a truly loving breed that forms deep bonds with a human family. Unfortunately, it shares with its English relative a variety of inherited disorders, including epilepsy, eye conditions, skin complaints, and kidney problems. Responsible breeders will assess their dogs for each of these disorders before breeding from them.

TRICOLOUR COAT

Silky-soft perfection
The American Cocker Spaniel's luxuriously profuse, soft coat mats easily and requires daily attention to achieve the beauty of this well-cared for individual.

TIBETAN TERRIER

SIZE 8–13.5kg (18–30lb), 36–41cm (14–16in)
GROOMING Time-consuming
TRAINING Average
COLOURS Variety of colours

Despite its name, this breed is not and never has been a working terrier intended to go to ground after small animals. The first Westerners who saw it were simply reminded of these dogs familiar to them at home, but its Tibetan name is the Dhoki Apso, which can be translated as "long-haired watchdog". Traditionally, it was kept by monasteries as a companion and a vocal guard dog, both roles that it still fulfils well today. Dogs were considered lucky, and were given as gifts or tributes, which is how the breed came to the West. A medic working in India in the 1930s, Dr Greig, was given puppies by a grateful patient, with which she established

a breeding kennel in Britain. Although gentle, affectionate, and surprisingly lively, the breed has never become as popular as its smaller compatriot, the Lhasa Apso.

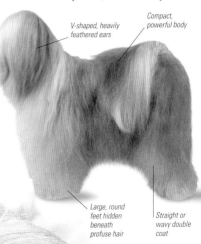

V-shaped, heavily feathered ears

Compact, powerful body

Large, round feet hidden beneath profuse hair

Straight or wavy double coat

Long, heavy hair
The Tibetan Terrier's long hair parts naturally in the middle of the head and falls forwards and to the sides. This dog has had some of its facial hair clipped to improve its vision.

SEPARATION ANXIETY

Tibetan Terriers suffer from separation anxiety – becoming noisy or destructive when left alone for long periods – proportionally much more than other breeds. While whining and yapping can be controlled, howling is a more difficult problem to eradicate. It is not known whether the problem has genetic origins or is triggered by the types of people who choose this breed as pets.

SMALL MÜNSTERLÄNDER

SIZE 14.5–15.5kg (32–34lb), 47–55cm (19–22in)
GROOMING Average
TRAINING Easy
COLOURS Brown and white

This engaging and intelligent breed was originally used centuries ago to flush birds for nets and hawks. The role earned it one of its other German names, Heidewachtel, or "heath quail" dog. It is also classified under the names of Kleine Münsterländer Vorstehhund or, more succinctly, Spion.

When hawking declined, the breed was used as a pointer and retriever, and later as a household companion. In the early 20th century a concerted effort was made to revive the breed, using crosses with other European gundogs to increase numbers. Today the Small Münsterländer is gaining a wider audience, and is favoured by hunters in North America, where it is listed in working rather than show registries.

Alongside its natural working abilities, the companion traits that saw it through its period of unemployment are still present, and this is a happy, affectionate, lively dog that asks for nothing more than leadership and entertaining exercise.

DIMINUTIVE HUNTERS

The slightest of all gundogs, the Small Münsterländer still makes an enthusiastic and efficient hunter. It readily uses its voice when tracking game, and experienced hunters can interpret from the tone of voice what type of quarry is being tracked. The breed has an especially soft mouth when retrieving birds, as the dog shown here demonstrates.

Distinctive coat colour
The Small Münsterländer's coat may be brown and white or, as seen here, brown roan with brown patches. Some individuals have areas of tan hair on the muzzle or around the eyes.

LARGE DOGS
20–40KG (44–88LB)

Closest in size to the Asiatic wolf, large dogs are the most numerous in variety, although many breeds were developed for only two primary purposes: to work with the hunter, finding and retrieving game, or to work with the farmer protecting his livestock. Today, these trustworthy breeds include some of the world's most popular canine companions.

RETRIEVING AND TRACKING

Gundogs had to be open to instruction from the hunter and to be willing learners who enjoyed working as team-mates with people. The European breeders who created the great variety of spaniels, setters, pointers, and retrievers unwittingly also created breeds that became some of our most reliable, obedient, and easy-to-train family companions.

Some large breeds thrive on teamwork with the hunter, while others enjoy greater rein. From Europe to Scandinavia to the US, specialist scent hounds were developed wherever there was game to be tracked. Elsewhere, sight hounds, the

Farm hand
A dependable and intelligent breed, the German Shepherd's first use was as a farm dog. Military service roles in World War I showcased the breed's versatility, leading to a global profile.

speed merchants of the canine world, developed in locations as diverse as Europe, Asia, and Africa.

While medium-sized dogs are ideal for driving livestock, larger dogs are better for protecting flocks from predators such as wolves. Many of today's shepherd dogs emerged in the late 1800s, on farms in the region of Europe where Belgium, the Netherlands, and Germany meet. Of these adept guards, only the malleable German Shepherd has gone on to achieve worldwide stardom. Today, it is matched in numbers only by the Labrador Retriever, with the Golden Retriever set to join them as top dog within a decade.

Flexible friend
The English Pointer is a superb example of the malleability of the dog. Pointers are bred to ignore their natural chase-and-kill instincts, and instead indicate prey to the hunter.

Blood ties
The dog evolved from the Asiatic wolf and it is no surprise that several large dog breeds, including the Chow Chow, are a similar size to their wolf ancestor.

EAST SIBERIAN LAIKA

SIZE 18–23kg (40–51lb), 56–64cm (22–25in)
GROOMING Average
TRAINING Time-consuming
COLOURS Solid sable, red or brown of any shade, grey, black, black and white

The indigenous spitz dogs of Siberia were first selectively bred in the 19th century, and remain genetically close to the wolf.

In the mid-20th century, the biologist K.G. Abramov wrote the first breed standard for the Vostochno-Sibirskaia Laika, encompassing both the lighter dogs used for pulling sleds and more powerful individuals used for hunting large game. Some variation remains in the breed today, which is defined as much by its working abilities as its appearance, but it is essentially a large, strong dog with a dense double coat. This breed is calm and even-tempered, and makes a good companion, even in the city. It can also be trained in obedience.

Tightly curled tail held close; it keeps dog warm while resting

Muscular neck gives holding power when dog attacks animals

Medium-short topcoat covering dense, waterproof undercoat

Small, erect ears covered by short, insulating fur

Well-insulated thick paws

WEST SIBERIAN LAIKA

SIZE 18–23kg (40–51lb), 56–64cm (22–25in)
GROOMING Average
TRAINING Time-consuming
COLOURS White, pale red, red, wolf-grey, black

This is historically the most popular of the Laikas, prized for its great hunting abilities and striking looks. Lenin's companion when he was exiled to Siberia may have been a West Siberian Laika. It has been used mainly for hunting large game, such as elks, reindeers, and bears, but can also be trained to hunt

small game, and makes a fine sled dog. It originated in the Khantu and Mansi areas of Russia as two slightly different types of dog: the former sturdier, the latter speedier. Both variations still exist today, with performance in field trials being rated as important as appearance in the breed standard. A good guard and hunting dog, this breed does not adapt easily to the role of household companion. Laikas thrive on strenuous physical activity.

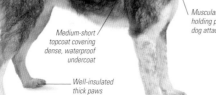

Ears well covered with insulating hair

Short, dense double coat

Dense undercoat

Thick skin covering well-boned legs

RUSSO-EUROPEAN LAIKA

SIZE 21–23kg (46–51lb), 53–61cm (21–24in)
GROOMING Average
TRAINING Time-consuming
COLOURS Black and white

Laika, meaning "barker", was once a name for all the athletic, fearless spitz-type dogs renowned for hunting, guarding, and sled-pulling in Russia. From the mid-20th century, the Soviet authorities, who annexed the Finnish area of Karelia as part of the Soviet Union, developed this regional type into a breed, the Russko-Europiskaia Laika, also called the Karelian Bear Laika. Originally, wolf-grey coats similar to the Siberian Laikas predominated, but the black-and-white pattern is now the only one allowed. Early crosses with the (possibly mythical) Utchak Sheepdog may have given this breed its fierce nature, making it an ideal working dog but unsuitable as a companion.

Small, brown, fiery eyes

Tail uncurling as dog relaxes

Muscular shoulders sloping forwards

> ### EARLY LEARNING
> The work ethic is deeply ingrained in the Russo-European Laika. Early and frequent contact with other dogs and people is vital if pups are to develop into reliable, controllable adults that stand any chance of shaking off their hard-core hunting traits.

KARELIAN BEAR DOG

SIZE 21–23kg (46–51lb), 48–58cm (19–23in)
GROOMING Average
TRAINING Time-consuming
COLOURS Black and white

Also called the Karelsk Bjornhund or Karjalankarhukoira, this breed is typical of the big, tough, intrepid dogs bred in Karelia for hunting large game. The black-and-white coat is unusual for northern spitz-type dogs, making these and the Russo-European Laika distinctive. They spring from essentially the same stock, but the Karelian Bear Dog was adopted and bred in Finland and has achieved greater international recognition, although numbers fell sharply in the 1960s. It is an unrelenting hunter, and not a peaceable household companion.

Ready, willing, and able
Although used mainly in the pursuit of elk, this tenacious and powerful breed is willing to take on virtually any game animal.

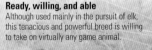

SIBERIAN HUSKY

SIZE 16–27.5kg (35–60lb), 51–60cm (20–24in)
GROOMING Average
TRAINING Average/time-consuming
COLOURS All colours, for both coat and eyes

Siberian or Arctic Huskies were used for centuries to pull sleds by the Chukchi and possibly the Koryak and Kamchadal peoples of Siberia. Genetically close to the wolf, they seldom bark but howl as a pack. Fur traders first brought them to Alaska in 1909, and continued for the next two decades until the Soviet Union closed the border in 1930. Siberian Huskies were used for draught work, but also excelled in racing, being smaller and lighter than other dogs then in general use. The breed's hour of glory came in 1925, when it helped carry diphtheria serum across Alaska in record time in the "Great Race of Mercy", saving the city of Nome from an epidemic. Ideally suited to long-distance endurance work, they are still used for sledding, as well as in the newer sports of skijoring and ski-pulka, in which they pull a skier wearing a special harness. Bred as pack animals, they need lavish amounts of company and activity, and make fine, gentle companions.

Skijoring to success

While the Siberian Husky's stamina and tolerance of extreme cold suited its role as a draught dog, successful breeding of certain lines for speed means teams now also compete at the top level in purebred sprint races.

Medium-length muzzle

Thick, bushy tail

Strong, deep chest

Relatively long legs

Well-furred, slightly webbed, oval feet

GREENLAND DOG

SIZE 30–32kg (66–70lb), 56–64cm (22–25in)
GROOMING Average
TRAINING Average
COLOURS All colours

Extremely powerful jaws

Typically dense, spitz-type coat

Well-feathered legs

Thickly furred toes with large, strong pads

This dog is typical of the northern spitz-type breeds that have existed throughout the Arctic since antiquity. It may be descended from dogs brought over from Siberia 12,000 years ago. Numbers have diminished with the rise of motorized transport, but this tireless breed is popular with hikers in Norway and Sweden. Also known as the Grünlandshund, it is steadfastly loyal and will follow its leader to the ends of the Earth – literally, if given the chance.

SWEDISH LAPPHUND

Erect and pointed ears

Thick, wiry topcoat; waterproof undercoat

Strong, vertical forelegs

SIZE 19.5–20.5kg (43–45lb), 40–51cm (16–20in)
GROOMING Time-consuming
TRAINING Time-consuming
COLOURS Black, brown, sometimes with small white markings

The discovery in Norway of 7,000-year-old skeletal remains similar to today's Lapphund shows just how long these dogs have been established. Lapphunds were used by the Sami people to herd and guard their reindeer, but as the Sami way of life changed in the 20th century, the breed declined. A revival programme in the 1960s gave us today's dog. The breed is becoming more popular elsewhere in Scandinavia, and in Britain, as an active, steady companion.

FINNISH LAPPHUND

SIZE 20–21kg (44–46lb), 46–52cm (18–21in)
GROOMING Average
TRAINING Average/time-consuming
COLOURS Range from black to red brindle

Tail curling over back

Very straight hind legs

Short forelegs in comparison with rest of body

In the 20th century, both Sweden and Finland laid claim to this Sami working dog, and as a result two breeds developed: the Swedish Lapphund, or Lapland Spitz, and the Finnish Lapphund, or Lapinkoira. Both are sturdy, active dogs with a strong herding instinct and insulating double coats. The Finnish breed was originally used to herd reindeer. Today, as well as usually herding sheep and cattle, it is more often kept as a companion.

SWEDISH ELKHOUND

SIZE 29.5–30kg (65–67lb), 52–65cm (21–26in)
GROOMING Time-consuming
TRAINING Average
COLOURS Shades of grey

Large, erect, pointed ears

Outside English-speaking countries, this breed is known by the name of Jämthund, after its native region of northern Sweden. At one time, virtually every valley in Scandinavia had its own variety of elkhound. The Swedish Elkhound became the national breed.

The Swedish Elkhound probably started its existence hunting bears, but it became a successful hunter of lynx, wolves, and moose, running its prey to a standstill and then guarding it until the hunter caught up.

This versatile breed has also done service as a herder, watchdog, sled dog, and military dog. A good companion breed, it is popular in Britain, the Netherlands, and North America.

Broad, roomy chest

Very powerful hind legs

NORWEGIAN ELKHOUND

SIZE 20–23kg (44–51lb), 49–52cm (19–21in)
GROOMING Average
TRAINING Average
COLOURS Shades of grey

Stone Age remains confirm that dogs of this type have been in existence for at least 5,000 years, but the standards for this breed date back only to the late 19th century. The most popular of the Scandinavian elkhounds, the Norwegian Elkhound is a versatile breed used to hunt not only large game but smaller prey, as well as to round up farmyard fowl and act as a guard dog. Today, it is primarily a gundog and companion breed. A steady, loyal dog, sometimes reserved with strangers, it is both alert and active and needs plenty of exercise to keep it occupied.

NATIONAL FAVOURITE

The Norwegian Elkhound is also known as the Gra Elghund, a name that describes both its colour and its primary prey – Elg is the Norwegian word for "moose". It is cherished as a family pet in its homeland. A similar but completely separate breed, the Black Norwegian Elkhound, or Sort Elkhund, also exists. Developed in the border region between Sweden and Norway, it is much less common than its grey relative.

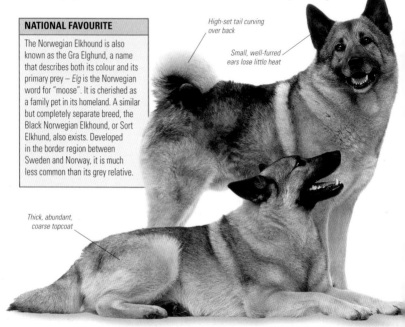

High-set tail curving over back

Small, well-furred ears lose little heat

Thick, abundant, coarse topcoat

GERMAN WOLFSPITZ

SIZE 27–32kg (59–70lb), 46–50cm (18–20in)
GROOMING Time-consuming
TRAINING Time-consuming
COLOURS Shades of grey

Spitzes probably arrived in
Germany over 1,000 years ago,
and were used as herding dogs.
Once there were many spitz breeds
in Germany, and different colours were
associated with different regions. Today,
all are increasingly rare. The German
Wolfspitz, also called the Chien Loup,
is an outgoing companion dog, but it does
have a tendency to nip. Although not an
easy dog to obedience train, its willingness
to bark and impressive appearance make
it an excellent watchdog.

*Medium-length tail
bending over back*

*Long, dense
coat needing
a lot of care*

KEESHOND

SIZE 25–30kg (55–66lb), 43–45cm (17–18in)
GROOMING Time-consuming
TRAINING Average
COLOURS Mix of grey, black, and cream

In some countries, no distinction is made between this
breed and the German Wolfspitz, while other countries
treat them as separate breeds. The name Keeshond
comes from a dog that was the constant companion
of Kees de Gyselaer, who led a Dutch rebellion in the
late 18th century. The dogs were a favourite on Dutch
barges, and were also used as guards
and vermin hunters. In the 20th
century they proved steady and
good-natured enough to move
into the role of companion and
domestic watchdogs, and
remain one of the most
popular large spitz breeds.
They are assertive dogs,
and need firm handling.

*Small, close-
set ears*

*Fairly short,
narrow
muzzle*

*Profuse coat,
densest in ruff
around neck*

Thermal insulation
The combination of a profuse
topcoat of guard hairs and an
equally abundant undercoat
means cold weather is never
a problem for the Keeshond.

JAPANESE AKITA

SIZE 35–50kg (77–110lb), 60–70cm (24–28in)
GROOMING Time-consuming
TRAINING Time-consuming
COLOURS All colours

Every Japanese dog (inu) is classified as large (akita), medium (shika), or small (shiba) (*see* Shiba Inu, p.99). There are many small and medium breeds, but this is the only large one and so is simply called Akita, or sometimes Akita Inu. It was once bred for fighting, and when this sport declined it was used for hunting. By the 1930s, its numbers had fallen to the point where it provoked the formation of the Society for the Preservation of Japanese Breeds to save it. Today it is kept as a companion or a guard and used as a police dog in Japan. Imposing presence and obvious power have helped make these dogs popular, and American servicemen took them home after the war. The Akita is an imperious, strong-willed, aloof dog, and is potentially aggressive with other dogs and sometimes humans. Given its strength, it is best left to experienced handlers, and as with all dogs, it should never be left unsupervised around children.

Erect ears carried in line with back of neck

Stout, straight tail carried over back

Strong, straight forelegs

BLACK MASK ON RED COAT

Strong, broad muzzle

Clear, well-defined coloration

BLACK MASK, RED-AND-WHITE COAT

Grey elegance
This handsome dog's colours are typical of the diversity seen outside Japan. In its homeland, only red, red and white, or brindle dogs are shown. They look like large Shibas.

CHOW CHOW

SIZE 20–32kg (44–70lb), 45–56cm (18–22in)
GROOMING Time-consuming
TRAINING Time-consuming
COLOURS White, cream, fawn, red, blue, black

To some, this truly ancient breed, one of the first to diverge from the wolf, resembles a teddy bear. To others, it looks like a lion. It would be wise to think of it as the latter in terms of personality. In the past, blue-tongued dogs of the Chow Chow type were eaten and their skin used for clothing in China. They were also employed as guard dogs and sled dogs, and none of these uses required a friendly or relaxed personality. This is a stubborn, independent breed with a tendency to snap aggressively, and it needs a firm and experienced owner.

OUT OF THE BLUE

The Chow Chow's blue tongue and gums make it difficult for vets to examine the mouth for visual signs of anaemia, low blood pressure, or shock. Alternative sites of inspection during routine examinations are the vulva or prepuce, which aren't blue.

Broad, flat skull

Small ears blending with the ruff

SAMOYED

SIZE 23–30kg (51–66lb), 46–56cm (18–22in)
GROOMING Time-consuming
TRAINING Easy
COLOURS White, cream, white and biscuit, silver tipped

This dog, also called the Samoyedskaya, accompanied the Samoyed people across the far north of Asia for generations as both a hunter and a herder of reindeer. First introduced to the West in 1889, it has made a smooth transition to the role of household companion and become a popular, firmly established breed due to its striking looks and engaging personality. This is a remarkably friendly and gentle breed, which according to the British standard "displays affection to all mankind".

EXCELLENT FAMILY DOG

This makes it an excellent family dog, but limits its usefulness as a guard. Obedience classes are still advisable, as Samoyeds can be stubborn, in their own dignified way.

Deep-set, dark eyes contrast with white hair

Solid, muscular legs

Very long tail

GREYHOUND

SIZE 27–32kg (59–70lb), 69–76cm (27–30in)
GROOMING Easy
TRAINING Average
COLOURS Black, black or red brindle, red, fawn, white, bicolour

The fastest of all dogs, capable of reaching almost 72km/h (45mph). This gentle breed makes an ideal family companion that chooses to spend its leisure time on the sofa. When something small, fluffy, and moving enters its field of vision, however, the Greyhound undergoes an instant personality change. Regrettably, the racing industry produces a constant surplus of retired individuals in need of new homes.

GREYHOUNDS

The name "greyhound" in English is a misnomer. *Grei* is an old Saxon word meaning fine, or beautiful, and there is perhaps nothing finer or more beautiful in the canine world than a Greyhound running at full throttle. Confirming the antiquity of this breed, these speed merchants are depicted in Egyptian tombs almost 5,000 years old. No one knows where they were first developed, but representative breeds from India, Hungary, Poland, and Britain show that their values and attributes are recognized the world over.

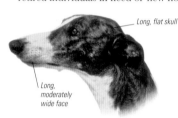

Long, flat skull

Long, moderately wide face

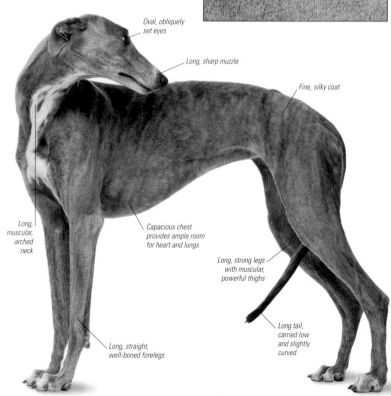

Oval, obliquely set eyes

Long, sharp muzzle

Fine, silky coat

Long, muscular, arched neck

Capacious chest provides ample room for heart and lungs

Long, strong legs with muscular, powerful thighs

Long, straight, well-boned forelegs

Long tail, carried low and slightly curved

HUNGARIAN GREYHOUND

SIZE 22–31kg (49–68lb), 64–70cm (25–28in)
GROOMING Easy
TRAINING Average
COLOURS All colours

Seldom seen outside Hungary or the Transylvania region of Romania, this breed shares the personality attributes of its British cousin (*see opposite*). Although a lively chaser, it is otherwise a placid and retiring dog, not given to shows of emotion. The short coat offers scant protection from the elements, and greyhounds may need insulating coats in cold or wet weather.

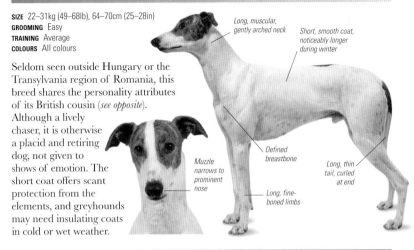

Long, muscular, gently arched neck

Short, smooth coat, noticeably longer during winter

Muzzle narrows to prominent nose

Defined breastbone

Long, thin tail, curled at end

Long, fine-boned limbs

POLISH GREYHOUND

SIZE 23–32kg (51–70lb), 68–80cm (27–31in)
GROOMING Easy
TRAINING Average
COLOURS All colours

Called the Chart Polski in its homeland, these dogs were used by Polish nobility for hunting hares and foxes. During the war and subsequent Communist era, the breed was driven virtually to extinction, but it has been revived. Strong, with a reserved disposition, this dog is also bred in North America.

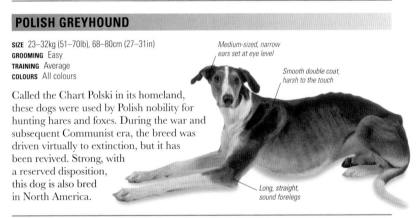

Medium-sized, narrow ears set at eye level

Smooth double coat, harsh to the touch

Long, straight, sound forelegs

RAMPUR GREYHOUND

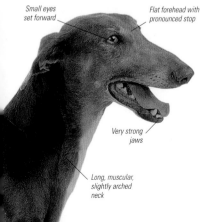

Small eyes set forward

Flat forehead with pronounced stop

Very strong jaws

Long, muscular, slightly arched neck

SIZE 23–32kg (51–70lb), 56–76cm (22–30in)
GROOMING Easy
TRAINING Average
COLOURS All colours

An indigenous sight hound of the Indian subcontinent, this breed is named after the state of Rampur, where it probably originated. English Greyhound blood was introduced in the 1800s, considerably altering the breed's form. Along with the Rampur, two other distinct sight-hound breeds remain today: the Banjara and the Mahratta Greyhound. Rarely seen outside India, the powerful Rampur Greyhound is an instinctive courser, seldom kept as a companion and unsuitable for urban living.

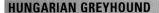

AFGHAN HOUND

SIZE 22.5–27.5kg (50–61lb), 64–74cm (25–29in)
GROOMING Time-consuming
TRAINING Time-consuming
COLOURS All solid or shaded colours

Of all the sight hounds, the Afghan is perhaps the most regal in appearance, with an expression that can seem to look straight through you. Although they are somewhat aloof, they are loyal and affectionate, and exuberant when playing or exercising. The aristocratic expression and luxurious coat of this breed have made

CARAMEL COAT

CHANGING APPEARANCE

The Afghan Hound's luxuriant coat is a result of selective breeding. The breed achieved official recognition in the late 1920s, and the dogs pictured here are typical of early show-quality dogs, before selective breeding to exaggerate length and density created today's dramatic coat.

it a fashion accessory and show dog in the West, but in its native Afghanistan, where there are also short-haired and fringed variants, it is still used to guard flocks and to hunt foxes and wolves. The world's first ever cloned dog, Snuppy (an acronym of "Seoul National University puppy"), was an Afghan pup born in Korea in 2005.

Afghan racing
Increasingly popular, Afghan racing consists of four hounds competing against each other at a set distance.

SLOUGHI

SIZE 20.5–27.5kg (45–61lb), 30–70cm (24–28in)
GROOMING Minimal
TRAINING Average
COLOURS Sand to fawn, sometimes with black shading and/or white markings

This lean, racy hound, also known as the Arabian Greyhound, originated in North Africa, although it is probable that nomadic Arab tribes brought its ancestors there over 1,000 years ago. In the desert environment, the Sloughi's sand-coloured coat provided perfect camouflage when hunting hares, gazelles, and Fennec foxes. It was more than just a hunting dog, however, and was treated very much as a member of the family.

It makes a quiet, dignified companion, but is a little too highly strung for some family households. A naturally vigilant breed, this dog can react aggressively to strangers. Sloughis have tremendous stamina, and need plenty of exercise.

Large, dark, gentle eyes

Pendant ears with rounded tips

Long, thin tail with slight curve at end

Very straight, well-boned forelegs

AZAWAKH

SIZE 17–25kg (37–55lb), 58–74cm (23–29in)
GROOMING Minimal
TRAINING Average
COLOURS Light sable to dark fawn, with white

Sometimes called the Tuareg Sloughi, this alert, independent dog was bred in Mali by the Tuareg people of the southern Sahara as a hunter and a guard. Azawakhs can still be found sleeping on the low straw roofs of their owners's house, and jump down and form packs to see off intruders.

This little-seen breed resembles the Sloughi in many ways, not least its turn of speed: it can reach speeds of up to 60km/h (37mph). The two breeds are also similar in their needs for plenty of exercise and a calm household, ideally without young children.

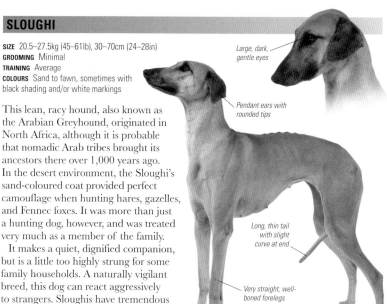

Elongated, muscular neck

Well-dropped, flat, muscular thighs

Well tucked-up abdomen

Deep, powerful chest, reaching to the elbow, with well-sprung ribs

Long, lean, elegant, straight forelegs

AMERICAN STAGHOUND

SIZE 29.5–45kg (65–99lb), 63–84cm (25–33in)
GROOMING Average
TRAINING Easy
COLOURS All colours

Also known simply as the Staghound, this dog is not recognized by any registry, but has been bred selectively for as long as many "official" breeds. The name "Staghound" is misleading. Pioneers in the American West needed dogs that could tackle wolves and Coyotes,

and this dog was the answer, developed from the Scottish Deerhound (*see* p.245), Irish Wolfhound (*see* p.245), and English Greyhound (*see* p.166). It has speed, stamina, and strength, together with an irrepressible urge to hunt, and, although relaxed with other dogs, it cannot be trusted around other small pets. It is now increasingly valued as a companion breed.

Rough, hard topcoat covers dense, fine undercoat

Long tail reaches well below hocks

Long, powerful jaws

LURCHER

SIZE 27.5–32kg (60–70lb), 69–76cm (27–30in)
GROOMING Minimal
TRAINING Average
COLOURS All colours

The Lurcher not only has no written breed standard or official recognition, it is historically a dog of crosses, with each new generation a new cross of greyhounds and collies or terriers. Today, Lurchers are bred to Lurchers, but many coursing competitors are still first-generation crosses. Their distinguishing

characteristics are lightning speed, boundless energy, and an unstoppable urge to chase and kill small game. Although not suited to confined city living, it makes a fine, non-aggressive family pet for those who can keep up with it.

Alert, round, dark eyes

GYPSY DOGS

In Britain and Ireland, the alert and versatile Lurcher is associated with Romany people (Gypsies). Its name may come from *lur*, the Romany word for thief, because of its fame as a poacher's dog. The short-haired Lurcher was historically more prized than the long-haired, its greyhound ancestry providing a useful turn of speed for rabbit and hare poaching.

Strong hind legs

Deep chest provides lung capacity for endurance

LONG-HAIRED VARIETY

IBIZAN HOUND

SIZE 19–25kg (42–55lb), 56–74cm (22–29in)
GROOMING Minimal
TRAINING Time-consuming
COLOURS White, shades of red from lion to chestnut, solid or in combination

The ancestors of this lithe, finely built dog were brought to Ibiza in the Balearic Islands by traders thousands of years ago. Since then, the breed seems to have had more names than it needs. Called the Balearic Dog, Ca Eibisenc, Podenco Ibicenco, and Charnique, to their owners these dogs are often affectionately known as Beezers. They are somewhat reserved with strangers, but demonstrative with their family. As hunting dogs, used for coursing or in packs to hunt rabbits and hares, they are fairly relaxed around other dogs, but pursue other small animals on sight. Both short-haired and wire-haired varieties of the breed exist.

SHORT-HAIRED VARIETY

Large ears funnel sounds to assist in hunting

Strong, lean thighs, well suited to bursts of speed

Steep, rather short shoulders

Long, straight legs

Well-arched toes with light-coloured claws

WIRE-HAIRED VARIETY

PHARAOH HOUND

SIZE 20.5–25kg (45–55lb), 53–63cm (21–25in)
GROOMING Minimal
TRAINING Time-consuming
COLOURS Tan with restricted white markings

The English name of this breed evokes its similarity to the ancient dogs of the Middle East, which Phoenician traders may have spread around the Mediterranean. Its original Maltese name of Kelb-tal Fenek means "rabbit dog", which sounds much less poetic but describes this dog's historic role as a hunter, pursuing small game by sight, smell, and sound. It is still used as a hunter, but since it was "discovered" by breeders in the 1960s, it has become the most popular of the Egyptian-type hounds. It is a calm, affectionate household companion, but it does require plenty of exercise.

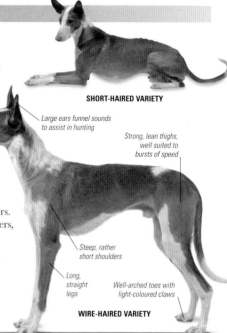

Long, lean, chiselled face

Shoulders laid well back

Short, glossy, but slightly harsh coat

Mobile ears, carried erect when alert

White feet

Long, lean legs

Elegant, lean, muscular neck

GRIFFON NIVERNAIS

SIZE 22–25kg (49–55lb), 53–64cm (21–25in)
GROOMING Average
TRAINING Average
COLOURS Black, fawn, grey

Built for endurance as well as speed, the Griffon Nivernais is occasionally somewhat obstinate when it comes to obedience training. They may descend from rough-coated hounds brought to central Europe up to 800 years ago by Mediterranean traders. The Griffon Nivernais, and its relatives the two Griffons Vendéens, thrived in the central regions of France, where hunting large game was a popular sport among the nobility. Today, the Griffon Nivernais is more often kept as a family companion.

Slight beard on chin

Fairly long head with bristly eyebrows

Long, slightly conical ears

Shaggy, coarse-textured coat

Strong legs covered with dense hair

GRIFFON FAUVE DE BRETAGNE

SIZE 18–22kg (40–49lb), 48–56cm (19–22in)
GROOMING Average
TRAINING Average
COLOURS Red, gold, wheaten, fawn

Shorter in height than the Nivernais, this ancient breed descends from the Fauve de Bretagne. Brittany farmers once used this strongly built dog to track wolves. In the late 1800s, when the breed nearly became extinct, breeders used Briquet Griffon Vendéen bloodlines to revive it, hence its close resemblance to that breed. It makes an affable and excellent house dog.

FRENCH GRIFFONS

The rough-coated, long-legged French hounds probably descend from crosses between greyhounds. The word "griffon" comes from the old French word *greffier* or clerk, as one of the first breeders of griffons was clerk to the French monarchy. These breeds are all larger than the French basset griffons (*see* pp.110–111). Jan van Eyck portrayed a small, griffon-type dog in this 1434 work, *The Arnolfini Marriage*.

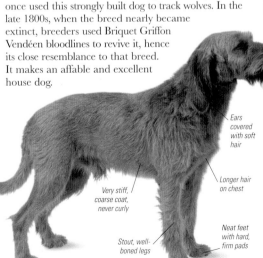

Ears covered with soft hair

Longer hair on chest

Very stiff, coarse coat, never curly

Neat feet with hard, firm pads

Stout, well-boned legs

BRIQUET GRIFFON VENDÉEN

SIZE 22–24kg (48–53lb), 50–55cm (20–22in)
GROOMING Average
TRAINING Average
COLOURS Tricolour, orange and white, cream

Almost wiped out by the ravages of World War II and still relatively unknown, even in France, this adaptable dog was developed from the larger Grand Griffon Vendéen. Breeders say that some individuals have a tendency to be stubborn, but they usually adapt well to urban living if raised in a city environment.

Large, dark eyes

Large, black nose, surrounded by facial whiskers

Dense, wiry coat is never woolly

Narrow, pendulous ears

Thick-boned, muscular legs

Thick-soled feet

GRAND GRIFFON VENDÉEN

SIZE 30–35kg (66–77lb), 60–66cm (24–26in)
GROOMING Average
TRAINING Average
COLOURS Tricolour, orange and white, cream

Probably descended from both the Griffon Nivernais and the St Hubert Hound, this is the largest of the French griffons, the size of an average Golden Retriever. Its coat needs regular brushing, not only to prevent tangles but to avoid a build-up of strong, natural dog odour. After World War II, this breed was revived using bloodlines from the Billy and the Anglo-Français (*see* p.176 and p.174).

Ears shaped like an elongated oval

Large, black nose with moustache

Relaxed expression to eyes

Sabre-like curve to tail

Muscular, robust, well-proportioned thighs

Grass seeds catch easily in dense fur between toes

Dense, insulating, protective coat

GRAND ANGLO-FRANÇAIS BLANC ET NOIR

SIZE 34.5–35.5kg (76–78lb), 62–72cm (24–28in)
GROOMING Minimal
TRAINING Easy
COLOURS Black and white

While the Tricolore (*see box*) is perhaps the most popular household companion of all the large French hounds, the powerful Blanc et Noir is almost solely used for hunting large game such as red deer, roe deer, and wild boar, and is very rarely kept as a companion. All three colours of the Grand Anglo-Français were redeveloped after the turbulence of the French Revolutionary period by crossing imported English Foxhounds, with local, old-type hounds such as the Poitevin and Gascon-Saintongeois.

GRAND ANGLO-FRANÇAIS TRICOLORE

This gentle breed is partly descended from the Poitevin and English Foxhound and is kept both as a companion and as a worker. A third colour, orange and white, is extremely rare.

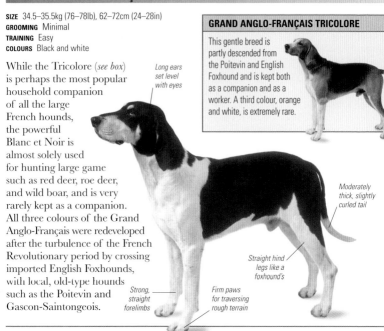

Long ears set level with eyes

Moderately thick, slightly curled tail

Straight hind legs like a foxhound's

Strong, straight forelimbs

Firm paws for traversing rough terrain

FRANÇAIS BLANC ET NOIR

SIZE 34.5–35.5kg (76–78lb), 62–72cm (24–28in)
GROOMING Minimal
TRAINING Easy
COLOURS Black and white

Moderately domed head

Rugged short coat with extensive black saddle

Long, strong neck

Long, muscular legs

As kindly and as gentle as it looks, the Français Blanc et Noir and its cousin the Tricolore make affable companions. They were recreated last century to embody the attributes of historic large French hounds. A French breeder, Henri de Falandre, produced the Blanc et noir by crossing English Foxhounds with the Bleu de Gascogne. Powerfully built with a superb voice, these dogs are excellent small-game hunters, easy to train and energetic. Seldom seen outside France, these breeds are not suited to city life.

FRANÇAIS TRICOLORE

The Tricolore was created by crossing the English Foxhound with the Poitevin and Billy. Both colour variants of the Français seem to have endless stamina and thrive on work. As with many scent-trailers, they are calm with other dogs.

GRAND BLEU DE GASCOGNE

SIZE 32–35kg (70–77lb), 62–72cm (24–28in)
GROOMING Easy
TRAINING Easy
COLOURS Black, tan and blue

Originating in Gascony, by the Spanish border, and probably descended from hounds brought to that region by Phoenician traders, this handsome scent tracker is now more numerous in the United States than in its French homeland. In the southern US it is used to track raccoons and deer, while in Europe its original purpose as a wolf tracker has been superseded by work tracking deer or wild boar. It is also increasingly popular in Europe as a calm but extremely vocal household companion.

LARGE FRENCH HOUNDS

Medieval France was at the forefront of developing an enormous variety of large scent hounds, with vast packs hunting through the parks and forests of the King and his nobles. This tradition ended abruptly with the French Revolution of 1789; some packs were taken to England but the majority were lost. Most of today's dogs are modern re-creations. *A PACK OF HOUNDS, C.O. DE PENNE (1832–97)*

GRAND GASCON-SAINTONGEOIS

SIZE 30–32kg (66–70lb), 63–71cm (25–28in)
GROOMING Minimal
TRAINING Easy
COLOURS White and black

Bred in the 1840s as a roe-deer pack hunter, this muscular, leggy dog is still a popular pack hunter for large game in southwest France near the Pyrenees. Although the breed has never been bred solely for the role, if raised in a family home it makes a gentle companion: easy to train, not given to aggression, and safe and amenable with children and other dogs. However, it does have a magnificent voice which it willingly uses if bored and not given the opportunity to exercise frequently.

Clear tan markings restricted to head

Well-set, round tail

Long, straight, well-boned legs

Rather large, oval feet

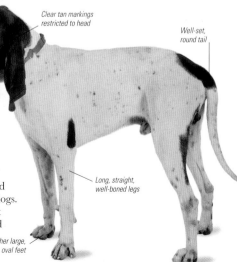

ARIÉGEOIS

SIZE 25–30kg (55–66lb), 53–61cm (21–24in)
GROOMING Minimal
TRAINING Easy
COLOURS Black and white

Supple skin covered with fine hair

Flat, muscular thighs for propulsive power

Slightly smaller than the Grand Gascon-Saintongeois, this easy-going and affectionate breed was produced in Ariège, southwest France, in the late 1800s as a small game hunter. Today it is mostly a soulful-looking household companion, but its hunting instincts have not been diminished. Often seen in Paris and other French cities, its southern origins also allow it to adapt well to warm climates.

BILLY

SIZE 25–33kg (55–73lb), 58–70cm (23–28in)
GROOMING Minimal
TRAINING Easy
COLOURS White with orange or yellow

Short coat, hard to the touch

Very deep, narrow chest

Strong, well-boned forelegs

Named after the Château de Billy in Poitou, this breed is rare even in Poitou. Today's whole population descend from two dogs that survived World War II. It was originally created by one man, Hublot du Rivault, who combined three now-extinct local breeds, the Céris, Larrye, and Montaimboeuf. Today, this relaxed dog with a deep voice is primarily a family companion.

POITEVIN

SIZE 25–34kg (55–75lb), 58–69cm (23–27in)
GROOMING Minimal
TRAINING Easy
COLOURS Tricolour, orange and white

Thin ears hang with slight fold

Long, slender, well-muscled neck

Long, straight, densely-boned legs

Also from the Poitou region, most of the few packs that survived the French Revolution were destroyed in a local rabies epidemic in 1842. The breed was rejuvenated using English Foxhound bloodlines, but remains rare today. Like all the other large French scent hounds, the gentle and friendly Poitevin adapts well to family life when raised from puppyhood in a home environment.

French hunting pack
Hunting with pack hounds remains both popular and legal in France. These French hunters, dressed in the traditional colours of their local hunt and carrying hunting horns, attend a local game fair with their pack of Poitevins.

FOXHOUND

SIZE 25–34kg (55–75lb), 58–69cm (23–27in)
GROOMING Minimal
TRAINING Average
COLOURS Black, tan, white, in any combination

Called the Foxhound in its homeland and the English Foxhound elsewhere, this is the classic modern hunting breed. As pack dogs, they are relaxed with other dogs and friendly with people, but are rarely kept as companions. Their athletic speed and capacity for sudden sprints, combined with a strong urge to pursue anything that looks like a fox, can turn walks into chases. Developed from French and English hounds as fox hunting's popularity grew in the 14th century, their working future is in doubt since hunting to kill with dogs in Britain is now banned.

Long, but never thick, neck

Colour and markings highly variable between individuals

Thickly boned legs with short, straight pasterns

AMERICAN FOXHOUND

Leggier than its English counterpart, and descended from English, Irish, and French hounds, this ardent and strong-voiced dog tends to work individually rather than as a group. Used for fox hunting in northern states, it is also used for night time scent-trailing in southern states. Unlike the English Foxhound, most of these dogs are raised as both family and working dogs.

PORCELAINE

SIZE 25–28kg (55–62lb), 53–58cm (21–23in)
GROOMING Minimal
TRAINING Easy
COLOURS White with a few spots of yellow or orange

Few of this endearing breed survived the Reign of Terror following the French Revolution of 1789. Those that did, mostly in regions by the Swiss border, were bred by Swiss breeders, using additional Swiss laufhund bloodlines. Numbers are small and limited to France and Switzerland, where they make fine family companions.

Reflective, smooth glossy coat

Powerful hind legs with well-muscled thighs

Broad feet with well-arched toes

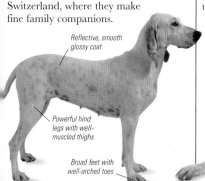

HARRIER

SIZE 22–27.5kg (49–60lb), 46–56cm (18–22in)
GROOMING Minimal
TRAINING Easy
COLOURS All colours

The name Harrier, from the French *harier*, or "hunting dog", perfectly describes this dog. Records of Harriers go back to the Penistone pack in the west of England in 1260, but it is not formally recognized in its native country. It came close to dying out in the 20th century, and was revived using Foxhound crosses; Bloodhounds and Beagles may have been used in its earlier breeding. Relaxed and gregarious, it is reliable with children.

Very level, powerful back

Chest broader than deep

BASSET HOUND

SIZE 18–27kg (40–60lb), 33–38cm (13–15in)
GROOMING Minimal
TRAINING Average/time-consuming
COLOURS Black, tan, lemon, white in any combination

Long, low-set ears

Slightly sunken eyes with soft expression

Weight born heavily on centre of paws

Short but massive, the Basset (from the French word *bas* for low) is a hound once used to hunt in packs. Originating in France and possibly descended from dwarfed Bloodhounds, selective breeding shortened the legs so that human hunters could keep pace. They are mild and affectionate by nature, with tuneful voices.

It may be the hound described by Shakespeare in *A Midsummer Night's Dream*: "their heads are hung/With ears that sweep away the morning dew/Crook-knee'd, and dew-lapp'd like Thessalian bulls". This singular appearance has a practical function: the long ears sweep the ground, stirring up scent on a trail, while splayed feet give stability. Lighter examples still take part in field trials, but the majority of Bassets are now to be found lounging langorously in family homes. Exaggerated breeding for excessively long backs and ears has, to some extent, been reduced, but there is still a higher-than-average incidence of back pain and irritating eye conditions. Paw problems are also common in older individuals.

CREATURE COMFORTS

The Basset's lugubrious expression has made it popular as a comedy turn in drawings and occasionally on film. The *Fred Basset* cartoon strip has run in the *Daily Mail* newspaper in the UK for over three decades and has also become a success across the Atlantic. These dogs have even been used to advertise shoes, an association that unfortunately pushed the breed's popularity to the point where it suffered problems due to irresponsible breeding, a common drawback with breeds subject to fads.

Sophisticated Hush Puppies.

HUSH PUPPIES SHOES

Expert hunter
Taking a break from following a trail, this Basset's lifted head displays the folds of skin under the chin that help to trap and retain the scent.

FINNISH HOUND

SIZE 20–25kg (44–55lb), 56–63cm (22–25in)
GROOMING Minimal
TRAINING Average
COLOURS Tricolour

This is Finland's most popular native working breed, also called the Finsk Stövare or Suomenajokoira. Summer hunting dogs have been known in Finland since at least the 18th century, but this hound is the result of a 19th-century breeding programme using Swedish, German, and French hounds. The result is a friendly breed that follows scent and calls a hunter to shot gamebirds, but does not retrieve. Gentle with children and calm with dogs, it makes a good household dog but needs plenty of company and exercise.

Lean, noble-looking head

Dense, coarse coat

Long, high-set ears

White facial blaze

Powerfully built limbs

Tough, resilient pads

OTTERHOUND

SIZE 29.5–54kg (65–120lb), 58–69cm (23–27in)
GROOMING Average
TRAINING Average
COLOURS All colours

Otterhounds have been known in Britain for at least 1,000 years. The exact breed origins are obscure, but may have involved Bloodhound, rough-coated terriers, ancient foxhounds, or the French Griffon Nivernais (*see* p.172). The Otterhound's job was to follow otters into rivers and their dens on day-long hunts. Consequently, it is a cold-hardy, tireless breed that loves water, happiest in a home with access to a river. In character, it is cheerful and even-tempered, and now that otters are protected rather than hunted, efforts are being made to increase its limited numbers and establish it as a household companion. In Britain the Otterhound is considered an "endangered breed".

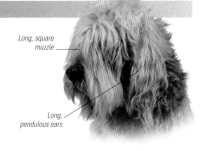

Long, square muzzle

Long, pendulous ears

Harsh, bristly topcoat covering woolly undercoat

Well-muscled hindquarters

BLACK-AND-TAN COONHOUND

SIZE 23–34kg (51–75lb), 58–69cm (23–27in)
GROOMING Minimal
TRAINING Average
COLOURS Blue, brindle

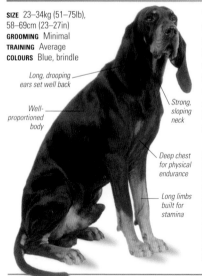

Long, drooping ears set well back

Well-proportioned body

Strong, sloping neck

Deep chest for physical endurance

Long limbs built for stamina

The most popular of all the coonhounds, the Black-and-tan is a common rural companion in the states on the Eastern Seaboard with its popularity extending well into Canada. It is also the most frequent sufferer of a serious condition called coonhound paralysis, a medical complaint first reported in coonhounds but occasionally seen in other breeds. Black-and-tans are vocal, friendly companions.

AMERICAN COONHOUNDS

The Coonhounds, descended from large French, Irish, and English hounds, are among the world's more specialized breeds. They vocally follow the scent trail of a raccoon or opossum until their quarry is cornered up a tree and then change the tone of their baying voice to one that the hunter recognizes as "It's here!"

REDBONE COONHOUND

SIZE 23–32kg (51–70lb), 53–66cm (21–26in)
GROOMING Minimal
TRAINING Easy
COLOURS Red, red and white

Broad muzzle

In action, tail is held upright

The Redbone is named not after its colour but after Peter Redbone of Tennessee, an early breeder. It is the only solid-coloured coonhound, although some individuals have white hair on the feet and chest. As with all the coonhounds, this makes a gentle and affectionate companion if raised from puppyhood in the home.

Strong forelegs

Well-proportioned, robust physique

ENGLISH COONHOUND

SIZE 18–29.5kg (40–65lb), 53–69cm (21–27in)
GROOMING Minimal
TRAINING Easy
COLOURS All colours

Long, pendant ears

Powerful, muscular shoulders

Ticked areas apparent in coat

Most often seen in redtick colour, these hounds were developed in Virginia, Tennessee, and Kentucky. Smaller than the Black-and-tan, they are popular as family companions and are typically relaxed and gentle with children. As with all the coonhounds, females are considerably smaller than males. Unlike all other coonhounds, any colour is acceptable within the breed.

RED TICK

Sturdy, straight forelegs

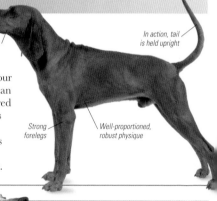

Drooping lips help capture scent

BLACK TICK

BLUETICK COONHOUND

SIZE 20.5–36kg (45–79lb), 51–69cm (20–27in)
GROOMING Minimal
TRAINING Easy
COLOURS Tricolour

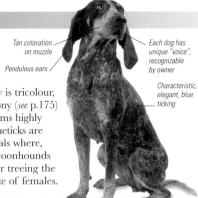

Tan coloration on muzzle

Pendulous ears

Each dog has unique "voice", recognizable by owner

Characteristic, elegant, blue ticking

This dog's elegant coat, which technically is tricolour, suggests that hunting hounds from Gascony (*see* p.175) played a part in its development. This seems highly likely considering its Louisiana origins. Blueticks are frequent participants in licensed night trials where, over three hours, teams of three to four coonhounds track and tree raccoons. Points are lost for treeing the wrong game. Males can be double the size of females.

TREEING WALKER COONHOUND

SIZE 22.5–32kg (50–70lb), 58–69cm (23–27in)
GROOMING Minimal
TRAINING Easy
COLOURS Tricolour, bicolour

Long, thin muzzle

Clearly defined areas of colour

Smooth, fine, glossy coat

Compact feet with thick pads

Most similar in looks to the English Foxhound, this breed is named after Thomas Walker who imported English Foxhounds into Virginia in 1742. Its task of "treeing" involves confining an opossum or raccoon to a tree, then altering its howl, telling the hunter that game is cornered. As do all coonhounds, this makes an elegant family companion when raised from puppyhood in a home environment.

Large, broad ears hang down back of head

PLOTT HOUND

SIZE 20.5–25kg (45–55lb), 50–60cm (20–24in)
GROOMING Minimal
TRAINING Easy
COLOURS Blue, brindle

Deep-set eyes with dark, drooping eyelids

This breed bears the name of the Carolina family that has bred it for almost 250 years. It is kept for hunting raccoons in the eastern United States and mountain lions further west. Alone among American coonhounds, its ancestors were German hounds, and it has an unusual high-pitched voice. In other respects it is a typical coonhound: lean, muscular, tireless, needing plenty of exercise. Also reliable, it makes a good household dog, but is usually kept as a hunter's companion.

Lean, powerful thigh muscles

Strong feet with webbed toes

HYGENHUND

SIZE 20–24kg (44–53lb), 47–58cm (19–23in)
GROOMING Minimal
TRAINING Average
COLOURS Tan and white, chestnut, yellow, chestnut and black

Kept primarily as a hunting dog rather than for companionship, this Norwegian hare hunter is named after its first breeder. It was developed from local hounds crossed with imports from the German–Danish border region. It makes a reliable watchdog, gets on moderately well with other dogs, needs vigorous exercise, and has a tendency to snap or bite. It is not a city dog, and when the weather permits, it is content to live outdoors, although it is a breed that needs protection from very cold conditions.

Wedge-shaped head

Ears stand away from head

Deep chest

Well-arched toes

Smooth, dense coat

Straight, lean forelegs

POLISH HOUND

SIZE 25–32kg (55–70lb), 56–66cm (22–26in)
GROOMING Minimal
TRAINING Easy
COLOURS Black, grey, brown, black and tan

This friendly hunting breed dates back to the 18th century, although its origins remain obscure. Its conformation and locale suggest that it is a relative of the St Hubert Hound, and was then crossed with German hounds. World War II very nearly made the breed extinct, but Polish hunters successfully found enough survivors to perpetuate this rustic dog. Remaining rare outside their homeland, Polish Hounds are excellent trackers, persistent and enduring, using their medium-toned voices when latching on to a scent trail of large game. They make easy-going if energetic household companions.

Deep, broad, chest

Black saddle marking

Thick tail

A RECENT REVIVAL

Today's Ogar Polski, as it is called in Poland, was developed after World War II by Colonel Kartwik, using surviving dogs from the Polish Nowogrodek region. A similar smaller dog, the Gonczy Polski, no longer exists.

HALDENSTÖVARE

SIZE 23–29kg (51–64lb), 51–64cm (20–25in)
GROOMING Minimal
TRAINING Average
COLOURS White with black-and-brown markings

This breed takes its name from its place of origin, near Halden, in southern Norway. Remaining relatively obscure, even in Scandinavia, it is a young breed, created in the early 20th century from crosses of English Foxhounds and local hounds, and was recognized in 1950. Like other Norwegian hounds, it was developed to hunt singly with its owner rather than in a pack. It is a calm and friendly breed that thrives on human companionship. Although the very fine coat needs little attention, the Haldenstövare should be protected from extreme cold.

Long, curved neck

Smooth, shiny, very fine coat

Deep chest

Oval feet, with well-arched toes

HAMILTONSTÖVARE

SIZE 23–27kg (51–60lb), 46–60cm (18–24in)
GROOMING Minimal
TRAINING Average
COLOURS Tricolour

Although there have been hunting hounds of this kind in Sweden since the Middle Ages, this breed was first shown in only 1886. It can be traced back to crosses of Swedish hounds with English Foxhounds and German Beagles. These crosses were made by Adolf Patrick Hamilton, the founder of the Swedish Kennel Club. The Hamiltonstövare is one of the most populous breeds in Sweden, used singly rather than as a pack hunter for tracking and flushing hares and foxes. It is even-tempered and reliable around children and other dogs, and it has gained a foothold as a companion breed in Britain.

TRACKER, GUNDOG, AND COMPANION

Long, powerful neck merges with shoulders

Long muzzle tipped with large, black nose

Deep chest

White markings on feet, muzzle, and chest

Tail thick at root, tapering to tip

SEGUGIO ITALIANO

SIZE 18–28kg (40–62lb), 52–58cm (20–23in)
GROOMING Minimal
TRAINING Easy
COLOURS Black and tan, shades from wheaten to deep red, limited white markings

Low-set, long, folded ears

Dense, short, glossy coat

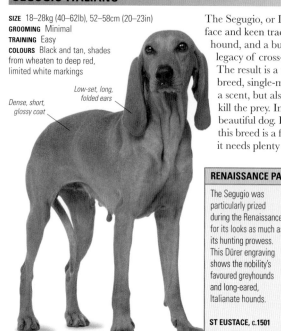

The Segugio, or Italian Hound, has the face and keen tracking ability of a scent hound, and a bulkier frame that is the legacy of cross-breeding with mastiffs. The result is a wonderfully versatile breed, single-minded in pursuit of a scent, but also keen to capture and kill the prey. In addition, it makes a beautiful dog. Reliable and affectionate, this breed is a fine companion, although it needs plenty of physical activity.

RENAISSANCE PAINTING

The Segugio was particularly prized during the Renaissance, for its looks as much as its hunting prowess. This Dürer engraving shows the nobility's favoured greyhounds and long-eared, Italianate hounds.

ST EUSTACE, c.1501

SABUESO ESPAÑOL

SIZE 20–25kg (44–55lb), 46–56cm (18–22in)
GROOMING Minimal
TRAINING Average
COLOURS Red and white, black and white

This breed has an ancestry of mastiffs and Bloodhounds, possibly extending back to the extinct Talbot Hound, and was bred in isolation from other northern European hounds on the Iberian peninsula. It is a tracker of great stamina that thrives on hard work and is used alone, rather than in packs. Also known as the Spanish Hound, sizes of the breed vary considerably; a smaller variant, the Lebrero, is now virtually extinct. It does not make an ideal companion, as it can be troublesome around unfamiliar dogs. As with all breeds of dog, however, early socialization diminishes this potential concern.

Long ears extending to, or beyond, tip of nose

Large dewlap

Fine, glossy coat and loose, flexible skin

Short legs in relation to body

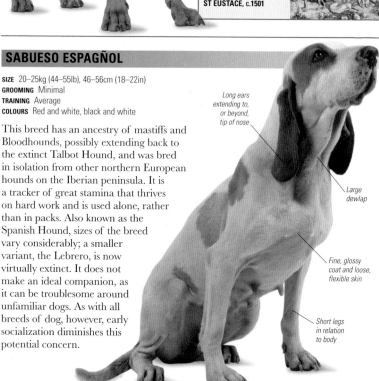

BAVARIAN MOUNTAIN HOUND

SIZE 25–35kg (55–77lb), 50cm (20in)
GROOMING Minimal
TRAINING Easy
COLOURS Fawn, red, red brindle, black brindle

This breed is very rarely seen except as the working companion of game wardens and hunters in Germany and the Czech and Slovak Republics. It is also known by its native name of the Bayerischer Gebirgsschweisshund. It is a hound of unsurpassed scenting ability and agility, developed by crossing the Hanoverian Hound with short-legged Bavarian hounds. This tenacious but amenable and level-headed breed is often used to follow cold trails in the forests of Bavaria where other dogs have failed; the honour code of the middle-European hunter instructs that no animal should be left to die on its own.

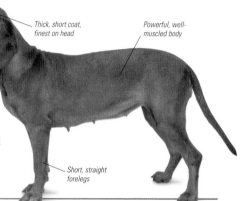

Thick, short coat, finest on head

Powerful, well-muscled body

Short, straight forelegs

TRANSYLVANIAN HOUND

SIZE Short-legged: 22–25kg (49–55lb), 45–50cm (18–20in)
     Long-legged: 30–35kg (66–77lb), 55–65cm (22–26in)
GROOMING Minimal
TRAINING Easy
COLOURS Black and tan, tricolour

This somewhat reserved breed, also called the Erdelyi Kopo, was developed to hunt small and large game and comes in two sizes. It has probably been in Transylvania since the Middle Ages, arriving west from Russia or north through the Balkans. After 1,000 years in the region, it nearly died out during World War II. Worse was to come when, in 1947, the dogs were exterminated on government orders, since they were reminders of the Hungarian "occupation" of Romania. Fortunately, there were a few survivors in Slovakia and Hungary, and breeders in these countries are gradually reviving the breed.

Long head with slightly rounded skull

HANOVERIAN HOUND

SIZE 38–44kg (84–97lb), 51–61cm (20–24in)
GROOMING Minimal
TRAINING Average
COLOURS Black, black-brindle, red

Affable, calm, and relaxed, this northern German equivalent of the French St Hubert hound, or the English Bloodhound, is thought of as a professional's dog. It can frequently be seen accompanying German foresters and game wardens. Once a pack hound, it now works singly and is rarely seen outside Germany. Its docile disposition means it is well suited to family life, but a powerful instinct to track game (and people) make it a challenge to train.

Heavy, pendulous lips

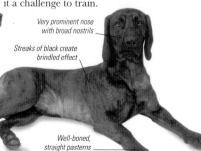

Very prominent nose with broad nostrils

Streaks of black create brindled effect

Well-boned, straight pasterns

GERMAN SHEPHERD DOG

SIZE 28–44kg (62–97lb), 55–66cm (22–26in)
GROOMING Average to time-consuming
TRAINING Easy
COLOURS Black and tan, white, black, and sable

Probably the world's most numerous breed of dog, all of today's millions of German Shepherd Dogs descend from a small population of working shepherd dogs from northwest Germany. Only a hundred years ago, there was a great

Lustrous, long hair covering slightly shorter undercoat

BLACK LONG-HAIRED

Tail carried down with a slight curve while resting

Straight, strong forelegs

variety of coat types and body shapes among shepherd dogs in northern Germany. A retired German cavalry officer, Max von Stephanitz, was to change that. With a stockman's keen eye and an entrepreneur's confidence, he purchased a local shepherd dog, and, with the help of a colleague, set up the German Shepherd Club (Verein für Deutsche Schäferhunde, or SV), registering the world's first German Shepherd. Von Stephanitz was a superb publicist. When the Great War broke out in 1914, he offered some of his dogs for military service, and by the end of the war, 48,000 had served in Germany's armed forces. The success of these dogs as message carriers, telephone

Ever alert
Erect, forward-facing ears and intense eyes give this German Shepherd the classic look of the watchful, ever-vigilant companion.

Travelling companion
German Shepherd Dogs bond firmly with their families and enjoy participating in all their activities, especially outdoors.

line layers, and scouts was noted by Allied troops, and soldiers returning to Britain and North America took German Shepherds with them. The reputation of the breed was enhanced further through Hollywood films such as *Strongheart*. Already the most popular breed in Germany, by the 1950s, the TV series *The Adventures of Rin Tin Tin* had made it one of the most prized dogs in North America and the UK.

WHAT ARE ALSATIANS?

When British soldiers brought German Shepherds to the UK after World War I, anti-German feeling was still intense. Breeders decided it would be diplomatic to rename the breed after the province of Alsace, which was German until the war but is now part of France. Enmity towards Germany continued and it was not until the late 1970s that British breeders recognized the breed by the name used worldwide and re-named their club The German Shepherd Dog (Alsatian) Club.

Medium-sized, erect ears, wide at base

Muzzle half the length of head

Hard, straight topcoat with dense undercoat

BLACK-AND-TAN SHORT-HAIRED

By the early 1970s, there were well over a million German Shepherds in the United States alone, with over 100,000 registered there annually. However, breeding was no longer in the hands of dedicated people who bred for reliable character and sound health. The virtues and soundness of the breed started to decline, and so too did its numbers. In the press it became a "devil dog". But the problem of aggression in the breed was never a genetic problem; it was a social phenomenon. Today, the German Shepherd is acknowledged as the world's most successful police and military dog.

This is a strong, agile, and ever-alert dog, friendly within a family, but often cautious with strangers. With its rhythmic gait, it is an all-round action dog that participates in herding and tracking and excels at agility and obedience. German Shepherds shed hair profusely. Sadly, they may also suffer from medical problems, including chronic degenerative radiculomyelopathy (CDRM) and hip dysplasia, causing incurable progressive loss of use of the hind limbs.

THE BERGER BLANC SUISSE, OR WHITE SHEPHERD

The colour white is "undesirable" according to UK standards, but downright "verboten" in the United States, where dogs of that colour are disqualified from the show ring. Nevertheless, creamy-white pups are not rare in German Shepherd litters. In 2002, Swiss breeders sought and achieved recognition from the FCI for a "new" breed, the Berger Blanc Suisse. This breed is also recognized by one of the American canine registries, the United Kennel Club, as the White Shepherd. Elsewhere, it is still simply a German Shepherd Dog (white).

Agility champions
With natural athleticism and complete
trust in its handler, a German Shepherd
leaps fearlessly through a flaming hoop.

GIANT SCHNAUZER

SIZE 32–35kg (70–77lb), 60–70cm (24–28in)
GROOMING Average
TRAINING Easy
COLOURS Pepper and salt, black

Developed by increasing the size of the standard Schnauzer (*see* p.126), the Riesen-schnauzer, as it is also known, was once commonly found as a herding dog in southern Germany. The breed was first shown in 1909 under the name Russian Bear Schnauzer. At one time its extensive feeding habits led to a waning in popularity, but it regained some ground as a butcher's dog. Its territorial instincts and considerable power mean that this breed is not always suitable for a household with other dogs in it, but it makes a good guard dog. Arthritis in the shoulders and hips can be a problem.

Strong, rather square profile

Robust, slanting upper thighs

HOVAWART

SIZE 25–41kg (55–90lb), 58–70cm (23–28in)
GROOMING Average
TRAINING Average
COLOURS Golden, black, black and gold

The first mention of the "Hofwarth", an estate guard dog, is in Eike von Repgow's *Sachsenspiegel* of 1220. In the late 19th century, a group of breeders decided to re-create the Hovawart, using farm dogs from the Black Forest and Harz mountain regions. These may have been crossed with the Hungarian Kuvasz, Newfoundland, and the German Shepherd. The elegant results were first recognized in 1936, and

Domed head
Straight muzzle
Dark, oval eyes

BLACK-AND-GOLD COAT

All-weather dog
Vigorous and athletic, the Hovawart thrives on physical activity. The dense double coat provides excellent thermal protection in cold climates.

the Hovawart is now established in several European countries. A reserved dog, it is easy to train and generally sociable with children and other dogs, but some strains are prone to fear biting.

DUTCH SHEPHERD DOG

SIZE 29.5–30kg (65–66lb), 55–63cm (22–25in)
GROOMING Average
TRAINING Easy
COLOURS Range from black brindle to red brindle

This breed developed in the 19th century as an adaptable, all-purpose farm dog for herding, guarding, and pulling small carts. It comes from the southern part of the Netherlands, especially the province of Brabant, and from neighbouring Belgium. The breed shares similar origins with the Belgian Shepherds (*see* pp.192–193) and German Shepherd Dog (*see* pp.186–189). Curiously, it has not gained the popularity of these breeds, remaining rare even in its native land and almost unknown outside it.

The Dutch Shepherd Dog is one of the most competent of the shepherd breeds, excelling in trials and used as a security and police dog. As a companion it is loyal and dependable, but still playful and highly energetic, and makes a good family dog or guard dog. The breed was divided into Long-haired, Short-haired, and Wire-haired versions when showing started at the turn of the 20th century. All three coats are fairly hard and offer excellent protection against the cold.

Hard, wiry hair with close, dense undercoat

WIRE-HAIRED VARIETY

POLICE TRAINING

The Royal Dutch Police Dog Association (KNPV) trains Dutch Shepherd Dogs in all aspects of police dog work. The dog shown here is responding to the "Attach" command, which is actually a form of "Retrieve" training. Many police forces, including Britain's Metropolitan Police, train police dogs to retrieve an object, often a cricket bat inside the sleeve of a coat. Police dogs graduate from retrieving this "heavy sleeve" to retrieving the sleeve of a person wearing protective clothing.

Triangular, erect ears set high on head

Medium-length muzzle with prominent nostrils

Protective hair growing between toes

Long, parallel, well-muscled forelegs

SHORT-HAIRED VARIETY

BELGIAN SHEPHERDS

SIZE 27.5–28.5kg (61–63lb), 56–66cm (22–26in)
GROOMING Time-consuming
TRAINING Easy
COLOURS Grey, through fawn and red to black

Classifying the Belgian Shepherds is not easy because national kennel clubs cannot agree on how to name them. In 1891, Professor Adolphe Reul, of the Belgian School of Veterinary Science, conducted a field study of all the existing sheepdogs in Belgium. Eventually, four different breeds came to be recognized nationally. In many countries, these are classified as varieties of one breed, namely the Belgian Shepherd. In the United States, however, the Groenendael is the Belgian Shepherd, while the Malinois and Tervueren are recognized separately, and the Laekenois not at all. These dogs are all similar in type, differing only in terms of their coloration and coat length. Not naturally aggressive, the Belgian Shepherds are excellent family companions, although they can be wary of strangers and timid.

From the Malines region of Belgium, the Malinois is one of the least common of the Belgian shepherds. It is, however,

Neck broadens close to shoulders

Hindquarters fringed with longer hair

Forelegs held close to body

MALINOIS

the first to have a written breed standard, and the closest in conformation to the German Shepherd Dog and the Smooth-haired Dutch Shepherd (*see* pp.186–189 and p.191). The Malinois is both a highly successful scent detector and police dog.

Enduring stamina
While many breeds thrive on physical activity, Belgian Shepherds such as this Malinois have enormous energy and endurance, whether at play, in the agility ring, or in police work.

The breeding of the Groenendael began in about 1890, almost by chance. Nicholas Rose, the owner of the Belgian Café du Groenendael, bred a black puppy, and obtained another. This pair formed the basis of the distinctive, long-haired breed.

The shaggy, rustic-looking Laekenois is the rarest of the Belgian Shepherds. A favourite of Queen Henrietta of Belgium, it acquired its name from the Château de Laeken, a residence she frequently visited. It is fairly easy to obedience train and a superb companion, and therefore hard to explain why it is not more popular.

The Tervueren is accorded separate breed status, although Groenendael matings occasionally produce Tervueren puppies. This variety of Belgian Shepherd has become enormously popular as a drug-detecting dog. Easy to train, it is equally successful on the agility trials circuit.

What the Belgian shepherds perpetuate is the great coat variety dating back to when dogs were bred for utility and function. You can see it in the Groenendael's long, black hair, the Tervueren's long, tawny coat, the Malinois's short, tawny coat, and the Laekenois's wiry-textured coat.

Dark eyes and rims contrasting with lighter coloured hair

TERVUEREN

Bristly, feathered muzzle

Dense hair, bushy on tail, with no distinct feathering

Long, smooth, black hair, especially abundant around shoulders, neck, and chest

LAEKENOIS

MULTI-PURPOSE DOGS

Regardless of coat length or texture (revealed by recent studies as the only significant genetic difference between these four breeds), Belgian Shepherds are champion multi-taskers. Some individuals thrive in the obedience ring, while others are champions in the agility field. A Belgian Shepherd may be superb at Flyball and equally adept at moving sheep; a star in the show ring and at the same time a vigilant home companion. With these all-round qualities, its worldwide popularity is unsurprising.

Long feathering extending from foreleg to wrist

GROENENDAEL

BOUVIER DES FLANDRES

SIZE 27–40kg (60–88lb), 58–69cm (23–27in)
GROOMING Time-consuming
TRAINING Average
COLOURS Range, from fawn to black

Bouviers are cattle-herding dogs, and there was once a wide range of these across Belgium. The Bouvier des Flandres is the best known of the three surviving breeds, with the Bouvier des Ardennes still very

Powerful neck muscles

Chest descends to level of elbows

Powerful jumpers
As well as having a great herding instinct, in France, Belgium, and the Netherlands Bouviers participate in agility trials. The breed is also trained as a police dog.

rare, and Bouvier de Roulers on the verge of extinction. The muscular Bouvier des Flandres does not resemble either of the other two, which are far more rangy, and may have been created from crosses of the old-type Beauceron and griffons. It was used in the medical corps of the French Army during World War I, and numbers were very low afterwards. The intervention of the Belgian Kennel Club saved the breed, which is now popular as a companion in several countries, particularly the United States. It is generally amiable, but its aggressive side can come out around other dogs, and it makes a good guard dog. The distinctive, rough double coat and beard need a lot of attention and regular clipping.

BERGER PICARD

SIZE 23–32kg (51–70lb), 55–66cm (22–26in)
GROOMING Time-consuming
TRAINING Easy
COLOURS Grey, fawn, gold, black

Picardy has been a cruel place for dogs in the 20th century. Trench warfare in the region in World War I diminished numbers, and the ravages of World War II drove the breed to near extinction. Because it has never gained popularity on the show circuit, the Berger Picard survives primarily on farms in northeastern France. Its thick, weatherproof coat is ideal for the damp climate, while the ease with which it can be obedience trained and its natural inclination to herd and guard sheep make it a reliable but underestimated breed, unfortunately on the verge of extinction.

Erect, high-set ears, wide at base

Thick eyebrows do not shield eyes

Dark nose

Harsh coat, crisp to touch

Solidly boned legs

BRIARD

SIZE 34–34.5kg (75–76lb), 58–69cm (23–27in)
GROOMING Time-consuming
TRAINING Average
COLOURS Shades of fawn or grey, black

With an ancestry that may include the Beauceron and the Barbet, this breed is named after the French province of Brie, although it is far from certain that it originated there. The Briard has been a shepherd's guardian for centuries, becoming more widely popular in the latter part of the 19th century, and is one of France's most popular companion breeds today. Used by the French army in World War I, it was taken to the United States by returning soldiers, but took 50 years to become established there. Breeders have worked to eliminate shyness and aggression, and the best Briards make lively but well-mannered companions and guard dogs.

Ears covered by long hair

Square muzzle with black nose

Slightly wavy, very dry coat

BEAUCERON

SIZE 30–39kg (66-86lb), 64–71cm (25–28in)
GROOMING Minimal
TRAINING Average
COLOURS Black and tan, black, harlequin

Also from Brie, and with double dewclaws like its different-coated but genetically close relative the Briard, this physically imposing, powerful, and agile dog is now found throughout northern France. With a history of hunting and boar herding, today it is kept as a companion and guard. A reliable working dog, the Beauceron is also increasingly popular on the European show circuit. Because of its imposing size, first meetings with other dogs should be carried out under supervision.

Powerful neck

Long muzzle with black nose

Rough, short, dense coat

Reddish-tan colour on legs

Double dewclaws on hind feet

PORTUGUESE CATTLE DOG

SIZE 23–34kg (51–75lb), 51–61cm (20–24in)
GROOMING Average
TRAINING Time-consuming
COLOURS Range, through grey to shades of brindle

Originating in the region of the town of Castro Laboreiro, the Cão de Castro Laboreiro, as it is called in Portugal, is a natural guardian, used to a more limited extent to herd sheep and cattle. The breed is inclined to give its opinion through its voice, a deep growl proceeding to sharp, threatening barking. This sentinel behaviour makes it an equally good watchdog. Rarely seen outside its native land, it is typical of the livestock guardians that exist in the Iberian peninsula and the Balkans, and these dogs willingly use threatening behaviour to intimidate predators, including people. A rugged, powerful dog, it requires experienced, firm handling.

Large narrow head

Medium-sized ears

Medium-sized, almond-shaped eyes with slightly severe expression

Wide, deep, powerful chest

Straight, well-boned legs

CA DE BESTIAR – MALLORQUIN SHEPHERD

SIZE 35–40kg (77–88lb), 62–73cm (24–29in)
GROOMING Average
TRAINING Time-consuming
COLOURS Black, black brindle

Another no-nonsense livestock guarding and herding breed, the Ca de Bestiar developed in the Balearic Islands off the coast of Spain and has always been bred for its practical uses. Larger than the Portuguese Cattle Dog, it fulfils the same two functions, protecting and moving sheep and cattle. The breed can be found in South America, working as guard dogs on family estates, and some have been trialled in the American northwest for use in coyote control on sheep ranches. What this enthusiastic breed lacks in visual appeal it makes up for in companionship.

Thickly rooted, tapering tail extending to hocks

Finely chiselled facial features

Jet-black nose at end of medium-length muzzle

Smooth, short, hard coat

ISTRIAN SHEPHERD – KARST SHEPHERD

SIZE 26–40kg (57–88lb), 50–60cm (20–24in)
GROOMING Average
TRAINING Time-consuming
COLOURS Iron grey

Recognized under the name Krasky Ovcar, this breed has protected flocks in Slovenia since the Middle Ages and is undergoing a revival today. It is a typical guardian breed, vigilant and instinctively distrustful, with no hesitation in taking on larger opponents should it see the need. It is not particularly suited to family life, but makes a fine, loyal guard for those willing to devote time and patience to proper training. This breed and the Illyrian Sheepdog were treated as one breed until 1968.

V-shaped ears lying flat to head

Lighter hairs in circles round eyes

Powerful chest

ILLYRIAN SHEEPDOG

SIZE 25–36kg (55–79lb), 56–60cm (22–24in)
GROOMING Time-consuming
TRAINING Time-consuming
COLOURS Iron grey, white, tan, black

Since being divided from the Istrian Shepherd, this breed has suffered. It has many names, including Yugoslavian Herder, Charplaninatz, and Sarplanina, and is officially called Jugoslovenski Ovcarski Pas-Sarplaninac, or Yugoslavian Shepherd Dog of Sarplanina, although its country of origin is given as Macedonia or Serbia-Montenegro. All of this reflects the violent chaos of its homeland, and its future rests with breeders in the United States and Canada, where it is used to control Coyotes. This is a powerful guard dog, not a pet.

Dense, medium-length coat

HELLENIC SHEPHERD DOG

SIZE 30–50kg (66–110lb), 65–78cm (26–31in)
GROOMING Time-consuming
TRAINING Time-consuming
COLOURS All colours

Often working as pairs guarding sheep and goats against predators, the Hellenikos Pimenikos, only recognized as a breed in 1999, is loyal to his shepherd and only his shepherd. A natural guard, these dogs are used only for protection, never herding or gathering the flocks. Hard-working, but suspicious of strangers, the Hellenic Shepherd Dog is suited only to experienced handlers, and early socialization is vital. Some breeders are now trying to breed for a more placid temperament, an achievable objective in any breed.

Powerful jaws with prominent flews

Thick coat, heavier at the neck, giving protection from the elements

Strong, muscular body with well-sprung ribs

ROUGH COLLIE

SIZE 18–30kg (40–66lb), 50–60cm (20–24in)
GROOMING Time-consuming
TRAINING Average
COLOURS Sable, sable and white, blue merle, tricolour

This breed originated in Scotland as a working dog, somewhat shorter than it is today, and for a long time it was virtually unknown elsewhere. In the 19th century, Queen Victoria acquired a Rough Collie as a companion, kindling interest in the breed and a shift in its looks to a more elegant, show dog appearance. In the 20th century, the Lassie films cemented the breed's international recognition and

THE BIGGEST STAR IN COLLIEWOOD

One of television's greatest animal companions and always the saviour of the day, Lassie was a heroic Rough Collie that became arguably the most famous dog in the world. Although playing the role of a girl, Lassie was actually Laddie, a male. The plucky Hollywood pooch is pictured here with co-star Timmy (Jon Provost) in an episode from the 1950s.

acclaim. Its working heritage has left it with a biddable nature, and it makes a fine, family dog, although the long coat is a major commitment.

Small, tipped ears

Abundant, smooth, shiny mane

SMOOTH COLLIE

Ears erect when alert, with tips hanging forward

Short, dense coat

Long muzzle with black nose

Powerful, arched neck

Long, slender forelegs

SIZE 18–30kg (40–66lb), 50–60cm (20–24in)
GROOMING Average
TRAINING Average
COLOURS Sable, sable and white, blue merle, tricolour

This breed was once regarded as the same as the Rough Collie, as both long- and short-haired individuals might occur in a litter. But the two have diverged, with all Smooth Collies traceable back to Trefoil, a tricoloured dog born in 1873, and they may have some greyhound in their heritage. This strain is less popular than the Rough Collie, and some breeders say it is more inclined to be both shy and a little fearful.

BEARDED COLLIE

SIZE 18–30kg (40–66lb), 50–56cm (20–22in)
GROOMING Time-consuming
TRAINING Average
COLOURS Grey, red-fawn, blue, shades of brown, black, solid or with white

Legend has it that this breed, a working dog since the 16th century, originated in a cross of Scottish dogs with Polish Lowland Sheepdogs (*see* p.132). It almost died out, but was revived in the mid-20th century, and is now firmly established in Britain and North America. The high-maintenance, long coat conceals a lean dog bursting with energy. A reliable, active companion for those who have the time and stamina.

Ears covered with long hair

Long hair forms beard, framing mouth

Medium-length, harsh coat

OLD ENGLISH SHEEPDOG

SIZE 29.5–30kg (65–66lb), 56–60cm (22–24in)
GROOMING Time-consuming
TRAINING Average
COLOURS Grey, blue, with limited white markings

The origins of the Old English are obscure, with probable descent from continental sheepdog breeds such as the Briard. Also called the Bobtail because it was usually docked, by the 19th century it was mainly a working dog, in use in southwestern England. Selective breeding for showing began in the 1880s. An amenable breed, it rarely shows its old aggressive instincts.

DIFFERENT STROKES

Since the 1960s, the Old English Sheepdog's appearances in television advertisements for a British brand of paint have given the breed an assured place in the public's minds and homes, although by the nickname of "Dulux Dog" rather than its official name. Sales of both paint and dog soared on the back of this publicity.

Small ears hidden by hair

Shaggy coat can be shorn in hot weather

SHORN COAT

SHOW TRIM

ENTELBUCH MOUNTAIN DOG

SIZE 25–30kg (55–66lb), 48–50cm (19–20in)
GROOMING Average
TRAINING Average
COLOURS Tricolour

This breed has been known in the Swiss mountains since antiquity, and takes its name from the Entelbuch or Entelbuch valley in the canton of Lucerne. It is also called the Entelbucher Sennenhund, or cattle dog. Its looks suggest that it may be descended from Roman mastiffs, but ultimately its origins are untraceable. In the 19th century, breeder Franz

Schertenlieb and show judge Professor Albert Heim scoured the Swiss valleys, searching out the many regional mountain dog breeds before they vanished. This is the smallest of the breeds they rescued from extinction. The muscular, compact, and eager-to-please Entelbuch is now popular in Switzerland as a happy and biddable companion, but it is still rare to see it outside its native country.

Short, hard topcoat; dense, fine undercoat

Muscular hips covered by thick skin and even thicker hair

Powerful, well-formed, long jaws

Flat skull

Small, V-shaped, pendant ears

APPENZELL MOUNTAIN DOG

SIZE 25–32kg (55–70lb), 48–58cm (19–23in)
GROOMING Average
TRAINING Time-consuming
COLOURS Tricolour

Possibly descended from warrior mastiffs that accompanied Roman soldiers through Switzerland 2,000 years ago, this breed's tail also suggests spitz ancestry. It has been

a versatile farm worker for centuries, known as the Appenzeller Sennenhund, or cattle dog. As well as its herding role, it undertook guard duties and was large enough to pull small carts to market. Numbers fell in the 19th century, and, although revived by breeder Franz Schertenlieb, the Appenzell is seldom seen outside Switzerland.

Tapering muzzle with symmetrical markings

Curled tail unique among Swiss mountain dogs

White blaze must be present on head

Short, dense, glossy coat with dense undercoat

AIDI

SIZE 23–35kg (51–55lb), 53–60cm (21–24in)
GROOMING Average
TRAINING Time-consuming
COLOURS White, tawny, red, black, black and white

This dog has protected herds of sheep and goats for Moroccan nomads since the Middle Ages; it is suitably adapted to baking daytime temperatures and bitter nights. It has also been used with the Sloughi for hunting – tracking game that the Sloughi then brings down. Also called the Chien d'Atlas or Atlas Sheepdog, it is similar to Turkish livestock breeds, such as the large Akbash, and may be related to the great white mountain dogs that spread from the East across Europe. It does not make the transition to household companion well, but is a fine watchdog.

Coarse, insulating double coat

Muscular neck

Straight, well-boned forelegs

BULLDOG

SIZE 23–25kg (51–55lb), 30–36cm (12–14in)
GROOMING Minimal
TRAINING Average
COLOURS Fawn, red, brindle, solid or with a black mask, or with white

When bear-baiting died out in Britain, the mastiff breeds used were crossed with terriers to create the Bulldog for the newer sport of bull-baiting. This powerful and tenacious dog would hang on to the bull regardless of injury. When this sport in turn became illegal in 1830, the breed was in danger of dying out, as it was physically ill-suited to dog fights. However, breeder Bill George undertook a programme to reduce aggression in the Bulldog, transforming the brawler into a companion breed. It had already become a symbol of the British nation, and by the 1880s a music-hall song dubbed British sailors "boys of the Bulldog breed".

Very short, broad nose

Undershot lower jaw with thick flews

WINSTON CHURCHILL

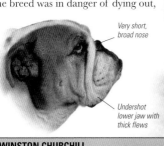

When Winston Churchill became Britain's wartime Prime Minister in World War II, his fortuitous resemblance to the breed was endlessly exploited in propaganda. Breeding to an extreme standard has sadly left the Bulldog with some serious health problems, but it is an engaging character.

BOXER

SIZE 25–32kg (55–70lb), 53–63cm (21–25in)
GROOMING Minimal
TRAINING Average
COLOURS Fawn and white, fawn,
brindle, occasionally white

The tallest of the flat-faced (brachycephalic) breeds, Boxers are dogs that never grow up. Ever. They are bouncy, energetic, fearless risk-takers, although males can be wary and circumspect with strangers. The typical Boxer's mantra is "All I wanna do is have fun." This is a breed for active families. They make superb companions for young children because they are, in thought and action, similar to perpetual three-year-old kids. Although the breed's muscularity, size, and intimidating appearance suits it to a role as house protector, these dogs are unfailingly gentle with children.

Boxers were first developed in Germany, probably from the Brabant Bullenbeisser (bullbiter) from Belgium and similar dogs from the Danzig region. Bavarian breeds and perhaps even the English Bulldog may have been used in its original development. By the turn of the 20th century, they were essentially as they are today. No one knows exactly how the name "Boxer" developed.

Unfortunately, there are serious health problems within the breed and these lead to a shorter-than-average life expectancy.

WHITE BOXERS

There have been white Boxers since the breed was first developed. It was not until 1925, when the German Boxer club banned their registration, that other clubs moved to reduce the numbers of white individuals. Today, in many countries white pups may be registered but may not be shown: in the United States, Boxers with more than one-third of their body covered in white are not eligible for showing. Sadly, mostly or wholly white individuals are also more prone to deafness.

Wrinkled brow giving impression of intense concentration

Short, straight, muscular back

Short, shiny, smooth hair covering extensive, deep chest

Turned-up, black nose

Strong, straight, firmly muscled forelegs

MOTHER AND PUPPY

In some countries tails are still amputated, leading to high-speed-metronome vestige-wagging and subsequent, often painful, bony changes in the vertebrae around the sacrum. Skin cancer occurs more frequently in Boxers than any other breed, and a heart condition causing a ballooning of the lower chambers, a "dilated cardiomyopathy", is regrettably all too common.

Thick, padded upper lip

Strong, muscular neck

Agility trials
Boxers aren't commonly associated with agility trials, but can participate in them, as well as in obedience trials. Early obedience training is a vital tool for success.

NEW ZEALAND HUNTAWAY

SIZE 18–29.5kg (40–65lb), 50–60cm (20–24in)
GROOMING Variable
TRAINING Easy
COLOURS All colours

This curious breed is not recognized by any registry, and has a very variable appearance, because it is defined by a single trait: its ability to herd sheep using its voice. The original sheepdogs exported from Britain to New Zealand had been bred to work silently, but some breeders decided to develop those that did bark into a new breed. The field trials were called huntaways, giving rise to the breed's name. The result is a healthy, highly responsive dog that can be trained to bark or not bark on command, which has been exported back to Britain and is used in field trials or as a very active companion.

Half-dropped, velvety ears

Round, alert eyes

Moderately long, muscular neck

Long, robust back

Powerful thighs providing bursts of speed

NORWEGIAN BUHUND

SIZE 24–26kg (53–57lb), 41–46cm (16–18in)
GROOMING Average
TRAINING Average
COLOURS Wheaten, red, black

The Norwegian word *bu* means a farm or homestead, and the Norsk Buhund (Norwegian Sheepdog) has been a farm worker for centuries.

DEDICATED TRAINING

As with virtually all the Nordic spitz breeds, the Buhund requires patient training to create a reliably obedient companion. Even so, its chasing instinct remains powerful, and given the opportunity it will chase livestock. Unlike the Border Collie, the Buhund's primary goal is to please itself rather than to please the farmer, or the pet owner for that matter. This is not an affection-demanding dog, nor is it one that slavishly worships its handler.

Curled tail set high on back

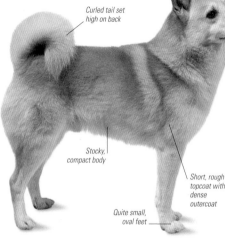

Stocky, compact body

Short, rough topcoat with dense outercoat

Quite small, oval feet

Perhaps because of this prosaic background, it did not receive the same attention as other Norwegian breeds until the 1920s, when a government official, Jon Saeland, made a concerted effort to save it. Since then the breed has become popular in Great Britain, and as a sheepdog in Australia, where it works tirelessly and does not appear to suffer in the heat. A steady, affectionate, and active breed, even tempered unless provoked, it makes a vocal watchdog and a fine companion for those who can keep up with it.

DOBERMANN

SIZE 30–40kg (66–88lb), 60–70cm (24–28in)
GROOMING Minimal
TRAINING Easy
COLOURS Blue, fawn, brown, or black, with red markings, sometimes with limited white markings

One of the best-known German breeds, the Dobermann was the creation of Louis Dobermann, a tax collector who often had to carry money through risky areas and wanted a dog to accompany him. He used the Weimaraner, Manchester Terrier, Rottweiler, German Pinscher, and English Greyhound to produce a loyal, alert bodyguard that is fearless and resourceful in combat. The breed was an instant success when it was first shown in 1876, and has since become established across Europe and also in North America, where it is called the Doberman Pinscher and is usually seen with cropped ears.

Its popularity as a guard dog has not always helped this sleek breed. Unscrupulous breeders have produced strains given to nervousness and fear biting, and careless owners looking only for a guard have not always socialized their dogs adequately. However, a Dobermann from a good breeder, integrated into the household, makes a fine companion. Unfortunately, heart disease is increasingly a serious problem for the breed.

Well-proportioned chest with good width and depth

LIVER-AND-TAN COAT

Small ears set high on head

Short, hard, thick, glossy coat

Compact, well-arched, cat-like feet

BLACK-AND-TAN COAT

RHODESIAN RIDGEBACK

SIZE 29.5–38.5kg (65–85lb),
60–69cm (24–27in)
GROOMING Minimal
TRAINING Time-consuming
COLOURS Wheaten to red

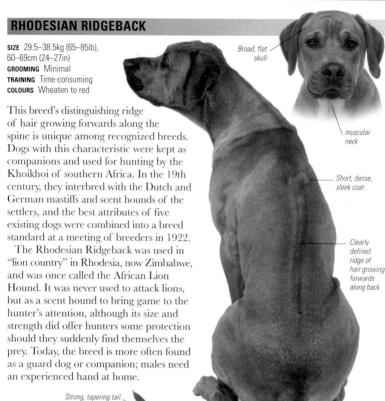

Broad, flat skull

muscular neck

Short, dense, sleek coat

Clearly defined ridge of hair growing forwards along back

Strong, tapering tail

This breed's distinguishing ridge of hair growing forwards along the spine is unique among recognized breeds. Dogs with this characteristic were kept as companions and used for hunting by the Khoikhoi of southern Africa. In the 19th century, they interbred with the Dutch and German mastiffs and scent hounds of the settlers, and the best attributes of five existing dogs were combined into a breed standard at a meeting of breeders in 1922.

The Rhodesian Ridgeback was used in "lion country" in Rhodesia, now Zimbabwe, and was once called the African Lion Hound. It was never used to attack lions, but as a scent hound to bring game to the hunter's attention, although its size and strength did offer hunters some protection should they suddenly find themselves the prey. Today, the breed is more often found as a guard dog or companion; males need an experienced hand at home.

THAI RIDGEBACK

SIZE 23–34kg (51–75lb), 58–66cm (23–26in)
GROOMING Minimal
TRAINING Time-consuming
COLOURS Silver, blue, chestnut, black

This breed was discovered relatively recently in Thailand, where it is known simply as Mah Thai or "Thai dog" and has been a companion and house guard for centuries. Dogs here have bred in isolation for centuries, rarely if ever crossing with breeds of European origin, and this distinctive dog combines the looks of ancient spitz-types dogs and primitive hounds. Thai Ridgebacks are not yet recognized by any major Western registry, but there is a club in Thailand devoted to ensuring the breed's future in its native land.

Loose, pliant skin on head and neck

Large, triangular, pricked ears inclining forwards

Large, black nose

Ridge of hair on spine growing in opposite direction

Tail tapering towards tip

STANDARD POODLE

SIZE 20.5–32kg (45–70lb), over 38cm (15in)
GROOMING Time-consuming
TRAINING Easy
COLOURS Any solid colour

Long hair covering ears

Well-proportioned, dignified head

Straight, parallel forelegs

SILVER POODLE IN PUPPY LION TRIM

Don't let those frivolous cuts deceive you. The Poodle has acquired the unfortunate image of an over-groomed fashion accessory, but the breed's names and its modern temperament tell a different story. Poodle probably comes from the old low German *pudeln*, to paddle or splash, and the French name of Caniche means "duck dog". This is a retrieving dog bred to work in water, and the elaborate "lion" clip of the coat was originally created to reduce water resistance, while still affording some insulation against cold water around the chest and the joints in the legs.

Although some registries regard this breed's home as France, where it is held in great affection and also called the Barbone, the evidence points to these curly-coated dogs originating in Germany in the Middle Ages and then influencing French breeds such as the Barbet, rather than the other way round. The Standard Poodle scores consistently high in canine "intelligence" tests, is amenable to training, good-tempered around children, and is still a working dog underneath it all. This breed is remarkably healthy. The only significant condition Poodles suffer from more than other dogs is the skin complaint sebaceous adenitis, which can be mistaken for allergy or other skin diseases. Stomach bloat, hip dysplasia, and various late-onset cancers are also potential concerns, but remain relatively rare. This is a superb breed, one of the best for urban or rural families.

Outdoor pursuits
In the 1980s and 90s, John Suter raced all-poodle sled teams before a change in rules disqualified them.

PUDELPOINTER

SIZE 20–30kg (44-66lb), 53–66cm (21–26in)
GROOMING Time-consuming
TRAINING Average
COLOURS White, fawn, chestnut, grey, black

Short, rough, waterproof coat

The Pudelpointer is the result of German sportsman Baron von Zedlitz's attempt to produce an ideal tracking, pointing, and retrieving dog by crossing poodles with various German pointers. The Baron was years ahead in his thinking. Today, successful crosses such as the Standard Poodle and Labrador Retriever, producing the Labradoodle, are highly prized, but the superb yet underrated Pudelpointer remains a handsome oddity even in its German homeland.

High-set ears with rounded tips

Bushy, coarse eyebrows covering eyes

Wiry beard

CORDED POODLE

SIZE 20.5–32kg (45–70lb), over 38cm (15in)
GROOMING Average
TRAINING Easy
COLOURS Any solid colour

The corded coat of this poodle provides excellent protection against the elements and also against predators, which is why it is most often found on herding breeds. The Corded Poodle is probably related to the extinct Schafpudel or sheep poodle, but was developed more for retrieving from water than shepherding work, and so gave rise to the more common Standard Poodle (*see* p.207). Although an excellent companion breed, it is extremely rare today, found mostly in France.

The distinctive cording is produced by the topcoat and the undercoat interweaving, and once corded the coat is quite easy to care for.

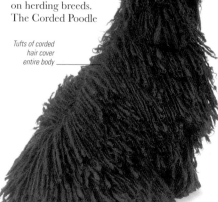

Tufts of corded hair cover entire body

High-set tail, raised when dog is active

Flat, broad ears, with round tips

Forelegs covered in abundant hair

IRISH WATER SPANIEL

SIZE 20–30kg (44–66lb), 51–58cm (20–23in)
GROOMING Average
TRAINING Easy
COLOURS Rich dark liver

The Irish Water Spaniel shows the influence of some curly-coated European water dogs, but exactly which is not known for sure. It might have been the Barbet or the Poodle, or possibly a Portuguese Water Dog brought to Ireland by sailors. This highly distinctive spaniel has a virtually waterproof coat, tremendous stamina, and Olympic swimming abilities, all making it ideal for winter work in wide river estuaries. Although it is gentle, quiet, and faithful, it has never become popular as a house dog, perhaps due to its apparently boundless energy, which makes it an excellent companion for hikers.

Large nose, the colour of dark liver

V-shaped patch of smooth hair

Straight, powerful forelegs

Tight ringlets of hair cover body

WIRE-HAIRED POINTING GRIFFON

SIZE 23–27kg (51–60lb), 56–61cm (22–24in)
GROOMING Average
TRAINING Average
COLOURS Grey with brown markings, chestnut, roan, white and brown, white and orange

Developed by the Dutch breeder, Eduard Korthals, from Dutch gundogs, German pointers, French griffons, and possibly English stock as well, this is an excellent all-purpose worker. Also called the Griffon d'Arrêt Korthals, this versatile breed was fittingly the first all-purpose European gundog to be formally recognized in the United States. Its comparative rarity is a mystery.

DALMATIAN

SIZE 22.5–25kg (50–55lb), 50–61cm (20–24in)
GROOMING Minimal
TRAINING Average
COLOURS White spotted with black or liver

One would imagine that such a distinctive dog would have a well-recorded history, but the origins of the Dalmatian are a matter of dispute. Greek friezes from over 4,000 years ago show similar dogs, but it may not have originated in Dalmatia, on the Adriatic coast and now part of Croatia.

Sleek, glossy coat with distinctive spots

DALMATIAN PUPPY

COACH DOGS

In the 1800s, in Europe and especially in Britain, it was the fashion for the carriages of the aristocracy to have "coach dogs" running alongside. Although their original purpose was probably to protect the occupants against highwaymen, they undoubtedly served a decorative purpose, and Dalmatians were in demand because of their eye-catching coat. This wood engraving from 1807 shows the custom's popularity in England.

Instead there is ample evidence that the breed arrived there with traders from India. In 1700, a similar dog was known as the Bengal Pointer in England.

Whatever its origins, the breed has worked as a hound, vermin catcher, bird dog, and herder, before it became famous as a carriage dog because of its unique willingness to walk or run beside carriages, clearing a way in populated areas. Today, it is a popular companion breed, in part due to its literary and cinematic fame, although owners must remember that the Dalmatian loves to run, and run, and run. Males are sometimes aggressive with other male dogs, and deafness affects some individuals of either sex.

Black nose preferred

Ears set level with eyes

Waterproof undercoat

PUPPY

CLASSIC WATER DOGS

Water is a natural element for Golden Retrievers. My travelling companion Macy, here on a beach in northern California, will cavort in and out of the water for hours when given the opportunity to do so. Although well insulated from cold, they are nevertheless still prone to hypothermia if excessively exposed to cold water.

Gradations of gold

This Golden Retriever in the US is a rich golden colour, the preference of dog show judges there. Show judges in the UK and other countries look for lighter, "champagne" shades, from deep yellows to almost bright white.

A big softie
Soft of mouth and affectionate by temperament, the Golden Retriever is an ideal companion for all types of families.

CLUMBER SPANIEL

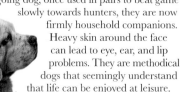

SIZE 29–36kg (64–79lb), 48–51cm (19–20in)
GROOMING Time-consuming
TRAINING Easy/average
COLOURS Tan and white

Dark amber eyes with soft expression

Square, flesh-coloured nose

This heaviest of all spaniels was developed by the Duke of Newcastle in the 18th century. Its ancestors may include the Basset Hound, bequeathing the long back, and the St Bernard, from which it gets its massive head. A laid back, easy-going dog, once used in pairs to beat game slowly towards hunters, they are now firmly household companions. Heavy skin around the face can lead to eye, ear, and lip problems. They are methodical dogs that seemingly understand that life can be enjoyed at leisure.

Long, vine-leaf shaped ears

Well-feathered tail

Short, well-boned legs

REVOLUTIONARY ORIGINS

The Clumber Spaniel may exist as a consequence of the French Revolution. Legend says that the French Duc de Noailles sent some of his spaniels for safekeeping to his English friend, the Duke of Newcastle, at Clumber Park in Nottinghamshire.

DUTCH PARTRIDGE DOG

SIZE 21–23kg (46–51lb), 58–66cm (23–26in)
GROOMING Average
TRAINING Easy
COLOURS Red and white, brown and white

From the once-isolated Dutch province of Drente, the Dutch or Drentsch Partridge Dog is a classic all-rounder, an all-purpose hunter, pointer, retriever, and companion. It is probably a good example of what the ancestors

Broad, powerful back is longer than it is high

Strong, sturdy legs with thick pads on feet

Fringes on ears

of today's setters and spaniels looked like, before dogs diversified into those separate uses and shapes, as its appearance has not altered in at least 400 years. While overall numbers of Dutch Partridge Dogs remain low, enough pups are born each year in the Netherlands to ensure the survival of this excellent companion. As with all small gene pools, there are potential medical concerns, and with this breed comes a high incidence of progressive retinal atrophy (PRA). A gentle and obedient breed, the Partridge Dog is an excellent companion.

LARGE MÜNSTERLÄNDER

SIZE 25–29kg (55–64lb), 59–61cm (23–24in)
GROOMING Average
TRAINING Easy
COLOURS Black and white

Biddable but sometimes opinionated, the Large Münsterländer exists for what was originally an aesthetic reason. German Long-haired Pointers once produced both liver-and-white and black-and-white pups. When that Pointer's breed standard was re-written to accept only variations of liver and white, some breeders in the Münster region of Germany set up their own club to perpetuate black-and-white coloured dogs. It has a typical pointer personality – occasionally a little intense and serious but capable of spirited humour as well – and it is an increasingly popular breed outside Germany, especially in Britain. Somewhat confusingly, despite the breed's name it is not related to the Small Münsterländer

Back sloping slightly downwards

Strong, muscular neck

Tapering tail carried in line with back

Well-feathered, straight forelegs

At home in the field
Most suited to pointing, the Large Münsterländer can also retrieve fallen game birds.

GERMAN SPANIEL

SIZE 20–30kg (44–66lb), 40–51cm (16–20in)
GROOMING Average
TRAINING Easy
COLOURS Black and white, brown and white, brown

Called the Wachtelhund ("quail dog") in Germany, this fine retriever and all-round bird dog has a vibrant personality that is very similar to the much more common English Springer Spaniel (*see* p.221). It was developed by German breeders in the late 1800s, who used English Cocker Spaniels and various local breeds in a successful attempt to recreate the Stober, an extinct German bird dog. Surprisingly rare even in its native Germany, it makes an excellent family companion.

Predominantly smooth coat on head

Elongated, but not pointed, muzzle

Long body compared with height

Long, rugged, thick, wavy coat

Close-set toes have tufts of hair between them

IRISH SETTER

SIZE 27.5–32kg (61–70lb), 64–69cm (25–27in)
GROOMING Average
TRAINING Easy/average
COLOURS Red

Once called the "Modder rhu", simply the "red dog" in Gaelic, the sheen and lustre of this handsome dog's coat is the envy of many human redheads. Irish Setters like to party. They are racy and can be rather rambunctious. They mature late, at over three years of age, and this probably accounts for their reputation as flighty, exuberant extroverts. Under the joyous exterior remains a hidden setter, and while it is now kept only as a family companion, it retains its natural abilities to set game. Fast and active, it thrives on canine company.

Abundant long, silky coat

Low-set, feathered tail

Long, lean head with square muzzle

Long, fine feathering on legs

IRISH RED-AND-WHITE SETTER

SIZE 27.5–32kg (61–70lb), 58–69cm (23–27in)
GROOMING Average
TRAINING Easy/average
COLOURS Red and white

Triangular ears, covered in short hair

Working Irish Setters were once chestnut and white as well as solid chestnut; the latter is the more popular. Because of this, red-and-white coloured Irish Setters declined to near extinction, but in recent years this colour has been rescued. The Red-and-white can be more tentative than its chestnut cousins, and often needs extra time spent on socializing and early training. Like all deep-chested dogs, it is prone to sudden, often fatal, gastric torsion, a twisting of the stomach.

WORKING SETTERS

On the continent, dogs that stopped and "pointed" were popular hunting aids, but in England, Scotland, and Ireland, breeds were developed to sit quietly when they scented game, waiting for the hunter to arrive. They called these specialized dogs "setters", and four breeds remain today.

ENGLISH SETTER

SIZE 25–30kg (55–66lb), 61–69cm (24–27in)
GROOMING Average
TRAINING Easy
COLOURS Tricolour, black and white, liver and white, lemon and white

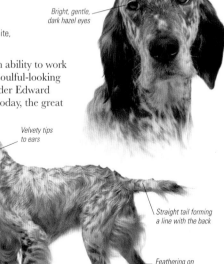

Bright, gentle, dark hazel eyes

Setters evolved from spaniels, with an ability to work as hunters. This leggy, elegant, and soulful-looking breed was developed by British breeder Edward Laverack. Seldom used for hunting today, the great majority of English Setters are quiet, warm-hearted, considerate, and easy-to-train companions. Allergic skin conditions are common, particularly in those with predominantly white coats. An inherited retina condition, which causes blindness, should be checked for before breeding. This breed requires a great deal of exercise, but makes an affable dog for families with children.

Velvety tips to ears

Straight tail forming a line with the back

Feathering on chest and legs

GORDON SETTER

SIZE 25–30kg (55–66lb), 62–66cm (24–26in)
GROOMING Average
TRAINING Easy
COLOURS Black and tan

Friendly and relaxed, the Gordon was developed in the 1700s in Banffshire, Scotland, on the Duke of Richmond and Gordon's estate. Black and tan has been a consistent colour in many varieties of British dogs, and black-and-tan setters existed long before this breed was formally developed. It is surprising, considering its fashion model long, lithe looks and its benign disposition, that it has never achieved the widespread popularity of its English and Irish relatives. More heavy-set than the other setters, the Gordon thrives on routine and vigorous exercise.

PICARDY SPANIEL

SIZE 19.5–20.5kg (43–45lb), 56–61cm (22–24in)
GROOMING Minimal
TRAINING Easy
COLOURS Grey and brown

Finer, longer hair on ears

A true setter in looks and abilities, this is one of the underrated stars among French dogs. Rarely seen outside northeast France and neighbouring Belgium, the elegant and refined-looking Picardy has a generous and giving personality, is easy to train, and is happiest when pleasing its family. While it is an excellent setter and retriever, working flatlands and marshes equally well, it also makes a very successful household companion.

LARGE FRENCH SPANIELS

In northern France a variety of large spaniels developed. These were invariably multi-purpose hunters, setters, and retrievers. Their exact origins are unknown, although they were probably similar to those of the Dutch and German dogs bred for the same roles. Only three of these breeds remain, all limited in number, and all deserving more recognition.

BLUE PICARDY SPANIEL

SIZE 19.5–20.5kg (43–45lb), 56–61cm (22–24in)
GROOMING Minimal
TRAINING Easy
COLOURS Blue roan

Medium-sized, broad head

Flat, straight coat with heavy white ticking

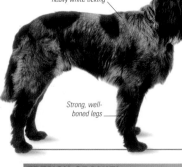

Strong, well-boned legs

A relaxed and good-natured dog, this breed's setter-like qualities come from its development through crossing blue-lemon flecked English Setters with Picardy Spaniels. Fun-loving and friendly, although a bit boisterous, it is used by local hunters in northeast France to retrieve snipe from marshes. More commonly it is a very successful family companion, especially where there are children. Breeders say it is not much inclined to use its voice, but it is quite demanding in its desire to participate in family activities.

Low-set ears covered with long, fine hair

FRENCH SPANIEL

SIZE 20–25kg (44–55lb), 53–61cm (21–24in)
GROOMING Average
TRAINING Average/time-consuming
COLOURS Chestnut and white

Long, flat, feathered ears

Low-set tail covered in long, silky hair

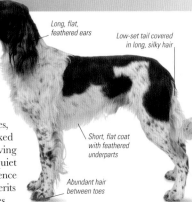

More setter than spaniel in looks, and rarely seen outside France, this is a gentle and elegant dog. Also called the Épagneul Français, it may be related to the Dutch Partridge Dog and certainly shares its abilities, although this typical gundog is seldom worked today and is more likely to be found as a loving household companion. Breeders say it is a quiet and sensitive dog that thrives on gentle obedience training. It copes well in cold weather and merits greater recognition than it presently receives.

Short, flat coat with feathered underparts

Abundant hair between toes

OLD DANISH POINTER

SIZE 18–24kg (40–53lb), 51–58cm (20–23in)
GROOMING Minimal
TRAINING Easy
COLOURS Liver and white, with ticking

This delightful dog, a popular field-trial participant in Denmark, is rarely seen outside that country. Shorter and lighter than the English Pointer, the breed was rescued from near extinction after World War II. It retrieves well, both on land and from water, and is a skilled tracker, successful in ordinance and drug detection. Its equable disposition and small size makes it a good urban family dog.

Short, dense coat with insulating undercoat

Broad, straight back

Developed, muscular chest

POINTING

When pointers scent or sight game they "strike a pose", pointing rigidly in the direction of the quarry. On the hunter's command they "flush", scaring the game out of hiding, and then after the hunter has shot the game, retrieve it from land or water. This pointer (a Vizsla) is pointing in the direction of its prey and is close enough for the hunter to see the quarry.

ENGLISH POINTER

SIZE 20–30kg (44–66lb), 61–69cm (24–27in)
GROOMING Minimal
TRAINING Easy
COLOURS Black and white, liver and white, orange and white, lemon and white

No longer commonly worked as a gundog, this breed retains the serious personality of a dog bred to behave unnaturally: to track and locate its quarry and then simply freeze, historically permitting the greyhounds to chase and capture, latterly allowing the hunter to shoot. The English Pointer has a kindly and biddable, although sometimes rather sensitive, disposition. It is stoic about life, easy to train, and great with children.

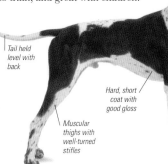

Tail held level with back

Hard, short coat with good gloss

Long, sloping shoulders

Muscular thighs with well-turned stifles

GERMAN WIRE-HAIRED POINTER

SIZE 27–32kg (60–70lb), 61–68cm (24–27in)
GROOMING Average
TRAINING Average
COLOURS Black or brown roan, white
with black or brown roan

By far the most numerous of all the
German Pointers in their native
land, breeders say the Wire-
haired can be more aloof and

Broad, long, robust muzzle with brown nose

Pronounced beard

Powerful muzzle

Prominent chest with prolonged sternum

Harsh, flat outercoat

Straight forelegs

headstrong than their short-
haired relatives, but equally
there are lines of this breed
that live to play. This is the
most recently developed of
the German Pointers. The
insulating, rough, double
coat was developed by
crossing the Short-haired
Pointer with French griffons and the now-
extinct German Broken-coated Pointer.
The protective coat helps in the field, while
its distinguished "beard" gives this breed
a dignified, imperial presence. Wire-hairs
thrive on routine and vigorous exercise.

GERMAN LONG-HAIRED POINTER

SIZE 27–32kg (60–70lb), 60–68cm (24–27in)
GROOMING Average
TRAINING Easy
COLOURS Chestnut and white, chestnut

German Long-hairs were developed by
breeding selectively from a variety of
spaniels, pointers, and setters, including
the French Spaniel, and
Irish and Gordon

Setters. This breed's standard was
established in 1879 and most of today's
lineage descend from a genetic base
of only five dogs. One of them, named
Kalkstein, was the only one with a brown-
and-white ticked coat, the favoured colour
today. German Long-hairs are the gentlest
of the German pointers, easy to obedience
train, and reliable with children. Although
sometimes timid, they can be surprisingly
vocal watchdogs.

Long, lean head, with sloping stop and straight muzzle

Well-spaced, gentle eyes

Laterally set, broad based ears covered with wavy hair

Long, straight forelegs fringed with soft hair

Profusely feathered tail

GERMAN SHORT-HAIRED POINTER

SIZE 20–30kg (44–66lb), 60–65cm (24–26in)
GROOMING Minimal
TRAINING Easy/average
COLOURS Brown roan

Until the early 1800s, German pointers were rather stocky in build. Crossing with English Pointers produced a lighter, more athletic physique with powerful muscling. They make superb trackers and retrievers, and will retrieve game and vermin such as raccoon dogs, in Eastern Europe, and foxes. Some are trained to retrieve deer- and elk- antler racks, now a valued find in the forest. The German Short-hair is a successful participant in field trials both in Europe and North America.

WORLD CHAMPIONSHIP PULKA RACING

As well as excellence in the field, German Short-hairs do well in winter sports. In skijoring and pulka races, at World Championship level, the most common breeds in recent years have been German Short-haired Pointers and hybrids of short-haired pointers and greyhounds. In this pulka race, a German Short-haired Pointer pulls the weighted, flat pulk (sledge) while his teammate skis behind.

Short, thick, hard coat, harsh to the touch

Chest deeper than it is broad

Broad, well-muscled, lean thighs

Docked tail
Traditionally, the working German Short-haired Pointer had its tail docked by 60 per cent, leaving enough tail to sit on. There is no advantage to a companion dog having its tail docked.

SPANISH POINTER

SIZE 25–30kg (55–66lb), 66–76cm (26–30in)
GROOMING Minimal
TRAINING Easy
COLOURS Liver and white

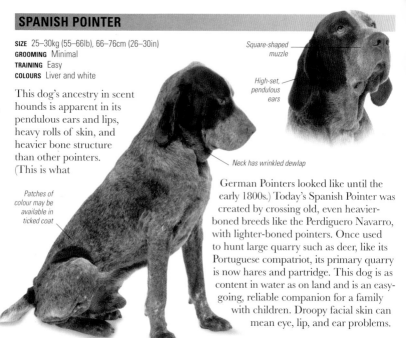

Square-shaped muzzle

High-set, pendulous ears

Neck has wrinkled dewlap

This dog's ancestry in scent hounds is apparent in its pendulous ears and lips, heavy rolls of skin, and heavier bone structure than other pointers. (This is what

Patches of colour may be available in ticked coat

German Pointers looked like until the early 1800s.) Today's Spanish Pointer was created by crossing old, even heavier-boned breeds like the Perdiguero Navarro, with lighter-boned pointers. Once used to hunt large quarry such as deer, like its Portuguese compatriot, its primary quarry is now hares and partridge. This dog is as content in water as on land and is an easy-going, reliable companion for a family with children. Droopy facial skin can mean eye, lip, and ear problems.

PORTUGUESE POINTER

SIZE 16–27kg (35–60lb), 52–56cm (20–22in)
GROOMING Minimal
TRAINING Easy
COLOURS Tan and white, chestnut, yellow

"Dish-face", similar to an English Pointer

HUNTING IN FOREST

This breed's local name of Perdigueiro Portugueso, which means "Portuguese Partridge Dog", explains its primary use today, but in ancient times its ancestors were probably hawking dogs, relatives of the extinct Spanish pointing hound, the Podengo de Mastra. This obedient and versatile dog, very popular in its homeland, is a probable progenitor of the English Pointer. Still used as a gun-dog, it is also a reliable family companion, equally at home in the garden or field. It is rarely seen outside Portugal, although some appear at Spanish dog shows. A long-haired coat type is now relatively scarce.

Strong forequarters and long, sloping shoulders

Short, broad body

Evenly spaced, well-arched toes

BRACCO ITALIANO (ITALIAN POINTER)

SIZE 25–40kg (55–88lb), 56–67cm (22–26in)
GROOMING Minimal
TRAINING Average
COLOURS Chestnut and white,
orange and white, lemon and white

This breed is rightly on the crest of a
wave of popularity. Once restricted to
the Piedmont and Lombardy regions
of Italy, where it worked as an efficient
tracker, pointer, and retriever, the soulful-
looking Bracco is now routinely seen at
dog shows throughout Europe. In some
ways similar in appearance to the smaller
Segugio (*see* p.184), it may descend from
crosses of Segugios and larger mastiff-type
breeds. Rather surprisingly considering its
relaxed looks, it can be a slightly stubborn
breed when it comes to obedience training.

In demeanour it is gentle and
sensitive, and remains a serious,
capable worker as well as a
fine family companion.

*Short, fine,
dense coat*

*Straight, firm forelegs
with robust feet*

ITALIAN SPINONE

SIZE 32–37kg (70–82lb), 61–66cm (24–26in)
GROOMING Average
TRAINING Average
COLOURS Chocolate, chestnut, orange, yellow and white

Another popular Italian dog, Spinones have
migrated successfully throughout Europe
and North America, where they are adored
family companions. Originally from the
northern Piedmont and Lombardy regions
of Italy, and rather doleful in appearance,
they are superb trackers and hunters. They
can develop a distinctive doggy aroma if
not brushed daily and the amount of

saliva some individuals produce in hot
weather can be hard to cope with. This is
a calm, reliable dog, easy to train, and
active in its own ambling way.

*Triangular ears, with
short, thick hair*

*Long, broad,
muscular
thighs*

*Thick, rough,
close-fitting
coat*

All friends together
This is a relaxed breed, not apt to theatrical displays with
other dogs. This group of four is typical both of the range of
colour varieties and of their naturally easy-going demeanour.

FRENCH GASCONY POINTER

SIZE 20–32kg (44–70lb), 56–69cm (22–27in)
GROOMING Minimal
TRAINING Easy
COLOURS Brown and white

In France this is the Braque-Français-type-Gascogne, the long-limbed variety of southern pointer favoured in the Gascony region. A classic pointer, this breed was saved from extinction early in the 20th century by two breeders, Dr Castets and M. Senac-Langrange. Still used as a working dog in Gascony and the Pyrenees, this calm and gentle dog thrives as much on human company as it does on vigorous exercise. Its undemanding attitude and enthusiasm for working with its handler makes it a great work and family dog.

Fine hair covering pleated ears

Robust, reasonably straight thighs

Long, straight, broad, well-muscled forelegs

Broad nose with wide-open nostrils

FRENCH PYRENEAN POINTER

SIZE 20–32kg (44–70lb), 47–58cm (19–23in)
GROOMING Minimal
TRAINING Easy
COLOURS Brown and white

Hunting in the rough terrain of the Pyrenees mountains called for a dog with shorter legs than other French pointers. This breed has legs that are 10cm (4in) shorter than its Gascony relatives. Rarely seen outside southern France, this dog's shorter limbs allow it to stand on its hind legs while sniffing the air for the scent. As with the other French pointers, it has an equable temperament, a responsiveness to obedience training, and a desire to pass time with its human family. Enthusiastic when working, off-duty it is happy to relax.

Pendant lips below prominent nose

High-set ears, barely folded

Long, well-muscled neck

Hair shorter and finer than French Gascony Pointer

Deep chest extending to elbows

FRENCH POINTERS

While British nobility preferred dogs that "set", meaning that the dogs sat and waited when they found game, their French counterparts favoured pointers, dogs that froze in a pointing pose when scenting or sighting game. Pointers were worked wherever men hunted, but war and revolution diminished both their variety and numbers. Today, only these four breeds survive in France.

SAINT-GERMAIN POINTER

SIZE 18–26kg (40–57lb), 54–62cm (21–24in)
GROOMING Minimal
TRAINING Easy
COLOURS Orange and white

Smaller than its southern cousins, the Braque St Germain, as it is called in France, has the size and colour of pointers in paintings from the time of King Louis XV. Intentionally decimated after the French Revolution, the breed was revived through breeding with English and French Gascony Pointers. Today, while some continue to work,

the majority are delightful companions, perhaps slightly tentative by nature, but trustworthy within families with young children and very easy to obedience train.

Supple ears set at eye level

Short, fine, thick coat

Well-arched toes with solid pads

BOURBONNAIS POINTER

SIZE 18–26kg (40–57lb), 55–57cm (22in)
GROOMING Minimal
TRAINING Easy
COLOURS White, with liver or fawn ticking

This pointer has existed in Bourbonnais since at least the late 1500s. The shortest of the French pointers, it is also the most relaxed and confident in temperament. It is not uncommon for pups to be born with no tails or just short stumps. Their popularity peaked over a century ago and they were driven to near extinction by the wars of

the 20th century. By the 1990s, efforts to restore the breed had been successful, although until recently this pointer was little seen outside France. It remains an all-purpose tracker, pointer, and retriever.

A POINTER TO WHAT THE FUTURE HOLDS

The Braque de Bourbonnais, as it is called in its homeland, remains an endangered breed with on average only 100 pups born there each year. Fortunately, there is developing interest abroad, in the United States in particular, where numbers almost equal to this are now being produced annually, helping to ensure this attractive breed's future.

Liver-coloured nose with well-developed nostrils

Dense, oily, but not glossy coat

Very straight forelegs

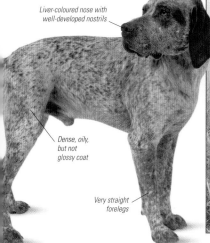

SLOVENSKY POINTER

SIZE 25–35kg (55–77lb), 56–68cm (22–27in)
GROOMING Average
TRAINING Easy
COLOURS Shades of mouse-grey to silver-grey

Czech and Slovak breeders were among the most active and successful in Europe at renewing and improving the variety of gundogs that survived World War II. This breed, the Slovensky Hrubosrsty Stavac, or Slovakian Wire-haired Pointing Dog, was created after 1945 by crossing German Wire-haired Pointers with Cesky Fouseks,

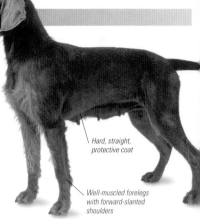

Hard, straight, protective coat

Well-muscled forelegs with forward-slanted shoulders

Amber eyes are initially blue

Long, upward-growing hair over eyes

Long, rounded ears

Distinctive beard of long, soft hair

before then crossing their offspring with Weimaraners. The breed was formally recognized in 1983. Until recently, they were rarely seen outside their native land, but representatives now appear in dog shows throughout Europe. With the attractive colouring of the Weimaraner, and insulating down under a wiry topcoat, this is a good all-weather, all-climate dog.

CESKY FOUSEK

SIZE 22–34kg (49–75lb), 58–66cm (23–26in)
GROOMING Average
TRAINING Easy
COLOURS Brown, brown and roan, brown and white

Used as a multi-purpose hunter in Bohemia since the early 1800s, this breed was reconstructed after World War II through the infusion

Long, large head

Bushy eyebrows covering large, yellow-brown eyes

Beard of long, thick, harsh hair

Well-developed thigh muscles

Powerful, straight forelegs with wispy feathering of hair

of German Short-haired and Wire-haired Pointer bloodlines. The result is a dog with a temperament not unlike the German Wire-haired Pointer, amenable and easy to train but occasionally headstrong and needing experienced control. As with so many wire-haired dogs, some males can be almost twice as heavy as the lightest females. This is a good family companion, very reliable with children, although still rarely seen outside the Czech and Slovak Republics.

WEIMARANER

SIZE 32–39kg (70–86lb), 56–69cm (22–27in)
GROOMING Minimal
TRAINING Average
COLOURS Shades of mouse-grey to silver-grey

A breed with athleticism, elegance, and show-stopping appearance. Named after the sport-loving Grand Duke of Weimar, the origins of this muscular breed are not known in detail. Breeders set its present looks and conformation in the late 1800s, and it was only in the 20th century that its popularity spread outside central Europe to northern Europe and North America.

The Weimaraner Vorstehhund, as it is officially called in Germany, can be opinionated; males in particular, because of their strength of body and personality, are best raised by experienced dog people. While it was developed as a dual-purpose tracker and retriever, and still occasionally participates in field trials and obedience work, the Weimaraner has become primarily a family companion, and is an excellent watchdog. The less common Long-haired Weimaraner differs strikingly in looks from its glossy, sleek brother, with endearingly long hair on its ears.

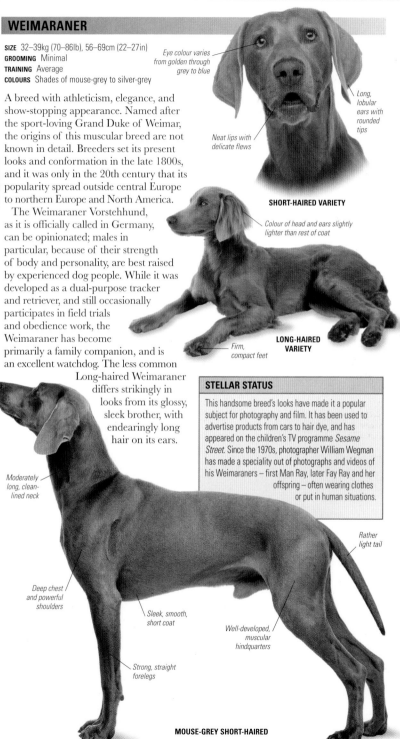

Eye colour varies from golden through grey to blue

Long, lobular ears with rounded tips

Neat lips with delicate flews

SHORT-HAIRED VARIETY

Colour of head and ears slightly lighter than rest of coat

LONG-HAIRED VARIETY

Firm, compact feet

STELLAR STATUS

This handsome breed's looks have made it a popular subject for photography and film. It has been used to advertise products from cars to hair dye, and has appeared on the children's TV programme *Sesame Street*. Since the 1970s, photographer William Wegman has made a speciality out of photographs and videos of his Weimaraners – first Man Ray, later Fay Ray and her offspring – often wearing clothes or put in human situations.

Moderately long, clean-lined neck

Rather light tail

Deep chest and powerful shoulders

Sleek, smooth, short coat

Well-developed, muscular hindquarters

Strong, straight forelegs

MOUSE-GREY SHORT-HAIRED

EXTRA-LARGE DOGS
40KG (88LB) PLUS

Early in the history of the dog's domestication, breeders selectively bred the largest of individuals, creating mastiffs, the giants of the dog world. The genes of these ancient breeds live on in nearly all of today's largest dogs. Physically breathtaking in size, mastiffs and related giants are generally easy-going in nature.

A BIG HELP

In ancient times, adaptable, heavyweight mastiff breeds acted as weapons of war, to guard livestock and property, and as fighting dogs. The Chinese and Babylonians used dogs in battle. So, too, did Alexander the Great. Later, mastiffs accompanied invaders and migrants as they moved from Asia into Europe. When the Europeans moved on to the Americas, they took their mastiffs – not as dogs of war, but as dogs used to intimidate both slaves and the native peoples encountered by the Europeans.

Giant breeds remain at work today. In most mountainous regions of Europe, breeds were developed to protect livestock from predators. And if it wasn't for the strength and warmth of huge breeds such as the Canadian Eskimo Dog and the Alaskan Malamute, the native peoples of these bitterly cold regions would never have survived. Another Goliath of a dog, the Komondor, has been exported to North America, where it protects sheep from Coyote predation, and to Namibia to guard farmers' livestock from lions.

Mastiffs today are also involved in dog fighting. Breeds including the Brazilian and Argentinean mastiffs and the Italian Cane Corso are still used in their own countries and others to satisfy the needs of

Komondor in command
The Komondor is well suited to its traditional role of guarding flocks. Its coat helps it to blend in with the sheep it protects.

those who enjoy this "sport". In the extra-large category of breeds exists one small anomaly. Geneticists say that Switzerland's greatest canine export, the life-saving St Bernard, descends from (or is a progenitor of) herding breeds rather than a member of the mastiff family. Purists can be assured, however, that the Newfoundland, that other life-saving breed, is a true genetic mastiff.

To the rescue…
The St Bernard, celebrated for its mountain-rescue ability, was first bred for draught work, hauling, and to make trails through fresh snow.

Swiss role
Perhaps typifying what most people picture when they think of an extra-large dog, the St Bernard is certainly a breed of imposing proportions. Tall, broad, and massively boned, it is a true gentle giant.

ALASKAN MALAMUTE

SIZE 39–56kg (86–123lb), 58–71cm (23–28in)
GROOMING Time-consuming
TRAINING Average
COLOURS Grey, black, sable, white

The largest of all the Nordic breeds, the Alaskan Malamute has been a favourite family companion for generations in North America. It is named after the Mahlemut Inuit people from the western coastal regions of Alaska and, like the Canadian Eskimo Dog, was used as a draught animal, pulling sleds, long before Europeans visited North America. Selective breeding for companionship successfully reduced the breed's natural inclination to establish a pack hierarchy and increased its willingness to engage with people. As with all of the Nordic breeds, this is not an overly demonstrative dog, but when raised in a family with children it is a wonderful participant in family activities. It is also a great athlete, excelling at sled-racing, where only the smaller Siberian Husky is more popular. Although most prevalent in North America, Malamutes are now ubiquitous around the world, with breed clubs in regions as diverse as Italy and Korea. Their dense double coat did not evolve for dogs living in tropical climates.

ALASKAN KLEE KAI

A small breed, the Alaskan Klee Kai has been created from bantam Alaskan Malamutes. Ranging in size from 4.5 to 9kg (10 to 20lb), it was formally recognized as a breed in 1997, with three categories: Toy, Miniature, and Standard. Though still rare, it is bred in the United States, Canada, and the United Kingdom.

Distinctive two-colour mask

Moderately broad chest

Insulating double coat

Relatively small, well-furred ears retain heat

Broad jaws with large teeth

Weather-resistant double coat

Outdoor companions
Although large in body, these dogs are surprisingly agile. They make ideal hiking companions, and are accomplished at freight-pulling, sledding, and racing.

CANADIAN ESKIMO DOG

SIZE 27–48kg (60–106lb), 51–69cm (20–27in)
GROOMING Time-consuming
TRAINING Time-consuming
COLOURS Variety of colours

Canadian Eskimo Dogs do everything – pull sleds, bark, eat, fight – with immense energy. While most Nordic breeds weigh just over 20kg (44lb), this breed can be well in excess of double that size. Indeed, the people of Arctic Canada, the Inuit, have survived in that harsh climate for over a thousand years only because of the versatility of this large, hard-working but aloof canine. Records show that in the 1950s they numbered around 20,000, and all Inuit used to keep a sled dog. However, the introduction of the snowmobile brought this breed to near extinction. By the early 1970s, with numbers reduced to fewer than 200, a breeding programme was initiated. Today, the Canadian Eskimo Dog is still endangered, with numbers in the low hundreds. This is the great husky as it was described in Jack London's stories.

Neat, wolf-like head

Fur between toes prevents pads from freezing

Dense coat protects dog from freezing temperatures

FREIGHT PULLING

The endurance of these powerful dogs is phenomenal, making them favourite sled dogs for arctic travel. On one polar expedition, a team of six dogs hauled a fully loaded sled and its occupant more than 50 miles each day for 14 consecutive days. Admiral Robert Peary, usually credited as the first man to reach the North Pole, in 1909, did so thanks to the efforts of teams of Canadian Eskimo Dogs.

Recreational activity
Dog-sledding as a winter tourist activity is increasingly popular in Canada. This new use will hopefully ensure the breed's survival.

BLOODHOUND

SIZE 36–50kg (79–110lb), 58–69cm (23–27in)
GROOMING Average
TRAINING Average
COLOURS Black and tan, red, liver and tan

Bloodhounds are known for their scent-trailing abilities, made possible by their vast nasal membrane. Indeed, the surface area of this membrane is greater than the surface area of all their skin. Droopy, moist lips help to trap scent particles, while the pendulous ears stir up dust. These affectionate, sensitive dogs are natural trackers, preferring the chase to the kill, and use their sonorous voices freely.

Nose to the ground
In its classic pose, the Bloodhound works the ground systematically, picking up the scent and, by its intensity, the direction to follow.

Powerful, muscular shoulders

Short, hard coat

Large, straight forelegs

BORZOI

SIZE 35–48kg (77–106lb), 69–79cm (27–31in)
GROOMING Average
TRAINING Average
COLOURS Variety of colours

In Russia, *borzoi* is a generic term for a sight hound. There are a variety of different regional types of borzoi in Russia and the Central Asian Republics; for example, the Chortai, Tasy, and Taigan. The breed recognized as the Borzoi probably descends from the Saluki and greyhounds crossed with lean sheepdogs.

Longer hair over chest and thighs

Long, hare-like feet

These graceful athletes were the pride of the Russian aristocracy, who used them for wolf-coursing, and were ruthlessly destroyed after the Russian Revolution, but numbers surviving outside the Soviet Union assured their survival. It makes an elegant, gentle, refined companion.

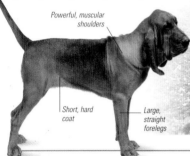

DEERHOUND

SIZE 36–45kg (79–99lb), 71–76cm (28–30in)
GROOMING Average
TRAINING Average
COLOURS Variety of colours

Ownership of this graceful, wistful-looking hound was once restricted to Scottish clan chieftains; when the clan system collapsed in 1746, the breed went into decline. It was eventually revived by a Scottish breeder, Duncan McNeil, and is now, rather oddly, much more common in South Africa than in its native land. While the Deerhound has the musculature and speed of the Greyhound, it also has a rough, weather-resistant coat that is suitable for the damp Scottish Highlands. It is an unassuming and gentle breed, with the short life expectancy typical of a giant canine, about nine and a half years. As with all deep-chested breeds, there is an increased risk of life-threatening rotation of the stomach.

Harsh, wiry, shaggy coat

Well-developed, strong neck

Lightly feathered legs with compact feet

IRISH WOLFHOUND

SIZE 40–55kg (88–121lb), 71–90cm (28–35in)
GROOMING Average
TRAINING Average
COLOURS Variety of colours

While wolfhounds had existed in Ireland for almost 2,000 years, they had entirely vanished by the mid-1800s. The breed was recreated by Captain G.A. Graham and is, with the Great Dane, now the tallest of all dogs. Irish Wolfhounds are on the whole calm, quiet, and surprisingly affectionate for such a large breed. However, they are the most predisposed to fatal cancers of all breeds and, according to pet insurance statistics, also have the shortest median life expectancy.

Deep chest

Powerful, muscular thighs

GREY COAT

Long back with powerful, well-arched neck

Sturdy, straight forelegs

Rough, wiry coat

BLACK COAT

TIBETAN MASTIFF

SIZE 64–82kg (141–180lb), 61–71cm (24–28in)
GROOMING Time-consuming
TRAINING Time-consuming
COLOURS Variety of colours

The mother of all mastiffs, this Tibetan dog was rescued from oblivion by British breeders in the late 1800s. Although its numbers remain small, it has been popular on European and North American dog-show circuits ever since. It is very likely that dogs similar to these, once used by Tibetan nomads to protect their homes and their flocks, provided the root stock for all of Asia's and Europe's giant livestock-guarding breeds. Over a century of selective breeding for show and companionship has resulted in a more easy-going temperament. Although this dog can be a little aloof, it makes a good family pet in either temperate or cold climates.

Long, straight coat with thick undercoat

Strong, muscular body

TIBETAN KYI APSO

The Bearded Tibetan Mastiff, the Tibetan Kyi Apso, from the remote, high-plateau region of Mount Kailish, is a smaller, regional variation, half the size of the Tibetan Mastiff and with a wiry coat. Once used by Tibetan nomads to guard their sheep and camps, it retains its traditional abilities while making a self-reliant, engaging family dog. First seen in the West in 1994, it is still very rare outside Tibet.

ENGLISH MASTIFF

SIZE 79–86kg (174–190lb), 70–76cm (28–30in)
GROOMING Average
TRAINING Time-consuming
COLOURS Brindle, fawn, silver, brindle or fawn and white

Mastiffs were being bred in Britain over 2,000 years ago and were prized exports to the Roman Empire, where they were used in both war and blood sport. The word "mastiff" probably derives from the old Anglo-Saxon word "masty", meaning powerful. English court documents from

500 years ago record the purchase of a "masty dogge". This giant canine needs exceptionally experienced handling, if only because of its size.

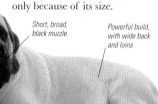

Short, broad, black muzzle

Powerful build, with wide back and loins

BULLMASTIFF

SIZE 41–59kg (90–130lb), 64–69cm (25–27in)
GROOMING Average
TRAINING Time-consuming
COLOURS Brindle, red, fawn

This unique British breed was produced by crossing the English Mastiff with old-fashioned Bulldogs. A powerful gamekeeper's assistant, its speed and strength enabled it to chase and subdue poachers without causing them lasting injury. While it is roughly the same size as the Rottweiler, its relative lack of popularity can be attributed to its boisterous stubbornness. Head halters work well to control the rather headstrong behaviour of males in particular. This is a breed suitable for experienced dog handlers only.

Short, black muzzle

Wide, deep chest

Well-spaced, powerful legs

DOGUE DE BORDEAUX

SIZE 36–45kg (79–99lb), 58–69cm (23–27in)
GROOMING Average
TRAINING Time-consuming
COLOURS Fawn, gold, mahogany

Rarely seen outside France until the 1989 film *Turner & Hooch* gave it worldwide recognition, the Dogue de Bordeaux was developed in Bordeaux at the time this French region was ruled by English kings. It was almost certainly created by crossing English Mastiffs with regional giant guard dogs. Males in particular can retain their formidable guarding instincts. Similar in many aspects to the Bullmastiff, this breed is best in the capable hands of experienced dog people. Its pendulous lips make it prone to considerable drooling.

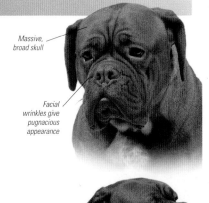

Massive, broad skull

Facial wrinkles give pugnacious appearance

Ears set well back on head

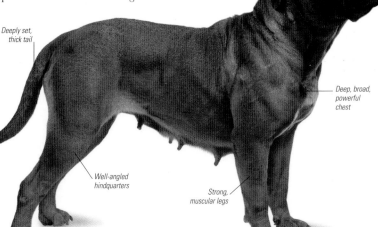

Deeply set, thick tail

Deep, broad, powerful chest

Well-angled hindquarters

Strong, muscular legs

CENTRAL ASIAN SHEEPDOG

SIZE 40–50kg (88–110lb), 60–71cm (24–28in)
GROOMING Average
TRAINING Time-consuming
COLOURS Variety of colours

Nomadic tribesmen throughout what are now the Central Asian republics of Turkmenistan, Uzbekistan, Kirghizia, Tadzhikistan, and Kazakstan have

> ### STUDENTS OF RED STAR
>
> The Central Asian Ovtcharka were, together with the Caucasian Ovtcharka, and the South Russian Ovtcharka at a later time, bred at the state-owned Red Star Kennels. They were to be used as police and army dogs, but also as guardians of large factories and warehouses. These Central Asian Sheepdogs were usually smaller than their livestock-guarding relatives.

Long, strong, broad back

Dense topcoat with woolly undercoat

Well-boned forelimbs with powerful shoulders

used mastiff dogs for centuries to protect their livestock. The fearless and bold Central Asian Sheepdog has lost popularity in Russia over the last 20 years, and is thought unreliable and difficult to train. Its official name, Sredneasiatskaia Ovtcharka, smacks of cultural imperialism to people in the Asian republics because the Russian word *ovtcharka*, meaning "sheepdog", is used rather than an Asian language word.

CAUCASIAN SHEEPDOG

SIZE 45–70kg (99–154lb), 64–72cm (25–28in)
GROOMING Time-consuming
TRAINING Time-consuming
COLOURS Variety of colours

Familiar in western Europe for their role as border guards in divided Germany, this breed, officially the Kavkazskaya Ovtcharka or Caucasian Ovtcharka, is Russia's most popular sheepdog. Its breed standard conforms to the bear-type sheepdogs from Georgia, a style favoured by Stalin. Thousands of them were abandoned as the Russian Army withdrew from East Germany after the fall of the Berlin Wall, and many of their descendants have been bred as family companions.

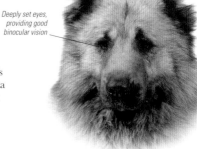

Deeply set eyes, providing good binocular vision

Thick, dense coat with profuse feathering

Hips slightly raised from line of back

MOTHER AND PUP

Finer coat than adult dog's

ANATOLIAN SHEPHERD DOG

SIZE 41–64kg (90–141lb), 71–81cm (28–32in)
GROOMING Average
TRAINING Time-consuming
COLOURS Variety of colours

Triangular ears, carried high when dog is alert

Slightly pendulous black lips

Short, flat coat with thick undercoat

It was not until the 1970s that breeders began to examine the variety of sheepdogs in the Anatolian region of Turkey. Here, sheepdogs are collectively called Coban Kopegi, and that remains a common name for this breed. So too is

Kangal Dog or Karabash Dog. The breed standard for the Anatolian Shepherd Dog is just one of the diverse forms of Coban Kopegi. These naturally protective and suspicious dogs are used as guardians to protect flocks of sheep and goats, rather than to herd. The smaller but equally strong-willed and independent Hellenic Shepherd (*see* p.197) is no doubt closely related, as is the smooth-haired variety of Central Asian Sheepdog. These powerful dogs have not yet been bred selectively for companionship. With careful early socialization they adapt to a family environment, but they must always be regarded as potentially aggressive, especially with other animals.

YOUTHFUL LEARNING

Success at almost every natural canine activity depends upon early learning. This Anatolian Shepherd Dog puppy is raised with goats and thinks of the flock as his extended family (he may even be shorn when they are). Later in life, when he is mature, he will naturally protect and defend his flock from predators.

Muscular thighs

Long, straight, wide-set forelegs

Strong feet with well-arched toes

AKBASH

V-shaped ears, slightly rounded at tips

Broad, slightly rounded skull

Thick, protective topcoat and undercoat

SIZE 41–55kg (90–121lb), 71–86cm (28–34in)
GROOMING Average
TRAINING Easy
COLOURS White

This Turkish sheepdog, also known by the names of Akbas or Coban Kopegi, is a light-coloured breed developed in western Turkey. Like the Anatolian Shepherd Dog, this breed is rangy in shape with a natural dignity and calmness, qualities that make it a superb livestock guard. Its passiveness should not be mistaken for a feeling of trust; it is innately suspicious of strangers and readily attacks other animals. In the 1970s, this breed was exported to North America, where it is successfully used to prevent Coyote predation on sheep and goat ranches in the Canadian and American Rocky Mountains.

SOUTH RUSSIAN SHEEPDOG

SIZE 55–75kg (121–165lb), 65–90cm (26–35in)
GROOMING Time-consuming
TRAINING Time-consuming
COLOURS White with yellow or shades of grey

This shaggy-haired breed is a tough guard dog. The South Russian Sheepdog arose when Asian and Caucasian sheepdogs met with shaggy white Spanish sheepdogs 200 years ago. These Spanish sheepdogs had accompanied Merino sheep across Europe to the Crimea, in what is now the Ukraine. Once a common breed (known in Russian as Ioujnorousskaia Ovtcharka), it was decimated during the 1917 Russian Revolution.

Fringe of hair hanging over face

Massive bone structure

A revival occurred, but World War II once more drove the South Russian Sheepdog near to extinction. It was revived using Komondor and Caucasian Sheepdog bloodlines. Rare outside the Ukraine and Russia, it is now a common sight at Russian dog shows.

Strong, straight back

Distinct moustache of hair on muzzle

Well-arched, oval feet covered in long hair

Waterproof, dense, insulating double coat

KOMONDOR

SIZE 36–61kg (79–134lb), 65–90cm (26–35in)
GROOMING Time-consuming
TRAINING Time-consuming
COLOURS White

The largest and most unique of the Hungarian guarding breeds, the ancestors of the Komondor probably accompanied the Magyar tribe from the East when they settled in Europe over 1,000 years ago. The breed's name was first used almost 500 years ago, although it was not until 1910 that the Komondor was firmly established as a modern breed. While its coat is now admired for its unusual appearance, it evolved for practical reasons, for protection from the elements and from the teeth and claws of wolves and bears as it protected its flock. The Komondor's guarding abilities led to its establishment in North America to protect sheep from Coyote predation. Pups are raised with sheep, move pasture with the flock, and, as adults, are even shorn when the flock is shorn. So effective is the breed at thwarting Coyote attacks on sheep, some ranches in British Columbia have eliminated livestock loss. The coat of the working Komondor is thick and protective, but it does not develop into a show-quality coat as illustrated here. This protective breed needs careful obedience training, but with early socializing, it makes a reasonable, if sometimes musty-odoured, companion.

Muscular upper and lower jaws

Corded coat with the sensation of felt

Muscular neck with grey-pigmented skin under hair

Heavy, coarse topcoat with dense, woolly, soft undercoat

Tail extends down to hocks

COAT CONCERNS

While this magnificently corded coat is wonderful to behold, it can create problems for the owner and also for the dog. Outdoors it acts like a magnet, picking up twigs, leaves, debris, and even insects. A wet coat can take almost a day to completely dry out. Komondors should only be bathed when medically necessary, and then thoroughly dried using a hand-held drier.

HUNGARIAN KUVASZ

SIZE 30–52kg (66–115lb), 66–75cm (26–30in)
GROOMING Time-consuming
TRAINING Time-consuming
COLOURS Creamy white

High-set, V-shaped ears

Large, black, open nostrils

This large mountain dog, taken to Hungary by Turkish nomads, can be ferocious. The name derives from the Turkish word *kavas*, meaning "armed guard". If raised from puppyhood in the home and socialized to other dogs and people, the Hungarian Kuvasz can make a good, although potentially formidable companion.

SLOVENSKY KUVAC

Broad head with fairly blunt muzzle

High-set, pendant ears

Thick topcoat over dense undercoat

SIZE 30–45kg (66–99lb), 55–70cm (22–28in)
GROOMING Time-consuming
TRAINING Average
COLOURS White with spots of other colours

Rescued from near extinction after World War II by a veterinarian, Professor Antonin Hruza of the Brno School of Veterinary Medicine, this is essentially a Hungarian Kuvasz that lives across the border in Slovakia. Its other name, Tatransky Cuvac, indicates it is also a close relative of the Polish Tatra Mountain Sheepdog. Selective breeding has made this dog a fairly reliable and affectionate companion for a family.

TATRA MOUNTAIN SHEEPDOG

SIZE 45–69kg (99–152lb), 61–87cm (24–34in)
GROOMING Time-consuming
TRAINING Time-consuming
COLOURS White

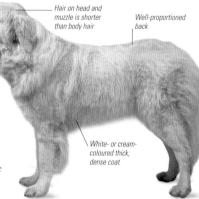

Hair on head and muzzle is shorter than body hair

Well-proportioned back

White- or cream-coloured thick, dense coat

The largest of the great white mountain dogs of Central Europe, the Tatra Mountain Sheepdog (Owczarek Tatranski) is a classic flock guardian, although it was also used occasionally to pull carts. Independent by nature, it can become firmly attached to humans when raised from puppyhood as a canine companion. Its popularity, in Poland in particular, but also elsewhere in Europe and North America, has soared dramatically in the last 15 years.

MAREMMA

SIZE 30–45kg (66–99lb), 60–73cm (24–29in)
GROOMING Time-consuming
TRAINING Time-consuming
COLOURS White

Uncommon outside Italy, except on the show circuit, the Italian name of this dog, Cane da Pastore Maremmano-Abruzzese, gives its location of origin in Italy, where it has long worked as a classic flock-guarding breed. Today, it also works in Australia. Although the Maremma is the smallest of the white mountain dogs, its personality is as firm and independent as its relatives to the east and west. Strong-willed, and a superb natural guard, this aloof breed often requires a knowledgeable handler to train it reliably.

V-shaped ears

Large, conical head

Sturdy shoulders and thick legs

PYRENEAN MASTIFF

SIZE 55–75kg (121–165lb), 71–80cm (28–31in)
GROOMING Time-consuming
TRAINING Time-consuming
COLOURS White with black and fawn

The Pyrenean Mastiff, also called the Mastin d'Aragon, shows obvious crossing between white mastiffs and lighter-coloured Spanish mastiffs. When working as flock guards, these dogs still wear the traditional *carlanca* – a spiked collar that protects the neck from attack by wolves. Selective breeding has made this a reliable companion for experienced dog owners.

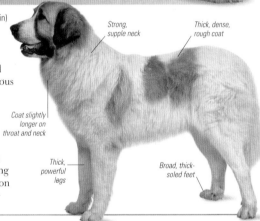

Strong, supple neck

Thick, dense, rough coat

Coat slightly longer on throat and neck

Thick, powerful legs

Broad, thick-soled feet

PYRENEAN MOUNTAIN DOG

SIZE 45–60kg (99–132lb), 65–81cm (26–32in)
GROOMING Time-consuming
TRAINING Time-consuming
COLOURS White, white with grey, pale yellow, or orange

The black, orange, or fawn colouring often present on the head of this dog can probably be attributed to crossbreeding between the relatively small number of great white mountain dogs that reached the Pyrenees and indigenous mastiff breeds. In the 1970s, when Pyrenean Mountain Dogs first emerged as family companions, there were problems with over-assertive personalities, but only a few generations of selective breeding produced dogs that are reliable with children and strangers.

BLENDING IN WITH THE FLOCK

SPANISH MASTIFF

SIZE 55–70kg (121–154lb), 72–82cm (28–32in)
GROOMING Average
TRAINING Time-consuming
COLOURS Variety of colours

Rarely seen outside Spain, the Spanish Mastiff (Mastin de Extremadura or Mastin de la Mancha) was taken to Spain by Phoenician traders over 2,000 years ago to what was then arid wasteland, but is today the wheat belt. The Spanish Shepherd's Association records that this bulky breed, a great saliva dribbler, has been protecting livestock from wolves for at least 600 years. Today, the majority of these dogs guard homes rather than livestock and, although males in particular can be aggressive with other dogs, they make reasonable family companions, and have surprisingly small exercise demands. Descendants of Spanish mastiffs exist throughout the regions of the former Spanish Empire.

Thick, fine coat, soft to the touch

Deep, wide chest

Short, firm-set feet, with neatly shaped toes

Ears set well back on head

VITAL NUTRITION

Extra-large dogs such as the Spanish Mastiff grow enormously quickly, and this has led to myths about their unique nutritional needs during puppyhood. Contrary to what is sometimes advised, these dogs do not need calcium supplements to grow healthy bones. In fact, adding extra calcium to an already balanced diet may actually cause developmental bone problems.

BRAZILIAN MASTIFF

SIZE 41–50kg (90–110lb), 61–76cm (24–30in)
GROOMING Average
TRAINING Time-consuming
COLOURS Variety of colours

Bloodhound ancestry is apparent in this dog's pendulous skin and ears and its superb tracking ability. One of two recognized Brazilian breeds (the other is the rare Brazilian Tracker), the Brazilian Mastiff descends from Portuguese and Spanish mastiffs taken to the Americas. It is used as a guard dog and large game tracker. Because it is used as a fighting dog in its native country, the breed is banned in Britain and elsewhere.

Thick neck with loose folds of skin

Short, dense, smooth, soft coat

Muscular chest

Powerful forelegs

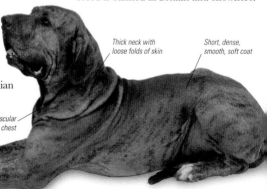

ESTRELA MOUNTAIN DOG

SIZE 30–50kg (66–110lb), 62–72cm (24–28in)
GROOMING Average/time-consuming
TRAINING Average
COLOURS Red or black brindle, fawn

This classic livestock guard is commonly seen as a guard dog or companion dog in Portugal, especially in towns in the Estrela Mountains, where it is known as the Cão de Serra da Estrela. The long-haired variety in particular has become popular in Britain. Its modern coat colours are a consequence of

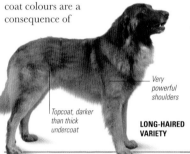

Very powerful shoulders

Topcoat, darker than thick undercoat

LONG-HAIRED VARIETY

crossbreeding with German shepherds in the 20th century, and this may also be why this breed is quite responsive to obedience training. Selective breeding has restored its shape to a form similar to what it was over 100 years ago. As with all the giant breeds, hip dysplasia is always a potential problem. This fast-growing breed is also prone to canine panosteitis, a condition causing growth pains during puppyhood.

PORTUGUESE WATCHDOG

SIZE 45–60kg (99–132lb), 76–77cm (30in)
GROOMING Average
TRAINING Time-consuming
COLOURS Variety of colours

Once commonly seen as a farm and estate guardian in rural regions of Alentejo in southern Portugal, this solemn and serious dog, also known as the Rafeiro do Alentejo, developed, probably randomly, through crosses of Estrela Mountain Dogs, Spanish Mastiffs, and local dogs. Numbers declined to near extinction in the 1970s, but recent breeding has

ensured the breed's survival. It is the largest of all Portuguese breeds and is seldom seen outside its native country. As its name suggests, this dog is a natural guard and requires careful, early socializing and efficient obedience training for it to become a reliable companion dog.

Short, stocky, powerful neck

Short- or medium-length coat

Long, curved, feathered tail

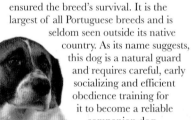

Triangular, folded ears hanging by cheeks

Broad, muscular hindquarters

ST BERNARD

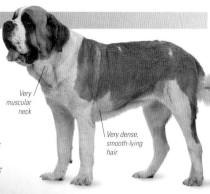

SIZE 50–91kg (110–201lb), 61–71cm (24–28in)
GROOMING Average/time-consuming
TRAINING Time-consuming
COLOURS Orange and white, orange, brindle

Descended from mastiffs that passed through Switzerland with the Roman army, this benevolent hulk is the world's largest dog. Named after the region of Switzerland on the Italian border where they have been kept by local Bernardine monks since the 1660s, the stories of their daring mountain rescues are as much mountain

Very muscular neck

Very dense, smooth-lying hair

myth as truth. However, these muscular dogs were certainly used as draught animals, able to pull heavy loads along icy ground, as well as to clear paths through snowdrifts. When their numbers declined to near extinction, the breed was revived using Newfoundland and Great Dane bloodlines.

It takes time to obedience train a St Bernard, and their massive size makes it a challenge for them to live primarily indoors in all but suitably spacious homes.

A true saint among dogs
Celebrated for its debatable history of rescuing snowbound alpine travellers, whatever the St Bernard's origins, this breed makes a kind, affectionate brute of a dog.

LEONBERGER

SIZE 34–50kg (75–110lb), 65–80cm (26–31in)
GROOMING Time-consuming
TRAINING Average
COLOURS Red-brown to gold-yellow

The Leonberger has bounced back from virtual extinction at the end of the second world war, reaching safe numbers in North America, Britain, Germany, and elsewhere. It was originally created by crossing the Newfoundland, St Bernard, and Pyrenean Mountain Dog, to resemble the lion on the Imperial

Coat of Arms of Leonberg in Germany. Its revival from a small genetic base has been associated with the dog world's highest incidence of two endocrine conditions: an underactive thyroid gland, and an underactive adrenal gland.

This handsome, genial breed is a superb swimmer.

Distinctive "lion" mane at throat and chest

Round feet with webbed toes

Rough, not shaggy, coat

GREAT SWISS MOUNTAIN DOG

SIZE 59–61kg (130–134lb), 60–72cm (24–28in)
GROOMING Average
TRAINING Average
COLOURS Tricolour

The largest of the tricolour mountain dogs of Switzerland, this was once a powerful draught dog, pulling milk carts from farm to market, or helping to drive cattle. All the tricolour dogs were traced and recorded at the turn of the 20th century by two men, Franz Schertenlieb and Albert Heim. They searched the Swiss valleys, recording the variety of draught and cattle dogs, or *Sennenhunden*, that they found there. While well muscled and heavy boned, this is an agile, all-round performer.

Broad, powerful chest

Dense, shiny topcoat with thick undercoat

Strong, broad thighs

Round, compact feet with well-arched toes

BERNESE MOUNTAIN DOG

SIZE 40–44kg (88–97lb), 58–70cm (23–28in)
GROOMING Time-consuming
TRAINING Average
COLOURS Tricolour

This is the most successful of the tricolour breeds, firmly established throughout Europe and North America as a popular family companion. While many are very affectionate towards people, some lines of Bernese can be aggressive. Breeding from a small genetic base has led to a high incidence of bone cancer and mast cell tumours. As a result, the Bernese has one of the shortest median life expectancies of all dogs, averaging only about seven years.

Long muzzle with distinctive markings

Abundant, long, glossy, black coat

White markings on feet, chest, face, and tail tip

Peak of health
These Bernese Mountain Dogs relax in the sunshine, looking resplendent in their glossy double coats.

NEAPOLITAN MASTIFF

SIZE 50–68kg (110–150lb), 65–75cm (26–30in)
GROOMING Easy
TRAINING Time-consuming
COLOURS Black, brown, brindle, blue, grey

With a massive skull and copious, pendulous skin around the neck and withers, this unique-looking breed probably descends from Roman warrior and fighting dogs. Dogs of this great size and shape have certainly been present in the Campania region of Italy for over 2,000 years, although its numbers declined to dangerously low levels in the mid-1900s. An inveterate saliva dribbler and a curiously messy eater, the Neapolitan Mastiff is also rather stubborn and needs early socializing if it is to be a good, well-rounded family companion.

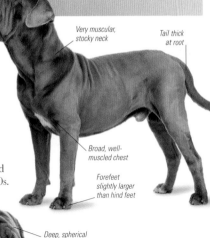

Very muscular, stocky neck

Tail thick at root

Broad, well-muscled chest

Forefeet slightly larger than hind feet

Deep, spherical shape to head

Short, dense, fine coat, with hard texture and good sheen

Long, broad thigh muscles

Stocky, well-boned legs

ARGENTINIAN MASTIFF

SIZE 36–45kg (79–99lb), 61–69cm (24–27in)
GROOMING Easy
TRAINING Time-consuming
COLOURS White

This breed is experiencing an international resurgence in popularity following the recent success of the film *Bombón el Perro*. Set in Patagonia, it tells the story of a red-eyed, crop-eared Argentinian Mastiff (Dogo Argentino) that gradually changes the life of his new owner for the better. This distinctive breed was developed by crossing Spanish fighting dogs and mastiffs, Boxers, Bulldogs, and old-style Bull Terriers to produce a puma and jaguar hunter. It instantly appealed to dog-fight organizers, and unfortunately it is still used to fight in South America and elsewhere. Its combative reputation has resulted in this breed being banned from a number of countries, including Britain. However, with early socializing to other dogs, and routine obedience training, the Argentinian Mastiff can make a loyal family companion for experienced dog handlers.

TOSA INU

SIZE 50–90kg (110–198lb), 62–65cm (24–26in)
GROOMING Average
TRAINING Time-consuming
COLOURS Dull black, red, fawn

The Tosa survived the ravages of World War II only because individuals had been exported previously to Taiwan and Korea. It descends from smaller Japanese fighting mastiffs that were selectively bred up in size through crosses with larger European breeds, such as the Great Dane. Today, it is very rare in Japan and even in the United States, and is banned in some countries due to its background. Males are dramatically larger than females, sometimes almost double their weight. Owing to their fighting ancestry, this breed can be formidably aggressive with other dogs unless socialized well when young.

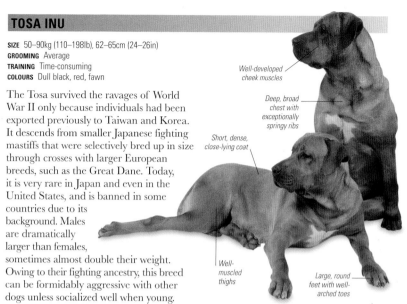

Well-developed cheek muscles

Deep, broad chest with exceptionally springy ribs

Short, dense, close-lying coat

Well-muscled thighs

Large, round feet with well-arched toes

CANE CORSO

SIZE 40–50kg (88–110lb), 60–68cm (24–27in)
GROOMING Average
TRAINING Time-consuming
COLOURS Various colours

Once a Sicilian cattle drover, then a butcher's dog, and no doubt also once a fighting dog, this breed (also known as Cane di Macellaio) is a classic mastiff, without the exaggerated skin features of its northern cousin the Neapolitan Mastiff. Like all mastiffs, the Cane Corso is prone to joint problems, in particular hip

dysplasia, and needs good, early socializing to ensure it is not a danger to other animals, including smaller dogs. Fortunately, it does not have excessive skin around its lips, so it doesn't suffer from the drooling common in other mastiffs, such as the St Bernard.

Powerful muscles
Healthy, strong dogs such as these two may take part in weight-pulling competitive events.

GREAT DANE

SIZE 50–80kg (110–176lb),
79–92cm (31–36in)
GROOMING Easy
TRAINING Time-consuming
COLOURS Fawn, black, blue, brindle, harlequin

This majestic and truly grand dog –
the tallest of all dog breeds – was
called the Grand Danois by the great
French naturalist the Comte de Buffon,
because he felt the strongest examples
came from Denmark. It was not
until 1880 that its other name, the
Deutsche Dogge, was established at
a dog show in Berlin. It is now Germany's
national dog. Like all mastiffs, the Great
Dane's origins are in Asia, and it is very
likely its ancestors, the Alaunts (mentioned
by Chaucer in the 1200s), were brought to
Europe by the Alans, a Scythian tribe that

Long, tapering, slightly curved tail

Short, dense coat

Well-turned stifles

originated in what is now Asian Russia.
The Great Dane, as we know it today,
was developed in the 1800s by crossing
the regional northern European mastiffs
with local greyhound stock. Great Danes
are enormously gangly as pups and then
develop into dignified and surprisingly
gentle adults, some of whom love to sit
on their owner's laps. A heart condition,
dilated cardiomyopathy (DCM), can be
passed by unaffected females to half of
their pups. Gene testing will eventually
make it easier to reduce the risk of this fatal
condition from developing. As one of the
deepest-chested of all breeds, it is prone
to life-threatening rotation of the stomach.

YOUTHFUL ACTIVITY

While adult Great Danes are typically moderate in
their desire for frenetic activity, during their youth
they can be enormously vigorous. A racing Great
Dane like this one is wonderful to watch, but needs
considerable space for manoeuvring. Care must
be taken when exercising young
dogs to prevent injury to
dog and bystanders.

A varied litter
Great Danes have large litters of pups. Eight is average
and twelve is not uncommon. Breeders often supplement
mother's milk to reduce the enormous demand on her
milk-producing capacity.

Round, fairly deep-set eyes

Long, flat skull

Thick, symmetrically hanging lips

ROTTWEILER

SIZE 41–50kg (90–110lb), 58–69cm (23–27in)
GROOMING Easy
TRAINING Average
COLOURS Black and tan

Bred in Rottweil in southern Germany as a droving and cattle dog, the Rottweiler's closest relative is probably the Great Swiss Mountain Dog. The two breeds share a variety of mental traits, including a relative ease of obedience training combined with a formidable protection instinct. It can be difficult to read a Rottweiler's body language, and this breed can be unreliable as a consequence – the mood can change

Coarse, flat, black topcoat, with tan markings

in a second from delight to anger, with the only visible sign being dilating eyes. High incidence of malignant bone cancer accounts for the foreshortened median life expectancy of only 9.8 years.

Working Rottweiler
Responsive to training, and possessing all the requisite traits of a guard dog – bulk, aggression, and a propensity to bark – the Rottweiler makes an ideal police dog.

Strong forelegs with forward-sloping pasterns

Broad, deep chest with well-sprung ribs

BROHOLMER

SIZE 40–70kg (88–154lb), 74–78cm (29–31in)
GROOMING Average
TRAINING Average
COLOURS Golden-yellow, occasionally black

Mastiffs arrived in Scandinavia as Viking plunder, but by the end of the 1800s all the indigenous mastiffs in Denmark, Sweden, and Norway had become virtually extinct. In Denmark, the last Broholmer, that country's mastiff breed, was registered by the Danish Kennel Club (DKK) in 1910. In 1974, DKK breeders started recreating the Broholmer and it was internationally recognized in 1998. Although it can now be sold outside Denmark, virtually the entire population lives within the country. The new Broholmer has been bred primarily for companionship.

Great Dane
The Great Dane is a lot of dog to keep indoors, but requires less outdoor exercise space than many smaller breeds.

RUSSIAN BLACK TERRIER

SIZE 40–65kg (88–143lb), 63–75cm (25–30in)
GROOMING Average
TRAINING Difficult
COLOURS Black, some grey hairs permitted

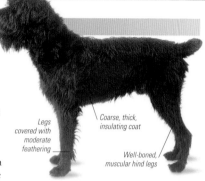

Legs covered with moderate feathering

Coarse, thick, insulating coat

Well-boned, muscular hind legs

It is difficult today to comprehend just how powerful Professor T.D. Lysenko was in Soviet Union science. His biologically impossible theory, which stated that acquired knowledge and learning could be passed in the genes from one generation to the next, had tremendous appeal to the Soviet authorities because it meant it only required the training of a single generation of communists to ensure the perpetuation of that philosophy. To show the gullible Party hierarchy how heredity could be broken down and moulded, he arranged for dogs to be selectively bred and then trained at the Red Star Army dog kennels in an ultimately unsuccessful attempt to prove his theory. The Russian Black Terrier, created by crossing the Giant Schnauzer, Airedale Terrier, and Rottweiler, is one result. This is a powerful dog, best in the hands of an experienced dog owner.

Russian exports
Increasingly popular outside the former Soviet Bloc countries, Russian Black Terriers make effective guard dogs, but most, like this pair, are now kept as companions.

DIFFICULT TO CLASSIFY

Breed registries around the world differ in how they classify the Russian Black Terrier. In Germany, for example, this pup is classed as a terrier, the European FCI places it within the Schnauzers and Pinschers class. Considering its history and utilitarian success as a guard dog, it would be reasonable to place it within the Working Dogs category.

NEWFOUNDLAND

SIZE 50–68kg (110–150lb), 66–71cm (26–28in)
GROOMING Time-consuming
TRAINING Easy
COLOURS Brown, black, grey, Landseer

Although genetic studies firmly prove that the massive Newfoundland (named after the Canadian province where it originated) is related to other mastiff breeds, such as the guarding dogs featured on previous pages, it is unlike many of them in personality. In fact, Newfoundlands (or "Newfies") can be the biggest softies of the dog world. While painful joint diseases, osteochondrosis dissecans (OCD), and hip dysplasia are serious problems within the breed, these are stoic dogs that benignly want to participate in family activities and thrive on human companionship. There is a colour variation of the Newfoundland, named after the 19th-century British painter Sir Edwin Landseer, who featured them in his work. The Landseer is black and white rather than primarily brown, black, or grey, and is recognized as a separate breed by some registries.

LANDSEER COLOUR VARIATION

SEA RESCUE

Newfies are inveterate swimmers, with an inclination to swim to anyone in the water. Their natural affinity for the sea has encouraged breed clubs to develop challenging water tests. These include taking lines or flotation rings to people in the water, boat towing, floating retrieves, and even underwater retrieves. French authorities have a number of trained, sea-rescue Newfoundlands at their disposal along the Mediterranean coast. This breed's lifesaving urge is so strong that the greatest problem may be stopping it from "rescuing" those not in difficulties.

Broad, massive head with short, square muzzle

Flat, dense topcoat, somewhat coarse, and oily

Very powerful hindquarters

Large feet with broadly webbed toes

KEEPING A DOG

CARING FOR A DOG

All dogs depend upon us for their physical health and psychological well-being. Living with a dog can make your life more interesting and enjoyable, but alongside the benefits come special responsibilities. Your canine friend is ever-reliant on you for food, security, health, and peace of mind.

THE CANINE CONUNDRUM

There is no other animal species, domesticated or wild, with such a tremendous variety of shapes, sizes, coats, and conformations. So how do you choose the right dog for you? Whatever your lifestyle, with a little thought and guidance, you can pick the perfect canine partner for a reciprocal relationship that will last a lifetime.

CARE AND CARE ALIKE

Dogs are creatures of routine, and this is an important consideration when caring for them. Every day, your dog relies upon you to make the right decisions about nutrition, for example.

Letting off steam
Although requirements vary with size and breed, all dogs need constructive daily exercise. Taking your dog for a walk is a great way for you both to keep healthy, happy, and to meet new friends, canine and human.

The right choice
Kitting out your dog need not be expensive, but you should choose items that are robust and suited to your pet. A dog's bed is his private den, so make sure it stands up to the job.

Dogs are good groomers, but they need continuing attention from you to keep their eyes, ears, mouth, paws, skin, and coat in prime condition. All dogs thrive on regular grooming from us, so make it part of your daily care drill. Consider also what other essentials a dog needs: permanent identification, regular health check-ups, bedding, collars and leads, and a varied selection of toys.

IN SICKNESS AND IN HEALTH

Routine body checks on your dog reveal potential problems before they become serious, while preventative care protects your dog, other dogs, and you. Elderly dogs in particular depend upon you to know when they are in pain or discomfort. And when emergencies occur – fortunately infrequently – the techniques you learned to assist people are easily adapted to giving first aid to a dog. The principles are the same, only the scale changes.

A clean bill of health
Regular veterinary examinations of your dog can catch future problems at an early stage when they are easier to treat.

The value of living with dogs

Dogs continue to have practical purposes – to guard and protect, to control vermin – but of all domesticated species it is the dog that today provides us with the greatest social, psychological, and emotional rewards. These are the modern values of living with a dog.

WHAT'S IN IT FOR THEM

It's obvious why dogs are delighted to live under our protection. And yet some people in the animal rights movement feel that dog ownership is a form of slavery and should be abolished. It certainly is, but exactly who's the slave? Can you imagine what an alien would make of it, landing on Earth, seeing how our dogs control our lives? At a dog's command – a bark or an unblinking stare – we feed them according to their biological

Taking the lead
Dogs generate positive energy, encouraging their owners to get off the sofa, step outside, and stay physically active.

clocks, often altering their diet according to their changing tastes. We chauffeur them to the park for their daily exercise. We follow them, sack in hand, cleaning up their poop! We wash and groom them, provide them with comfortable bedding, and take them to the vet's when they tell us they're unwell. We're putty in their paws, but we care for them as we do because the benefits of living with them are so profound.

OUR NEED TO NURTURE

While our relationships with our children and grandchildren evolve, we retain throughout our lives a perpetual need to nurture, to look after other living things. By gardening, for example. Or keeping pets. One of the greatest rewards of living with dogs is that they provide us with an outlet to care for

Reasons to be cheerful
Having dogs around is good for us. Studies prove that people living without pets are exposed to more persistent fears, stronger feelings of panic, experience more frequent headaches, and take more medication for stress-induced illnesses than pet owners.

A special relationship
The unconditional acceptance and love dogs give to their owners positively impacts on their owner's emotional health, particularly among the elderly.

because deep in the core of our being is the need to be needed. Owing to the lifestyle changes we chose to make in the 20th century – increased mobility, physical separation from the extended family, enhanced leisure activities – the source that would naturally fulfil our need to be needed isn't always there.

EMPTY NESTERS

Dogs are increasingly part of the lives of empty nesters, people whose children have grown up and left home. In my veterinary clinic, it is primarily women who bring pets in for health checks or medical attention, although I also see many couples over 60 years of age and lots of gay couples of any age accompanying their pooches. To many of these people, dogs are like surrogate children, filling a void in their lives that may be impossible to fill otherwise.

It's easy for cynics to belittle the intense relationship that can develop between an empty nester and his or her dog. It's easy to ask why people don't devote this surfeit of warmth towards other human beings. That's a societal problem for us to deal with. In the meantime, dogs are here – offering unconditional love and undivided attention to those who need it most – delighted to fulfil their role in helping people enjoy their lives to the full.

those who cannot care for themselves on their own. In turn, they care for us. The dog's effortless ability to raise our spirits ranges from reducing feelings of stress and anxiety to lowering blood pressure and helping us to lead healthier, more active lives. This care aspect is important,

Finding a dog

Before even thinking about acquiring a dog, ensure that you understand the long-term costs. Do you have the time, space, and energy to commit yourself to the demands of living with a canine companion, and have you researched the best places to get a dog?

CONSIDER THE COST

While the purchase price of a dog may range from nothing to over £1,000, start-up equipment and veterinary costs add, on average, another £400. Then there's food. Feeding a typical Labrador-sized dog costs at least £1 per day. Dogs are also living longer than ever before. With long life comes the additional cost of caring for the elderly canine. Health insurance averages out that cost over the years, but assume average annual veterinary and insurance costs of around £300. In total, running a typical dog for an average lifespan of 12.8 years will cost almost £12,000.

A HOME FIT FOR A HOUND

Is your home suitable for a dog to live in? Is it safe? Does it have enough living space for a dog to grow into throughout its life? Surprisingly, a dog's size is not the primary determining factor you need to consider. Some giant breeds, such as greyhounds and mastiffs, are content to laze around in relatively modest habitats, while smaller breeds, such as Border Collies and some terriers, relish larger home territories where they can release their high energy levels.

How does your home measure up?
Even a town apartment can be a suitable home for the right breed of dog. However, you will need to have a toilet area inside if your pup does not have access to a garden.

RELIABLE SOURCES OF DOGS

As well as coming in a variety of shapes and sizes, dogs also come from a variety of sources: some reliable, and some that should be approached with scepticism.
◼ The neighbour whose bitch has just had a litter is often an excellent source. Pups that are raised by amateur breeders may already be socialized and react well to the routines of family life.

RESCUING A DOG?

Make sure you ask the recycler the following questions about your prospective pooch:

	Yes	No		Yes	No
Is he obedience trained?	☐	☐	When left alone, does he:		
Is he house trained?	☐	☐	bark or howl?	☐	☐
Is he friendly with strangers?	☐	☐	dig or scratch?	☐	☐
Is he friendly with other dogs?	☐	☐	chew objects?	☐	☐
Does he behave differently on the lead?	☐	☐	urinate or defecate inappropriately?	☐	☐
Can you easily take a toy away from him?	☐	☐	pace constantly?	☐	☐
Is he worried when children are present?	☐	☐	Armed with these answers you'll have a better idea of any problems you may be inheriting.		

■While many professional breeders are involved because they love dogs, others breed canines simply to make money. Just because a breeder is registered with a kennel club does not ensure reliability. Look for pups raised in the home, rather than pups brought up in an outbuilding.

■Professional rescue centres examine all dogs that they recycle, not only for their health but also for their temperament. Wonderful individuals, including a large number of purebreds, can be obtained from pounds and dog homes.

■Notice-boards at veterinary clinics often advertise dogs for sale. These are invaluable sources because the staff at the clinic are likely to know the parent dog or its family personally.

■Consider homing a retired working dog, often available from charities such as Guide Dogs for the Blind. These intelligent dogs deserve a loving home after the responsibilities of their service roles, and often make excellent pets.

Dog breeder kennels
Take time to look round a breeder's facilities before buying your dog. These kennels are clean, comfortable, and the dogs are not crammed into their living spaces. A good breeder will want to assess your suitability as an owner: be prepared to answer as many questions as you ask.

WHERE NOT TO FIND A DOG

Avoid puppy farms, where unscrupulous traders sell cheaply and cruelly farmed animals. Avoid pet shops, which may be fronts for this trade. Avoid newspaper advertisements offering dogs for free. Avoid buying dogs off the Internet unless you can guarantee the validity of your source – while many websites offer excellent, fully vetted animals, some are fronts for the illicit trade in dogs. Avoid letting your heart rule your head while you're on holiday – don't rescue that poor moth-eaten stray. But if your options for getting a dog are limited to these means, be cautious, thorough, and sensible.

Choose your sources wisely
They may look cute now, but not knowing a puppy's ancestry or at least its early history could lead to extreme behavioural issues and exorbitant veterinary bills in the future.

Choosing a dog

Before looking at individuals, you need to make some important choices. Decide whether you want a pup or an older dog. Take into account the sex differences in canine behaviour, even in neutered dogs, and consider carefully what size and type of dog will suit you best.

PUPPY OR ADULT

Your first decision after you've agreed that a dog will be a welcome addition to your home is whether to get a malleable putty-in-your-hands pup or provide a home for an older dog that has already reached adolescence or adulthood. Pups are adorable but they remain pups for an amazingly short time. The advantage of getting a pup at around eight weeks of age is that this is the ideal time to socialize him to your lifestyle: travel, urban life, living with other animals, and so on. What some owners consider the greatest disadvantage is that you are responsible for the sometimes tedious, sometimes exasperating, house training. Many, but not all adult dogs, arrive already

Older and wiser
There may be many reasons why you decide that an adult dog will fit in better with your lifestyle than a puppy. But don't look on it as a soft option: any new dog requires a big commitment from the owner to forge a strong bond.

TESTING A PUPPY

It's difficult to assess a pup's personality on only one visit, but try the following exercises, ideally on a puppy around 6 weeks old. Give a score from 1 to 5 for each test.

Pick up the pup. Is he:

Shivering	Tentative	Relaxed	Resistant	Aggressive
(1)	(2)	(3)	(4)	(5)

Take the pup to a quiet area, put him on the ground, and watch him explore. Is he:

Shivering	Tentative	Relaxed	Inquisitive	Bustling with curiosity
(1)	(2)	(3)	(4)	(5)

Roll the pup gently on his back for a minute. Is he:

Terrified	Tentative	Relaxed	Wriggly	Annoyed
(1)	(2)	(3)	(4)	(5)

TEST A PUPPY AT 6 WEEKS OLD

Pups that score low are likely to be nervous or submissive. Pups with high scores are potentially strong personalities, best in the hands of experienced dog owners. Those who score somewhere in between these extremes are likely to be an easier addition to your household.

house trained, although there is always a degree of retraining in a dog's new environment. Adult dogs also often arrive already obedience trained. A drawback is that older dogs frequently come with unexpected emotional baggage, and a predisposition to separation anxiety is not uncommon in recycled adult dogs.

BOYS, GIRLS, AND NEUTERING

The difference is relatively simple. A rush of male hormone masculinizes male pups at the time of birth, whereas females are "neutral" until becoming "feminized" at puberty. Male dogs are more likely to be dominant, active, and destructive than females, as well as acting aggressively towards other male dogs. In general, female dogs demand greater affection and are easier to obedience train and house train. Whichever sex, there is no difference in their ability to watchdog bark.

If you are not planning to breed from your dog, consider neutering. It is a highly effective form of birth control, which offers several other benefits. Neutered males are less likely to urine-mark, pick fights

Bursting with energy
Male dogs are likely to be more active than females of the same breed, and may have greater exercise demands. As much depends on the individual, however, and ultimately, which sex you choose is a matter of personal preference.

Young and cute
Puppies entering a new household often form an especially close partnership with any children in the family.

with other male dogs, or wander off. Neutered females will not urine-mark (as they would at the onset of oestrus) or go off their food or attempt to escape (telltale signs of ovulation). Overly possessive behaviour is also prevented. They also live on average 18 months longer than similar females that are not neutered and the risk of mammary tumours and uterine infection is greatly reduced. The downside of neutering in females is that it may either increase the density of the coat (and so reduce its lustre) or lead to hair loss. One in three neutered dogs are also predisposed to weight gain.

S–M–L–XL

The size of dog you choose is up to you, although pet insurance actuarial statistics reveal that small breeds live longest. Small poodles, dachshunds, and Bedlington Terriers, for example, all have median life expectancies in excess of 14 years. At the other end of the spectrum, giant breeds have the shortest lives: Bernese Mountain Dogs live on average less than seven years. Although sizes are fairly similar at birth, growth rates are very varied, and the food needs of a growing giant breed are huge.

Opposite extremes
The Irish Wolfhound lives on average for seven years, whereas a Wire-haired Dachshund may reach double this age.

GROWTH CURVES

All breeds start life relatively similar in size. However, whereas the Yorkshire Terrier reaches its adult weight of 3kg (6.5lb) by 4½ months, a giant breed like the St Bernard will continue to grow rapidly for the first year, not attaining its full 60kg (132lb) until 18 months. Most breeds' growth curves fall between these two extremes.

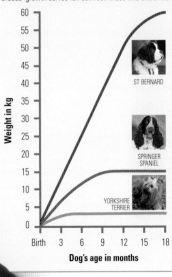

Weight in kg — 60, 55, 50, 45, 40, 35, 30, 25, 20, 15, 10, 5, 0

ST BERNARD

SPRINGER SPANIEL

YORKSHIRE TERRIER

Birth 3 6 9 12 15 18

Dog's age in months

Purebreds
As well as having pedigree good looks, a pure-bred pup holds few surprises as to its eventual size and temperament. Breed-specific medical problems are fairly common, however.

EXTENDING OUR OWN PERSONALITIES

While the size and the sex of a family companion are often easy choices, what you want your dog to look like is a more complicated question to answer. Guys often prefer short-coated, muscle-bound dogs, until they learn that a Chihuahua or a Yorkshire Terrier can compete in the thuggishness Olympics with the burliest Rottweiler. Purebred, crossbred, or random-bred is also a tough decision to make. There has been a gratifying cultural shift during the last quarter of a century or so regarding dog selection. Today, many families are actively choosing to give a home to an unplanned or unwanted dog, rather than buying a purebred with an impeccable pedigree or show-quality looks.

Random-breds
The majority of dogs living in rescue centres are random-breds, but the good news is that dog lovers are increasingly opting for mutts from shelters rather than purebred pets.

POSITIVELY PUREBRED

The advantage of getting a purebred is that you can accurately predict adult size, shape, and personality. Knowing your dog's ultimate size and temperament upfront is very handy – you're saving yourself from any unpleasant surprises. However, because of the consistent inbreeding necessary to create and perpetuate a breed, you also get known genetic predispositions to disease, for example skin allergy in West Highland Terriers or heart disease in Dobermanns and Cavalier King Charles Spaniels.

CROSSBRED DOGS

Only a decade ago, crossbreds, the progeny of two different purebred dogs, were considered "mistakes". It could be difficult to find homes for the results of unauthorized alliances between, say, a Bichon Frise and a Yorkie. Thankfully, this is no longer the case. Crossbreeding is now both planned and successful. It diminishes the risk of genetic diseases and often produces exhilarating results, such as Labradoodles and Cockerpoos. This success has led to some countries setting up breed registries for crossbreds.

MUTTS

Mutts are just about anything else – the result of random breeding. The look and shape of random-breds varies with dog stock from country to country. In parts of the United States, mutts have a hound-like appearance, while in regions of Britain there is an obvious element of sheepdog. Japanese mutts often have the appearance of Shiba dogs. From a medical perspective, one of the advantages of random breeding is the reduced risk of genetic disease. On the other hand, random breeding makes it more difficult to assess a pup's eventual adult size and personality.

Feeding a dog

Every single day of your dog's life you tend to the needs of your buddy's gastrointestinal system. During your dog's lifetime, you will spend more money on food and visit your vet more often to prevent or treat mouth and digestion problems than for any other reason.

DOGS ARE DIFFERENT

Your dog's nutritional needs are different from yours and because dogs no longer capture and kill their own food, but have constant access to tasty and nutritious meals, obesity has become a common canine condition. It is up to you to make the right choices for your dog to avoid these problems. The medical evidence is arresting. If you feed your dog a well-balanced diet, gradually altering it as your dog progresses through life, and if you ensure that his teeth and gums remain healthy, you can extend his life expectancy by, on average, 18 months.

TEETH, GUMS, AND INFECTION

Your dog has a carnivore's teeth, designed for capturing and killing prey, removing meat from carcasses, and chewing meat and roughage. Because we feed our dogs either commercially produced dog food or our own table food, dogs seldom have the opportunity to use their teeth as they evolved to be used. Gum infection, the cause of "dog breath", can spread via the bloodstream to other parts of the body.

SPECIFIC DIETS FOR DOGS

Canine nutrition is as susceptible to food fads as is human nutrition. One popular diet is called Bones and Raw Food (BARF). This diet consists of uncooked bones, muscle and organ meat, raw eggs, vegetables, fruit, and cereals. Whether it is wise to feed dogs this kind of diet, however, is contentious. Chewing on bones certainly massages the gums and scrapes the teeth, but swallowed bones are the most common foreign bodies vets end up operating on dogs for. What's more, raw meat and eggs are more likely than cooked foods to be contaminated by *Salmonella* or *E. coli* – bacteria dangerous to dogs and potentially transmissible to humans.

You can prevent gum disease through good nutrition and oral hygiene. Ask your vet about diet, compacted biscuits, chews, and toothbrushing to keep your dog's teeth and gums in good condition.

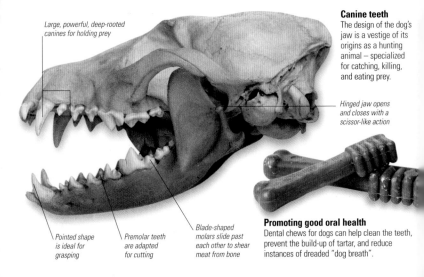

Large, powerful, deep-rooted canines for holding prey

Canine teeth
The design of the dog's jaw is a vestige of its origins as a hunting animal – specialized for catching, killing, and eating prey.

Hinged jaw opens and closes with a scissor-like action

Pointed shape is ideal for grasping

Premolar teeth are adapted for cutting

Blade-shaped molars slide past each other to shear meat from bone

Promoting good oral health
Dental chews for dogs can help clean the teeth, prevent the build-up of tartar, and reduce instances of dreaded "dog breath".

THE RISK OF BLOAT

Bloat is a life-threatening condition in which partial or complete rotation of the stomach prevents food from entering or leaving. The affected dog may drool, retch, wander restlessly, become listless, or show signs of pain. Symptoms of shock quickly develop.

Bloat affects mainly deep-chested large breeds, such as German Shepherds, Great Danes, Dobermanns and Weimaraners. If you have a dog that is known to be at risk of bloat, prevent the problem by limiting water consumption for an hour before or after each meal. Do not allow the dog to drain the bowl of its contents; water should be consumed in moderate quantities. Do not allow rolling or other exercise after meals.

THE STOMACH AND INTESTINES

A dog's stomach is essentially a holding tank. Its great capacity allows dogs to gorge on food, as they are naturally competitive and opportunistic feeders. Digestion is then a slow process. However, your dog's intestines house a dynamic ecosystem in which various competing "good" bacteria, taken in with mother's milk and supplemented by new bacteria from different foods, strike a balance that is optimum for digestion.

The dog is built primarily to digest protein and fat, which contain all the vitamins and minerals it needs. Dogs are superbly formed for an "Atkins-style", high-protein, low-carbohydrate diet. Carbohydrate is necessary for good

The burdens of obesity
Obesity is becoming a serious problem in domestic dogs. Among other ailments, the ability to exercise is reduced and the work of the heart increased.

intestinal health, but it is neither a natural energy source for dogs nor as nutritionally rewarding for dogs as it is for us.

ENERGY AND OBESITY

Plump pups look cuddly but they've manufactured excessive numbers of fat cells. Later in life, it's harder to reduce the number of fat cells than to shrink them in size. The evidence is dramatic and overwhelming. Lean dogs are likely to live, on average, 18 months longer than their plumper siblings. It's up to you to maintain your dog's healthy physique. Do so by offering any food in moderation. A commercial diet produced to help dogs lose weight usually contains around 15 per cent fewer calories than the manufacturer's regular food.

DIFFERENCES IN ENERGY NEEDS

The average daily kilocalorie (kcal) requirements for your dog depend on age, weight, and lifestyle. Dogs in colder climates will need a slightly increased energy intake depending on the amount of time they spend outdoors. Ask your vet about the specific energy needs of pregnant or lactating females.

Weight of dog (kg)	Daily energy requirements (kcal)			
	Active	Working	Inactive	Elderly
2–5	210–420	295–590	185–370	150–300
6–10	480–705	675–990	420–620	345–505
11–20	775–1,180	1,065–1,665	665–1,040	545–850
21–30	1,225–1,600	1,725–2,255	1,080–1,410	885–1,155
31–40	1,640–1,990	2,310–2,800	1,445–1,750	1,180–1,430
41–50	2,025–2,350	2,850–3,310	1,780–2,070	1,460–1,690

INGREDIENTS OF A HEALTHY DIET

Regardless of how you choose to feed your dog, he needs essential ingredients. A well-balanced diet, containing high-quality nutrients, is vital for good health. The essential components of a healthy canine diet are protein and fat. Proteins are complex molecules made up of a variety of amino acids, which are the building blocks for all body tissues and for all the enzymes that support the body's chemical reactions. The most natural source of protein is meat but, like us, dogs can get all the essential amino acids they need for a healthy life from vegetable protein.

Fat (or "oil" as it's usually described on food labels) contains essential fatty acids (EFAs). It is energy-dense, with around twice as many calories per gram as protein or carbohydrate. Both the aroma and taste of fat make food more palatable, but fat is also essential for transporting the fat-soluble vitamins A, D, E, and K. Dogs prefer animal fat, but vegetable fat can be equally nutritious. For example, linseed oil has similar nutritional benefits to fish oil.

Fibre is a natural part of a dog's diet, and is needed to promote good digestion and solid stools. In the wild, fibre is consumed when a dog eats the fur

UNDERSTANDING FOOD LABELS

Comparing protein, fat, and fibre levels in different commercial dog foods isn't easy because levels vary according to the food's water content. It is simpler to compare foods on a "dry-matter" basis – what remains if all moisture is removed. Here's how to calculate dry matter levels of protein, oil, and fibre.

A typical canned food label might say: moisture 80%; protein 8%; oil 6%; fibre 1%. This food is 80 per cent moisture so it is 20 per cent dry matter. Calculate the true levels of protein, fat, and fibre using this formula.

Dry matter nutrient content =
The label's nutrient percentage
x 100 ÷ Dry-matter content
percentage. Therefore:

Protein = 8 x 100 ÷ 20 = 40
Oil (fat) = 6 x 100 ÷ 20 = 30
Fibre = 1 x 100 ÷ 20 = 5

A good all-rounder
To be at his peak, your dog requires a diet that incorporates all of his nutritional needs. This diet will be dependent on his age, his health, and on any food allergies.

or intestine contents of other mammals. There are many types of fibre. They fall into two main groups: water-soluble and insoluble. Water-soluble fibre, from foods such as cooked vegetables and rice, increases the stickiness of food, slowing digestion and the absorption of nutrients from the small intestine. Insoluble fibre, such as bran and animal fur, retains water and makes faeces more bulky, helping waste to pass through the large intestine. The amount of fibre that your dog needs varies with its age and lifestyle; older dogs sometimes benefit from an increase in both soluble and insoluble fibre in their diet, to aid bowel function.

A constant supply of fresh, clean, easily accessible water is essential for life. Water is the largest component of most cells in your dog's genetic makeup. It is absorbed by fibre and carries the water-soluble vitamins – the B group, folic acid, and vitamin C – around the body. The daily amount a dog drinks will vary according to its diet, activity levels, and the weather conditions. Dogs fed on dry food will need more to drink than those fed on canned or home-cooked food.

ESSENTIAL FATTY ACIDS

Nutritional studies show that fats do more than simply provide energy. EFAs are involved in controlling a range of problems, such as allergies, arthritis, heart disease, and even cancer. There are two main groups of these fats: Omega 3 and Omega 6 EFAs. The larger group, Omega 6 EFAs, are essential for the walls of cell membranes to function efficiently. Omega 3 EFAs are associated with reduced cell inflammation. An optimum balance of Omega 3 and Omega 6 EFAs is necessary for strong, robust, healthy skin, efficient reproductive organs, and an all-round strong immune system.

FREE RADICALS

"Free radicals" are molecules and atoms that destroy cell membranes. The level of free radicals in the body increases with illness and age, but also with routine physical activity. "Free radical scavengers" are substances that sweep up and destroy dangerous free-radical molecules and atoms. Antioxidants, such as vitamins C and E and the minerals selenium and zinc, are free radical scavengers. So are

DIFFERENT NUTRITIONAL NEEDS

All dogs share the same dietary needs and digest food in the same way. What differentiates one breed from another are genetic factors that predispose the breed to medical or physical problems. For example, some large breeds are prone to arthritis and have a tendency to gain weight easily. Small breeds, like the Yorkshire Terrier shown here, will readily eat a meat-only diet if allowed, resulting in dangerously low levels of calcium. In that sense, diets formulated for specific breeds – and their respective sizes – may be beneficial.

substances called "carotenoids", such as lutein and beta-carotene. Diets high in free radical scavengers may help a dog's natural systems to destroy free radicals.

FOOD ALLERGIES

Dietary allergies in dogs are being increasingly diagnosed by vets. A food allergy occurs when a dog's immune system is abnormally sensitive to a particular component in its food. This may be a flavour or a colouring, but is more likely to be a nutrient, such as milk, beef, or other natural foods. The allergy usually causes a skin reaction, often itching; it may also affect the gastrointestinal tract and cause vomiting, diarrhoea, or both. Trying to discover what in the diet is causing a problem is time-consuming, but once the "allergen" is avoided problems resolve themselves.

Whether age- or health-related, any changes you do make to your dog's diet should be introduced gradually, over a 5- to 10-day period. This lets the digestive enzymes adjust to the new nutrients, and makes it easier to spot adverse reactions.

Your dog's diet

There is no such thing as a single diet suitable for all dogs. Each dog varies according to its own metabolism. Nutritional needs change as a dog matures from puppyhood through to old age, and energy demands vary according to the lifestyle your dog enjoys.

WHAT TYPE OF FOOD?

All dog diets should provide the correct balance of nutrients. After this, it's your call. If you want to cook for your dog, there are books and websites available to help you formulate a balanced, nutritious diet. If you choose a commercially produced dog food, whether to go for wet or dry food is a personal decision, based upon convenience for you and palatability for your dog. One texture of food is not nutritionally better than another, although manufacturers of pet food often produce their greatest variety of super-premium foods in dry form. Your vet can explain the pros and cons of different diets for your particular dog.

Food for thought
Good nutrition is as important to your dog's health as it is to your own. With a dizzying array of types of dog food to choose from, finding the right one for your pet isn't always easy. If in doubt, ask your vet for advice.

CHANGE THROUGH LIFE

During puppyhood a dog needs to grow as well as simply maintain itself. This demands more energy, ideally in the form of protein. Young dogs thrive on diets 20 per cent higher in protein than do mature dogs. Avoid feeding too much energy-dense food during puppyhood, however. Overweight pups are more likely to have lifelong weight problems.

Many commercially produced adult foods contain far more than enough nutrients, and are very tasty. If these nutrient-rich diets are fed freely, obesity is the natural outcome. Most of these commercial foods are formulated for mature dogs, but manufacturers' recommendations often advocate quantities that are directed at vigorous adults. To this end, your dog may actually benefit from eating smaller amounts than what the manufacturer suggests.

Contrary to what is sometimes written, healthy older dogs do not benefit from reduced protein levels in their diet. Most older dogs thrive on their adult diet simply reduced slightly in quantity and augmented with extra vitamins and minerals. Some may benefit from special "senior" diets, containing high-quality, easily digested nutrients and extra antioxidants to help the immune system, and extra nutrients for skin and gut health.

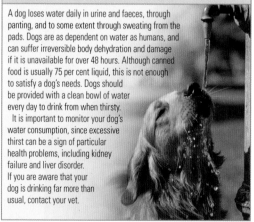

WATER

A dog loses water daily in urine and faeces, through panting, and to some extent through sweating from the pads. Dogs are as dependent on water as humans, and can suffer irreversible body dehydration and damage if it is unavailable for over 48 hours. Although canned food is usually 75 per cent liquid, this is not enough to satisfy a dog's needs. Dogs should be provided with a clean bowl of water every day to drink from when thirsty.

It is important to monitor your dog's water consumption, since excessive thirst can be a sign of particular health problems, including kidney failure and liver disorder. If you are aware that your dog is drinking far more than usual, contact your vet.

FRESH FOODS		NUTRIENTS PROVIDED	ADVANTAGES	SHORTCOMINGS OR LIMITATIONS
	Meat	Meat consists of amino acids in the form of protein, and fatty acids in the form of fat. Both are essential for life.	Meat, especially fatty meat, is tasty. It is also the food of choice for species, such as the dog, that evolved to capture and eat prey.	Meat is seriously deficient in calcium. A dog will eventually die of heart failure if fed a meat-only diet.
	Meat and vegetables	Protein, fat, and some vitamins and minerals from meat; carbohydrates, vitamins, minerals, and antioxidants from vegetables.	Vegetables balance the nutrients. The result is a diet closer to the dog's natural diet, which includes the intestinal content of prey.	Some dogs pick out the meat, leaving the vegetables. Finding the time to cook for their dogs can also be a problem for some owners.
	Vegetarian	Dogs can convert vegetable-derived protein and fat into essential amino acids and fatty acids.	Vegetarian dog owners need not bring animal-derived protein, fat, or carbohydrate into their homes.	Vegetarian diets must be carefully balanced to provide dogs with trace nutrients and prevent any deficiencies.
	Rice	White rice provides starch. Unmilled rice that retains its outer coating also provides fibre and nutrients such as magnesium, folate, and iron.	Rice is highly digestible, palatable to many dogs, and hypoallergenic. (The water it is cooked in contains many trace nutrients.)	Rice is an excellent source of calories in the form of starch, but contains few of the vitamins and minerals needed for a balanced diet.
PREPARED FOODS		NUTRIENTS PROVIDED	ADVANTAGES	SHORTCOMINGS OR LIMITATIONS
	Moist prepared food	All nutrients provided in moist prepared food are well above minimum levels, and moist food tends to be 75% water.	Often easier to digest than other types of food. Small dogs in particular may find moist food more palatable than dry food.	Moist foods can be more expensive than some dry varieties. Can stick to the teeth and gums, leading to dental hygiene problems.
	Semi-dry prepared food	Top manufacturers balance all nutrients to meet the dog's nutritional needs. Semi-dry prepared food is approximately 40% water.	This form of food is aesthetically pleasing to our eyes. It looks more like "real food" than dry food does.	Sugar gives this food its chewy consistency. High-sugar diets are both a risk to diabetics and may contribute to dental problems.
	Dry prepared food	Quality dry foods are routinely monitored by manufacturers and provide all the key nutrients a dog requires.	Many dog owners find it convenient to store and feed dry food, often available in bulk bags.	It takes longer for a dog to digest dry food than wet food. Antioxidant is added to dry food to prevent the fat it contains from going rancid.

Basic dog accessories

Shopping has become our most popular leisure activity, and shopping for your new dog is extra exciting. When buying dog accessories, make sure you choose items primarily for their practical use rather than solely for their design or cost.

THE BARE MINIMUM

All dogs have certain essentials: bowls for food and water, an ID tag, a collar and lead for security and control, and their own bed to call home. Almost as essential is a selection of toys, items to give mental and physical stimulation (*see* pp.314–315, The importance of play). Choose items that are designed according to your dog's needs. Some dogs, for example, are not the right shape for collars, and would benefit more from a body harness.

BEDDING

Before choosing a bed, think about both where your dog will sleep and his eventual size – you are buying bedding with an adult dog in mind and not a perennial puppy. Many dogs enjoy the security of a solid perimeter. Think of teething. Wicker looks wonderful but is very tempting to chew. Choose a bed large enough for your dog to lie on, on his side with his legs fully extended.

FOOD AND WATER BOWLS

Many individuals, particularly large dogs, don't eat their food – they vacuum it. The best food and water bowls are wide for easy access and either heavy or with non-slip bases to prevent sliding across the floor. Don't rely on your dog's tongue for bowl cleaning. Wash all feeding utensils daily after use, just as you wash your own.

FOAM-FILLED BED

WICKER BED

BEANBAG BED

Beds fit for a dog
A comfy, spacious, and hygienic bed is essential for your pet's well-being. Destined for years of service, the type of bed you choose now is all-important.

Bowled over
Before buying food and water bowls, consider your dog's needs: small breeds, such as the Yorkshire Terrier, will struggle to feed from a high-sided bowl.

Get collared
For the majority of dogs, a traditional nylon or leather collar is sufficient. Other options include sight hound collars, buckle collars, and quick-release flat collars.

COLLARS AND LEADS

By all means exercise your fashion sense when choosing a collar or harness for your dog, but always choose items that are practical and comfortable. Wide, flat collars are excellent for breeds with long necks such as whippets, while rolled leather is ideal for those with a long coat such as Golden Retrievers. You should be able to slide two fingers under a well-fitted collar. With all but the thickest-necked breeds, this means that the collar is comfortably loose but will not come off if your dog tugs backwards. If your dog's shape is not right for a collar, provide him with a body harness.

A full choke chain is commonly used as a safety device to prevent a dog from slipping its collar. Choke chains should never be used simply to control a dog's

behaviour, however, because they may cause compression of the windpipe, especially in small breeds. Head halters are ideal for controlling either giant or flamboyant individuals (*see* p.327).

Taking the lead
Choose a durable lead that is suitable for your dog's size and is comfortable in your hand. A good lead could last your pooch for its whole life.

Long training lead

In harness with your dog
Harnesses place less stress on the neck area of small breeds with wide necks, such as Pugs, or those with delicate windpipes, such as the Yorkshire Terrier and Chihuahua (*below*).

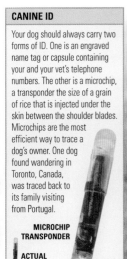

CANINE ID

Your dog should always carry two forms of ID. One is an engraved name tag or capsule containing your and your vet's telephone numbers. The other is a microchip, a transponder the size of a grain of rice that is injected under the skin between the shoulder blades. Microchips are the most efficient way to trace a dog's owner. One dog found wandering in Toronto, Canada, was traced back to its family visiting from Portugal.

MICROCHIP TRANSPONDER

ACTUAL SIZE

Additional dog equipment

There is an ever-increasing array of practical accessories available for your dog, designed to ensure that he is safe when he participates with you in your own leisure activities. Whether you're hiking, sailing, or just driving to the shops, make sure your dog is equipped for the event.

TRAVEL EQUIPMENT

A crate eases travel problems, as a sudden stop can turn your unsecured dog into a lethal missile. If you have an SUV, estate, or hatchback, a crate provides safe, secure transport for your dog. Alternatively, install a rigid dog guard. If your dog travels on the back seat, secure him to the seat belt anchor with a dog's seat belt harness. You should also carry a folding bowl so that you can stop every two hours to let your dog feed and have a drink of water.

Safe and sound
Using a crate when you travel by car ensures that your dog is secure and can't jump around, distract you from driving, or hang its head out of the window.

Eating on the run
Small enough to fit in a glove-box, a foldable, waterproof, lightweight bowl is an essential accessory for your dog if you do a lot of travelling together.

Belt up in the back
Your dog needs to be restrained if it is to travel with you as a passenger by car. Large dogs can wear special dog harnesses that attach to seat belts in the back seat.

HIKING BACKPACKS

It's up to you to carry your dog's gear if you're going on a short walk. Those walkers who cover more ambitious distances, however, can always accustom their dog to lightening the load by attaching a backpack to it to help carry bulky but lightweight items. A healthy, well-conditioned canine should be able to carry one-quarter of its own weight.

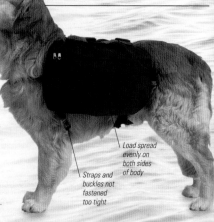

Load spread evenly on both sides of body

Straps and buckles not fastened too tight

Packed and ready to go
When attaching a backpack to your dog, ensure that the load is not too heavy, the fit is good, and that no straps or buckles will cause chafing to your dog's girth.

BODY INSULATION

It's easy for you and me to dress warmly, but dogs, like humans, can suffer from hypothermia, especially if they get wet. Short-haired dogs need cold-weather protection from wind, rain, and snow. Choose a coat that is comfortable, water-proof, provides great insulation, and looks good on your dog. Close-fitting neoprene garments are a very effective way of helping your dog preserve its own body warmth.

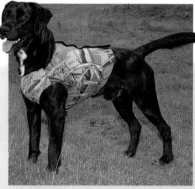

Wrapped up for winter
This dapper hound is protected from the elements by a highly breathable fleece coating.

Dressed for the job
This working dog wears a neoprene camouflage vest, helping to keep him warm and comfortable in the cold and rain or when diving into lakes and rivers.

FLOTATION DEVICES

Even the most inveterate Labrador can't swim indefinitely. If you take your dog with you while sailing, ensure he wears a flotation device. A doggy lifejacket will not only help him keep afloat, it will also help you find him if he falls or jumps overboard. A grab handle positioned on the dog's back makes lifting a sopping-wet pooch out of water easier.

Staying buoyant
Good swimmers they may be, but all dogs should be fitted with a canine life jacket if they will be near water for long periods.

FOOT PROTECTION

Shoes for dogs might seem a slightly frivolous idea, but in freezing weather, for example, breeds such as Boxers are prone to frostbitten feet. Burning hot sand is just as dangerous as ice and snow, so ensure your dog wears some form of foot protection in extreme weather. The neoprene rubber-soled dog boots pictured below also protect your pooch's paws from thorns, broken glass, and grass seeds.

NEOPRENE DOG BOOTS

DON'T DEMEAN YOUR DOG

There are lots of cute canine accessories you can buy, but are they really for your dog or are they there to satisfy our own vanities? Is it really in a dog's interest to wear a pink satin baby doll outfit or reindeer ears or a leather hat and goggles? By all means have fun with your dog, but laugh with him, not at him.

Preparing the household

With careful planning, caring for a new dog is a joy. But bringing a dog into your life includes responsibilities to your dog for its well-being and to your family, friends, and neighbours. There are several guidelines you should follow before bringing your new friend home.

NAMING YOUR DOG

The name you choose for your dog says as much about you as it does about your pet. It shows how you view your dog and your relationship with it. Choose as pretentious a name as you wish, but always use a one- or two-syllable word when speaking to your dog. Short, sharp names are best for getting your dog's attention. My dog's full name was Lexington, but always Lex or Lexy when speaking to her. Use your dog's name when getting its attention, but never for when you need to punish. That only teaches it to worry when it hears its name. Train everyone in your family always to use your dog's name when they want its attention.

Her first pet
The first few days you spend with your puppy sow the seeds for your future relationship together.

PREPARE FOR THE ARRIVAL

Dogs are born mischief-makers. Before welcoming one into your home, think about your new pet's indoor and outdoor environment. Remove any chewable and breakable items from your dog's territory-to-be. Make sure low windows are closed and outside doors latched. Ensure that all detergents, cleaners, insecticides, and fertilizers are out of reach. Tape down electrical wires, or spray them with taste deterrents. Check your back-yard fences for openings through which a puppy might escape; baby-guards are ideal for preventing a new dog from wandering out of its designated area. Even with perfect preparation, remain vigilant. Dogs are just amazing at finding the weaknesses in our best-laid plans.

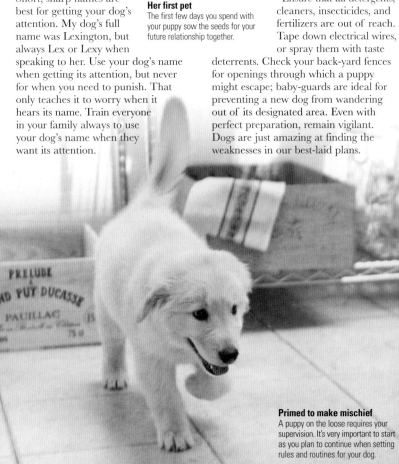

Primed to make mischief
A puppy on the loose requires your supervision. It's very important to start as you plan to continue when setting rules and routines for your dog.

MEETING THE FAMILY

Keep human activity to a minimum when your pup arrives in your home. Restrict him to a single room at first, but let him investigate it to his heart's content. Explain to children that they should be calm and quiet when they meet the new arrival.

A resident dog, especially an older one, can resent the arrival of a newcomer. Wait until your new addition is asleep and then let your resident canine take the initiative and sniff its new house-mate. Use the same approach with the family cat. Cats rule dogs and if your cat has the opportunity to hiss first he will establish his own ground rules. Make sure your cat's feeding bowl is inaccessible to your dog. Cat food always tastes better to canines than dog food.

SETTLING IN

For some dogs, moving home is very stressful. The stress increases the risk of illness, especially gastrointestinal disorders. Regardless of what you plan to feed your dog, get a sample of what

The security of his own bed

Your new arrival needs a safe, permanent place to retreat. Plan where your dog will eventually sleep, not just where she sleeps during her first weeks with you. Bedding should be hygienic, washable, comfortable, and protecting – an old duvet or a beanbag are ideal.

he's been eating and continue feeding that for the first few days, gradually switching it during the first week to the diet you have chosen. See pp.278–283 for more advice.

For the first eight weeks of his life, your dog snuggled in close with his mother and siblings when he slept. Where your dog sleeps now – in a crate in the kitchen, in the hallway, or in your bedroom – is your choice, but wherever it is be consistent. If he is to sleep alone, don't make a big fuss over him. Leave quietly and don't respond to howling or crying. If you do, he wins and he knows it. If you have thin walls, take your neighbours a box of chocolates and some earplugs, and offer an apology for any noise your dog may make. Only the rarest of canine individuals does not learn to sleep quietly alone within a week.

FURNITURE FANATICS

Dogs aren't dummies. Even the slowest pup knows that sofas and beds are more comfortable than the floor. And there's an added bonus for them: these places smell comfortingly of us. It's your choice whether you let your dog on your furniture or bed. If you don't want dog hair everywhere though, never, ever let them on furniture. To your dog, just once is enough to say it's always okay. Be firm from the outset and only let a sleeping dog lie where you say so.

Health and safety

Following your dog's arrival, over the next few days gradually introduce him to his new life within your family. When it's safe to do so, allow your dog outdoors, first into your garden, then into public areas. Car trips should be introduced as soon as possible.

CHECK OUT THE RISKS

Just as you planned ahead before you brought your dog home, make sure you're not exposing him to unnecessary outdoor risks. Before letting your dog into the garden, carry out a complete inspection. Is the fence or hedge escape-proof? Have you recently used any garden herbicides or insecticides? Are they safe if a dog is exposed to them? Can your dog create havoc with your barbecue? He'll want to investigate those scrumptious odours as soon as he smells them. If you're lucky enough to have a swimming pool, is it fenced off from access by your dog? When you take your dog outdoors, always visit his toilet area first (*see* p.316).

An outdoor adventure

Letting your dog out in the garden for the first time is an exciting moment for each of you. Before doing so, however, ensure that your garden is escape-proof and that no harm can come to your puppy or any other animals you may have.

DOGS ON HOLIDAY

While kennels and dog sitters are always available, it's great fun taking your buddy on dog-friendly holidays. However, take special precautions when travelling with your dog. Make sure his dog tag carries your mobile phone number, including the international dialling code if necessary. Include a local number when possible. Ensure you pack essential accessories and clothing, such as a life jacket (*below*). Check on risks where you're travelling; for example, there are poisonous snakes and scorpions in the American southwest, leishmaniasis in Mediterranean Europe, and tick-borne diseases throughout the world. Finally, check out physical risks, too, such as cliffs, strong local currents, or thorny, impenetrable undergrowth.

SAFETY IN PUBLIC PLACES

With puppies in particular, a wealth of experiences introduced early on is the ideal way to raise a well-socialized dog. Discuss with your vet the pros and cons of taking your dog to public areas before the age of 12 weeks – the age they are usually judged protected by vaccines from infectious diseases. Where I practice, the incidence of infectious diseases is now extremely low, and I tell my clients that the benefits of their dog walking on a lead along the streets and visiting public parks outweighs the minimal risk of coming in contact with canine infections.

Be sensible though: always keep your dog on his lead in circumstances where he could run away, such as an unfenced public park. And never leave your dog unattended outside a shop. Regrettably, young dogs are at risk of being stolen – sometimes, in my experience, for ransom.

Stay in control

By all means expose your dog to the great outdoors at an early age, but be sensible and keep him on a lead initially. A pup allowed to run free is a danger to itself and others.

TRAVELLING WITH YOU BY ROAD

My next door neighbour's new French Bulldog pup accompanies the family's children in the car when they are taken to school in the morning and is there waiting for them when the kids are picked up in the afternoon. She has done so since she arrived and thinks of the car as part of her home. However you plan to transport your dog, let her become accustomed to the car, the bus, even the basket on your bicycle, as soon as possible. By doing so you reduce the later risk of motion sickness or excitable behaviour when your dog travels.

Relaxed and ready to ride

For some dogs, car sickness is related to stress rather than the motion of the vehicle. Slowly acclimatize your dog to travelling by car by taking short journeys at first, always finishing with a positive experience, such as a long walk.

Grooming and bathing

Your dog's skin and coat need regular bathing and brushing, and occasional cutting or clipping. As well as making your dog feel clean and content, this kind of maintenance trains you to notice anything out of the ordinary that may indicate a medical problem.

GROOMING AND BRUSHING

When grooming and brushing your dog for the first time, keep sessions short and always reward him for his compliance. Most dogs look forward to grooming if it is carried out properly. Another bonus is that your actions – picking him up, holding him still, gently brushing him – help to reinforce your leadership role.

Use brushes and combs that are suitable for your dog's particular type of coat. A smooth coat like a Boxer's is the easiest to care for: use a rubber brush or a hound glove twice weekly, against the lie of the fur, to remove debris, dirt, and loose hair.

A short, thick coat like a Labrador Retriever's needs different tools. Use a slicker brush with the lie of the coat to clear tangles, then against the lie to

CLIPPING A DOG

Clipping and cutting is necessary in breeds with permanently growing hair such as poodles (*below*), but also in dense-coated breeds, such as schnauzers and spaniels, for warm-weather comfort. Unless you're a hairdresser, it's best to leave this form of grooming to the experts. However, you should occasionally trim your dog's coat yourself, to prevent tangles.

Shedding hair
All dog breeds shed, or moult, hair. Losing hair in this way is a natural process, occurring mainly in spring and autumn.

Different dogs, different brushes
Your dog's grooming kit should contain the right tools for the breed's coat type. A Boxer may only need a rubber brush, while other breeds will require a succession of brushes, from slickers to bristles and combs to finish off.

METAL COMB   BRISTLE BRUSH   SLICKER BRUSH   RUBBER BRUSH

remove loose hair. Use it twice weekly, followed by a bristle brush to remove any remaining dirt. Finish with a fine-toothed comb, concentrating on the neck and tail.

If the coat is slightly longer, like that of a Golden Retriever, it needs to be slicker- and bristle-brushed more frequently, preferably daily. The long hair around the feet, chest, and hind legs needs occasional trimming with scissors.

Some long-haired breeds, such as the Yorkshire Terrier, have no protective undercoat, and thin skin that is susceptible to laceration. This makes them sensitive to irritation from rough grooming. First, tease out tangles with a slicker brush, then use a bristle brush to position the hair. Follow by combing. Perform this routine daily.

WASH YOUR DOG REGULARLY

It's a myth that frequent shampooing dries out your dog's coat. Dog shampoos have come a long way; many are now made from natural ingredients, meaning they are kind to both skin and coat. In my experience, dogs are not washed enough. Washing your dog cleanses the hair and rids it of accumulated pollen and mould spores. It reduces the build-up of dead skin, making the coat less attractive to bacteria and parasites. Shampoos wash away accumulated sebaceous gland secretion, a common cause of "doggy odour". A washed dog smells better, looks more attractive, and has generally healthier skin than an unwashed one.

TYPES OF SHAMPOO

There is a wide range of shampoos specifically formulated for different coat textures and skin conditions. Your vet will be able to advise you about what type of shampoo is best for your dog's skin. Here are some of the shampoos available on the market:
■ Hypoallergenic – for dogs prone to itchy skin.
■ Antiseptic – kills surface skin bacteria.
■ Antibacterial – kills skin bacteria and prevents their multiplication.
■ Antiparasitic – prevents or kills skin parasites.
■ Humectant – adds shine to the coat.
■ Perfumed – to appeal to us, not dogs.

MATERIAL IN HAIR

All types of material can become stuck in a dog's coat – some too stubborn to disappear of their own accord. Hair is a magnet for chewing gum, burrs, tar, and paint, as well as for fleas and ticks. However, you should never use paint or tar remover to remove substances. For tar, paint, and chewing gum stuck in the coat, use scissors to cut out the substance and matted hair. Plant burrs are easiest to remove if you spray on a little cooking oil. Corn starch powder can help to untangle mats in your dog's coat, because it acts as a dry lubricant.

BATHING YOUR DOG

Dog hair is naturally self-cleaning – but not so self-cleaning that it only needs washing once or twice a year, as some people will tell you. Most dogs benefit from bathing about once a month; long-haired breeds may need more frequent attention, while smooth coats need less.

1 Brush your dog before bathing to remove tangles. Ensure there's a non-slip mat in the bath and that the hand-held shower is comfortably warm; run it first to get the right temperature. For general washing, use a "no-tears" baby shampoo.

2 Apply the shampoo all over the coat, then rinse very thoroughly, especially under each leg and the tail. Check that the coat is completely clean of any debris or dirt. If not, repeat the shampooing process before rinsing for a second time.

3 Have plenty of towels ready. Your dog will want to shake himself dry of all that water, and to make sure you get as wet as he is. For dogs with long or dense coats, a hair dryer can be effective for quicker drying, but use only a low temperature setting.

Routine body checks

Your dog depends upon you to carry out routine body checks for damage, disease, or infestation. Keep an eye on any changes in movement or behaviour. Contact your vet if your dog looks or acts any different from normal.

A DAILY ROUTINE

Virtually all of us touch or stroke our dogs every single day. We love it, and so do they. It's simple to turn this natural activity into a short and easy daily physical inspection. Start with the head and move down your dog's body. This is the simplest and most effective way to find potential problems when they are easiest to resolve.

BRIGHT EYES

Some breeds of dog, Yorkshire Terriers for example, develop sleep in their eyes overnight – small, hard crusts of dried tears that catch in the hair at the corners. Often it is easy to pick this off with your fingernails, but if it is firmly adhered, soften it with a cotton ball dipped in tepid saline solution or lukewarm water. If the eyes and skin around them do not look normal to you, consult your vet.

Eye inspection
Changes in a dog's eyes can signal more complex diseases elsewhere. Any conditions you can't treat yourself should be seen by a vet.

CLEAN EARS

Dogs with hair growing down their ear canals (breeds such as Poodles and many terriers) are prone to wax accumulation, leading to inflammation or infection. Lift each ear flap and check for unexpected odour, visible wax, or inflammation. Your vet will show you how to remove excess hair routinely from the ears. Sudden head shaking, especially when one ear is held slightly lower than the other, can mean a foreign object such as a grass seed caught in the ear canal.

HEALTHY TEETH AND GUMS

Lift your dog's upper lips each day and check that there is no unpleasant smell, and that the gums are a healthy pink colour. Dental plaque can build up surprisingly quickly – sometimes at only two years of age – especially in small breeds. Your vet can show you how to brush your dog's teeth effectively, using food treats to reward compliance.

NAIL CARE

Nails on medium- or larger-sized dogs usually wear down with exercise, but some small dogs, such as Chihuahuas,

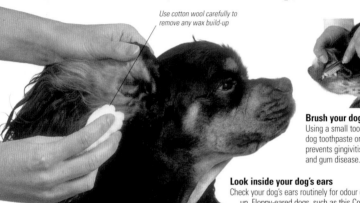

Use cotton wool carefully to remove any wax build-up

Brush your dog's teeth
Using a small toothbrush and dog toothpaste on your pooch prevents gingivitis, tenderness, and gum disease.

Look inside your dog's ears
Check your dog's ears routinely for odour or wax build-up. Floppy-eared dogs, such as this Cocker Spaniel, are more prone to ear problems because of the warm, damp climate in their ears.

Health check
Examine your dog's body, skin, and coat daily, feeling for any unusual lumps and watching for signs of pain.

need their nails trimmed routinely. Nails should never be brittle, but they soften when wet, so trim them after a bath. Cutting white nails is a simple process: cut in front of the visible pink "quick" in the heart of the nail. Cutting black nails is more problematic and needs special care because the quick, which is painful when cut, can't be seen.

FRESH SKIN AND COAT

Run your hands over your dog's whole body. There should be no lumps or bumps. Any resistance can be an indication of pain. The coat should smell and look fresh and clean. Any stickiness might indicate a site of skin infection or a penetrating injury. Frequently part the hair to examine the skin: it should look "quiet", without too much flaking dander visible.

CHECKING ANAL SACS

Here's the bit your dog won't appreciate. Accustom him to your checking his bum. It should be clean and odourless with no signs of swelling or inflammation. Dogs that drag their butts along the carpet or lick incessantly probably have blocked anal sacs, their scent-emitting marking glands. They normally empty naturally, but should be drained if they are full. (Full sacs feel like hard grapes.) Your vet can show you how to do so by gently squeezing both sides of your dog's anus.

DOG WITH BLOCKED ANAL SACS

EMPTYING ANAL SACS

Preventative medicine

It's a repetitive old mantra, but it's true: prevention is better than cure. It's easier and cheaper, too. There are simple, proven, and effective ways to protect your dog from infectious disease, parasites, unwanted pregnancies, and physical injuries.

PREVENTING INFECTIONS

Preventative vaccination is the single most important reason why dogs no longer die in massive numbers from infectious diseases such as distemper and parvovirus. Yet some dog owners are fearful of vaccinations, believing that inoculations are responsible for triggering other diseases. Any medical procedure has a possible risk associated with it, but the risk from effective and efficient vaccination, compared with the risk from the potentially lethal diseases dogs are vaccinated against, is minimal. Vaccination, or immunization, stimulates a natural and protective immune response against the agent in the vaccine. Vaccines contain killed or live but genetically modified pathogens. Some contain only parts

PREVENTING INJURIES

I've been in clinical practice long enough to see the life-sustaining value of simply walking a dog on a lead. Early in my career, when it was still common to let dogs wander off the lead, I treated at least two dogs each week for road traffic accident injuries. Today, these are thankfully rare. The best prevention of physical injuries to dogs is the use of a lead combined with basic obedience training.

of pathogens, the protein shells of viruses, for example. What your dog should be vaccinated against varies depending on where you live or where you visit. Vaccines against diseases such as rabies, distemper, hepatitis, and parvovirus give protection for at least three years, although some vets recommend annual booster shots. All puppies should start a course of "core" vaccinations against such diseases as soon as possible once they reach eight weeks of age.

Routine injections

As a responsible owner, you should inoculate your dog against infectious diseases. Discuss with your vet which vaccinations are appropriate for your dog's lifestyle and where you live, and how often booster shots should be given.

PREVENTING PARASITES

Internal parasites have evolved fascinating survival strategies, the most efficient of which is to become activated from a dormant state when a mother is pregnant and to pass to the pups in her first milk. That's why so many pups are born with worms, but these are easily and gently eliminated with the range of modern drugs that are available. The frequency of worming varies with where you live and the age and health of your dog. So too does the need for prevention of external parasites such as fleas and ticks. Fleas are one of the most common canine parasites, and besides causing itchiness can also spread roundworms if infected fleas are eaten. Ticks are particularly troublesome because they are capable

ADULT FLEA

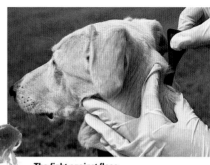

The fight against fleas
"Spot-on" treatments are a safe form of flea control. Applied directly to the skin, the treatment is quickly absorbed before it starts to kill the fleas.

of transmitting potentially lethal infections. In large parts of the world, mosquitoes transmit heartworms while sandflies transmit leishmaniasis. Using safe and effective oral or "spot-on" medications can prevent both internal and external parasitic diseases.

PREVENTING UNWANTED PUPPIES

Millions of dogs are killed each year because no one wants them. Preventing unwanted pups is our moral obligation, but neutering also brings wonderful fringe benefits in terms of increased life-span for females and reduced wanderlust for males. If you choose not to neuter your bitch, be vigilant when she is in season and keep her on a lead when outdoors to prevent unplanned matings.

PROBLEMS OF LIVING WITH DOGS

While rabies is the most dangerous disease dogs can transmit to us (see p.26), there are other less serious but nevertheless irritating drawbacks to owning a dog. Ringworm, a fungal infection, causes circular skin lesions in humans. If a dog eats raw, infected sheep offal, it can pass on hydatid disease to us via tapeworms. If swallowed by humans, the eggs of canine roundworms can cause blurred vision and trigger an allergic response in some children. Ticks can carry a range of bacteria, some of which can cause conditions like Lyme disease, resulting in enlarged lymph glands, joint inflammation, and pain.

ADMINISTERING TABLETS TO DOGS

The easiest way to give a pill is to hide it in a tasty treat: with any luck your dog will be none the wiser. Tasteless pills can be crushed and added to normal food. However, always check with your vet first; some pills are harmful if crushed or taken with food, and have to be given directly.

1 With the dog seated or restrained, use both hands to carefully prise open the jaws. Using the fingers of the lower hand, drop the tablet as far back into the mouth as it will go, past the "hump" of the tongue.

2 Hold the dog's mouth closed with one hand and tilt the head up slightly. Gently stroke or massage the throat to encourage the dog to swallow. Licking the lips shows that the tablet has been successfully swallowed.

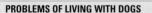

Allergies

Just as in children, allergies in dogs have increased enormously in the last few decades. So too have immune-mediated disorders, conditions in which a dog's immune system turns on a healthy part of the dog's body and damages or even destroys it.

THE SIGNS OF ALLERGY

Scarcely acknowledged before the 20th century, today we know that the body can experience an allergic response to almost anything, including foods, drugs, and chemicals. In the dog, two systems are primarily affected by allergy: the skin and the gastrointestinal system. The indicators of allergy are frequently mistaken for signs of other, often more common conditions. Itchy skin, and especially itchy ears, is commonly attributed to parasites, while food poisoning from scavenging is often erroneously thought to be the cause of either vomiting or diarrhoea.

WHAT DOGS ARE ALLERGIC TO

Most dog allergies are caused by allergens in the environment, with only 15 per cent caused primarily by food. The most common environmental causes are the house dust mite and, somewhat poetically, human dander. It is only since dogs were welcomed into our homes – and particularly into our bedrooms and beds – that they have experienced their greatest leap in the incidence of allergy!

Sleeping partners?

Letting your dog sleep with you on your bed may seem kind, but you are both at risk from allergens. Fleas and moulted hair may start you scratching, while your dog has to contend with dust mites and human dander.

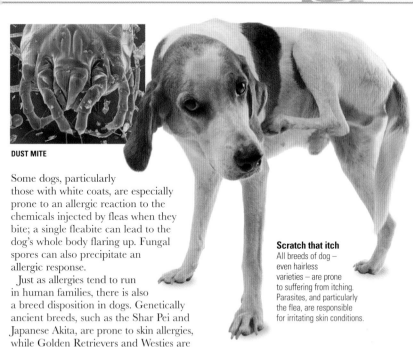

DUST MITE

Some dogs, particularly those with white coats, are especially prone to an allergic reaction to the chemicals injected by fleas when they bite; a single fleabite can lead to the dog's whole body flaring up. Fungal spores can also precipitate an allergic response.

Just as allergies tend to run in human families, there is also a breed disposition in dogs. Genetically ancient breeds, such as the Shar Pei and Japanese Akita, are prone to skin allergies, while Golden Retrievers and Westies are susceptible to gastrointestinal allergies.

Scratch that itch
All breeds of dog – even hairless varieties – are prone to suffering from itching. Parasites, and particularly the flea, are responsible for irritating skin conditions.

IMMUNE-MEDIATED DISEASE

At the same time that the incidence of allergy has increased (now affecting almost one in five dogs), numbers of immune-mediated disorders also appear to have risen. For example, Cocker Spaniels are particularly susceptible to hypothyroidism, where the immune system erroneously decides that the thyroid gland is "foreign" and destroys it, leading to medical and behavioural problems caused by low thyroid hormone levels. Reports of immune-mediated disease have increased dramatically over the last few years, but this could simply be down to better diagnoses.

REDUCING THE RISK OF ALLERGY

External parasite prevention, especially flea control, is high on the list of measures to reduce both the risk and the severity of allergic skin reactions. So too is routine shampooing. A terrier's rough coat, for example, is adept at capturing two causes of allergy, namely mould spores and pollens, but washing can remove them. The essential fatty acids found in fish oil or linseed oil added to the daily diet may also be beneficial in reducing the allergic response. And any dog that suffers from chronic allergy – skin or gastrointestinal – should be fed a unique, changed diet, such as fish and potato, for at least six weeks, to determine whether food is a complicating factor.

ALLERGIC TO YOUR DOG?

Contrary to popular belief, there are no dog breeds that pose a lower risk of allergy than others. All dogs carry the same protein (called Can F1) on flakes of their skin and in their saliva. This is what triggers the allergic response – runny eyes, sneezing, and even wheezing – in susceptible people. All breeds, including non-moulters such as poodles and hairless ones such as the Chinese Crested, produce Can F1. We are less likely to be allergic to dogs with clean skin and a regularly washed and clipped coat; these activities reduce levels of F1 production.

Symptoms of allergy
Streaming eyes and a runny nose can be prevented by keeping your dog clean and clipped.

The elderly dog

With age, a dog's body simply does not work as well as it once did. Many geriatric medical problems seem more frequent now because dogs are living longer than ever before. With good care and regular check-ups, however, many of them can be treated successfully.

AGEING AND THE SENSES

Dogs grow old gracefully, but their senses, it seems, can suddenly deteriorate. The lenses in the eyes go cloudy at around 10 years of age, a sign that the dog can no longer focus efficiently close up. He can see movement at a distance, but something lying in the grass in front of his nose is just a blur. His hearing may deteriorate quickly over a matter of months. Some owners feel that their dogs develop "selective hearing", but more often than not this is a genuine hearing loss, even a profound deafness. Many older dogs simply get confused, entering a room and then seemingly wondering why or how they have arrived there.

BODILY FUNCTIONS

With age, previously "clean" dogs can lose their toilet training. Sometimes there is a physical cause, such as sphincter muscle weakening that leads to urinary incontinence, but in other instances keeping the den clean ceases to be so important. A dog urinates or defecates in the home because it is no longer a priority to ask or wait to be let out.

SKIN AND COAT

Ageing causes the skin to lose its youthful elasticity, becoming thinner and more sensitive. Older dogs groom themselves

Signs of old age
Large breeds such as Golden Retrievers often suffer from hip dysplasia, a wearing down of the joint that leads to chronic pain. Older dogs of any breed are likely to suffer from deafness, poor vision, muscle shrinkage, and joint fluid drying up.

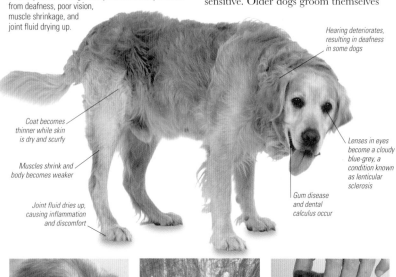

Hearing deteriorates, resulting in deafness in some dogs

Coat becomes thinner while skin is dry and scurfy

Muscles shrink and body becomes weaker

Joint fluid dries up, causing inflammation and discomfort

Lenses in eyes become a cloudy blue-grey, a condition known as lenticular sclerosis

Gum disease and dental calculus occur

LENTICULAR SCLEROSIS

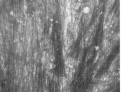

DRY, SCURFY SKIN

GUM DISEASE

His life in your hands
Disease control, good nutrition, and veterinary intervention mean dogs are living longer than ever before. However, yearly examinations are vital for older dogs.

less and resent our grooming them more. The skin also produces more secretions from the sebaceous glands, which can create either an oily or a dry, flaking condition. All this means that old dogs often become smellier than they were.

TEETH AND INTESTINES

"Dog breath" is so common in older dogs that it is often considered normal. Gum disease and dental calculus may be inevitable, but both are medical conditions requiring attention. Slowing down in older dogs is far too often attributed to ageing when, in fact, it is caused by chronic, treatable mouth infections. Dogs seemingly gain years in strength and vigour after these infections are tended to. Similarly, constipation and flatulence, other age-related problems, are often easily corrected by making changes to your dog's diet.

HEART AND LUNGS

There are some breeds of dog, Boxers and Labradors are often great examples, which never grow up. Whatever their age, they want to play games for ever and ever. Watch your dog's breathing. Does he tire more readily than he used to? Does he cough? Exercise tolerance naturally drops with age,

but cardiovascular diseases, which are treatable conditions, are as common in older dogs as they are in humans.

MUSCLES AND JOINTS

Don't delude yourself when you see an old dog getting up gingerly, walking slowly, or limping. He may not complain, but he's certainly in pain. Osteoarthritis is virtually inevitable if a dog lives long enough. Weight and pain control are at the core of improving his quality of life.

CANCER IN DOGS

Life-threatening cancers occur more frequently in some breeds than in others. Breeds most at risk include:

- Irish Wolfhound
- Staffordshire Bull Terrier
- Rottweiler
- Boxer

Breeds with the least risk of fatal cancers include:

- Border Collie
- Yorkshire Terrier
- Cocker Spaniel
- Mutts
- West Highland White Terrier

ROTTWEILER

AGEING AND YOU

While ageing is inevitable, there is ample evidence that with modifications to the diet, weight management, changes in exercise routines, maintenance of good health, and routine mental stimulation, the active years of an ageing dog can be dramatically prolonged.

A MANAGED DIET

As the years advance, what a dog eats becomes ever more important. Cell damage increases, which means an increase in free-radical scavengers becomes vital (*see* p.281). The ability of the intestines to digest food diminishes, so feeding higher-quality, more digestible protein is a simple way to guarantee continuing optimum nourishment.

A WEIGHTY ISSUE

Weight must be carefully managed; controlling a dog's calorie intake can make the difference between living a life of vitality and struggling with obesity. Some older dogs gain weight simply because they continue to consume the level of calories they've always done, but don't exercise enough to expend this energy. Other older dogs gain weight because of medical conditions, such as underactive thyroid glands.

The health risks of obesity
Obesity in dogs is a serious medical problem. Fat dogs are more prone to injury, and have more stress placed on their heart, lungs, liver, kidneys, and joints. They also run a very high risk of tearing the cruciate ligaments in the knees.

Once medical causes have been controlled or eliminated, alter your dog's calorie intake so that it is in line with his daily energy requirements (*see* p.279). This will help reduce strain on old joints, the most common site of age-related pain. If your ageing dog has become picky with his food, there's a medical problem. It may be as simple as gum disease, tooth pain, or diminished taste or smell, but it is just as likely to be caused by even more serious medical conditions. Your dog should be seen by your vet. In the meantime, warming food to body temperature releases aromas, improves flavour, and makes it more palatable.

CONTROLLED EXERCISE

Exercise is as beneficial to your older dog as it is for you, but it should be constant and routine. Avoid sudden increased activity. If your dog walks for half an hour a day and you plan to go for a four-hour hike at the weekend, then leave your golden oldie at home. Walking and occasional trotting is best. Avoid vigorous exercise. Leave ball catching to youthful canines, unless it's a simple toss straight to the mouth. Contrary to what you might read, walking up stairs is very good exercise and is safe for all but overweight dogs, who are prone to tearing knee ligaments.

ROUTINE GROOMING

While some older dogs groom less because they're either too fat to do so or have mouth pain caused by gum and tooth disease, others groom less just because they forget. Your intervening and grooming your dog not only keeps the skin and coat in fine condition, it also enhances skin circulation and massages the muscles. If you don't need to groom daily, give your dog a gentle all-over massage. Improved circulation keeps muscles in their best condition.

MENTAL STIMULATION

Yes, let sleeping dogs lie. Don't pester Old Faithful, but when he's awake and alert offer him mental stimulation: a food treat he has to get out of a hollow bone, a moving target he has to get his paw on to maintain physical dexterity. The longer he uses it the longer it will take for him to lose it.

THE REASONS WHY DOGS DIE

A recent pet insurance survey revealed illness – and not old age – as the primary cause of death in dogs. The full list of causes of death was as follows:

■ Natural causes	8%
■ Accidents	5%
■ Illness	35%
■ Euthanasia due to illness	29%
■ Euthanasia due to behaviour problems	2%
■ Euthanasia due to old age	21%

A QUESTION OF ETHICS

More than one-third of all dogs in the US, Canada, the UK, and Germany are over 10 years old. They're chronological geriatrics. In Sweden, however, where veterinary care and compassion for pets is equal to that of those aforementioned countries, only 17 per cent of dogs are over ten years old. In some countries there is an ethical debate on how far we should go to extend an older dog's life. Amputations, radiation therapy, and chemotherapy for cancers are common treatments in many countries, but in Sweden they are rare events. There is no universal interpretation of the words "quality of life". Decision-making is influenced by the culture you live in as well as your own principles.

EUTHANASIA

In Judaeo–Christian culture, the decision to euthanize an elderly dog for humane reasons is fraught with emotion, but is still a morally simple choice. In other cultures, where the value of a dog's "soul" is equal to that of a human's, for example in Hindu, Buddhist, and Buddhist–Shintoist cultures, euthanasia creates an intense moral dilemma. When a decision is made to euthanize, it is inevitably an easier process for the dog than for those attending to him. In most cases, an excess of barbiturate is given. The dog simply falls asleep and, while asleep, his heart stops.

A joint enterprise
Daily gentle exercise and an all-over massage can dramatically improve the quality of life of an old dog. Massage reduces pain by stimulating or relaxing the muscles and improving circulation.

Assessing injuries

Chances are, you'll never need to use life-saving first aid skills on your dog, but when emergencies do occur your dog depends on you to remain calm and to assess the priorities. Is he breathing? Is he in shock? Do you need to administer first aid for cuts or broken bones?

WHAT TO DO FIRST

Initially, you need to consider if your dog is in continuing or immediate danger. Are you in the same danger, or at risk from being bitten because of what has happened? Your first objectives are to:
- Save your dog's life.
- Prevent any further injuries occurring.
- Reduce pain and stress.
- Get your dog quickly and safely to a vet.

Lifting an injured dog
Grasp your dog gently under the neck and rump. Lift with a straight back, and bring your arms together to support the dog's weight.

AN EMERGENCY MUZZLE

Muzzle an injured dog if it looks frightened or has obvious painful injuries. A gauze bandage, a tie, or a pair of tights makes an efficient emergency muzzle. This should be 50–75cm (20–30in) long. Make a loop and slip it over the dog's nose. Gently tighten, draw the ends under the chin, cross them under the jaw, and tie in a secure bow behind the neck.

RESTRAINING YOUR DOG

After determining that you are not in danger, approach an injured dog with care, always speaking quietly and reassuringly. Reduce his fear by avoiding direct eye contact. Even the gentlest dog may bite because of fear or pain. If you can, loop a lead around his neck. A belt, tie, scarf, or any other available item can be used as an emergency collar and lead.

HOLDING YOUR DOG

Your dog should be held safely and reassuringly while you do an emergency examination. If your dog is large, wrap one arm around his neck and support him against your body. It may need two of you to hold and examine him. Hold smaller dogs gently but firmly by the muzzle, using the elbow of your free arm to press the dog's body against yours.

MONITOR YOUR DOG'S BREATHING

Large dogs normally breathe in and out around 10 times a minute, while the smallest dogs may breathe 30 times a minute. Pain, fever, heart conditions, and being in the early stages of shock all increase a dog's breathing rate. Note that breathing and panting are different. Panting increases with exercise, anxiety, and pain. Calculate breathing, not panting, by timing chest movements for 15 seconds and multiplying by four.

A large dog has a normal heart rate as low as 50 beats per minute; a small dog's heart beats up to 160 times per minute. An irregular heartbeat can indicate life-threatening advanced shock. To monitor the heart, press your fingers to the left side of the chest, just behind the elbow. On small dogs, grasp the chest on both sides and squeeze gently to find a pulse.

A precautionary measure
An injured dog may be very frightened or in severe pain, and its behaviour unpredictable as a consequence. You will need to muzzle it to avoid the risk of being bitten.

Hidden signs of shock
Shock is a hidden danger in all injuries and can be an unsuspecting killer. Signs of lethargy and weakness in your dog following an injury should be reported to your vet.

LOOK FOR SIGNS OF SHOCK

Shock occurs when blood fails to get transported throughout the body. Treating advanced shock is your top priority.

SIGNS OF EARLY SHOCK ARE:

- Faster than normal breathing and heart rate.
- Colour returns slowly to the gums after finger pressure applied and released.
- Persistently pale gums.
- Anxiety or restlessness.
- Lethargy and weakness.
- Subnormal body temperature

SIGNS OF ADVANCED SHOCK ARE:

- Shallow breathing and an irregular heart rate.
- Blue gums.

- Extreme weakness or unconsciousness.
- Very cool body temperature – less than 36.7°C (98°F).

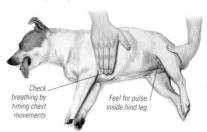

Check breathing by timing chest movements

Feel for pulse inside hind leg

Checking breathing
With an unconscious dog, your priority is to find a pulse and check the dog's breathing rate. Place your fingers either behind the left elbow or inside the hind leg.

TREATING SHOCK

If your dog shows any signs of shock, do not give him anything to eat or drink, or allow him to wander around. Keep him calm and do the following:

- Stop any bleeding and give heart massage and artificial respiration as necessary (*see* pp.306–307).
- Wrap him in a blanket to prevent further heat loss.
- Elevate his hindquarters to enable more blood to flow to the brain.
- Keep his neck extended (to help blood flow to the brain) and immediately transport him to the nearest vet.

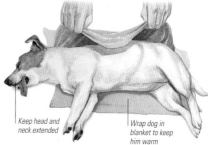

Keep head and neck extended

Wrap dog in blanket to keep him warm

Caring for a dog in shock
Shock reduces the blood flow around the body, and can dangerously lower body temperature, leading to failure of vital organs. Use coverings to keep a dog in shock warm.

Emergency treatment

In emergencies, heart massage can restart a stopped heart while artificial respiration puts oxygen into your dog's lungs, to be carried to his brain until he starts breathing again on his own. This combination is called cardiopulmonary resuscitation, or CPR.

MORE ABOUT CPR

Every living cell in your dog's body needs oxygen to survive. Oxygen is breathed into the lungs, picked up by red blood cells, and pumped by the heart around the body. Brain cells have a huge need for it – they use 20 per cent of the body's supply. If brain cells are deprived of oxygen, even for a few minutes, they are damaged or die. CPR saves lives by restoring and maintaining breathing and circulation, providing blood and oxygen to the heart, brain, and other vital organs.

GIVING ARTIFICIAL RESPIRATION

Only give artificial respiration if your dog has stopped breathing. Check the gums. If they are pink, the blood is still carrying oxygen around the body. If they are blue or white, artificial respiration may be necessary. If in doubt whether or not a small dog is breathing, place a small piece of tissue in front of a nostril and see if it moves. If breathing has stopped, give artificial respiration (*see opposite*). Give breaths every five or six seconds and check the pulse after every three breaths (*see* pp.304–305).

GIVING HEART MASSAGE

Give heart massage only if the heart has stopped beating. Check your dog's eyes – pupils dilate when the heart stops. Feel for a heartbeat or pulse. Check the gums.

LIFTING A CRITICALLY INJURED DOG

Take care when lifting or moving a critically injured dog. Always use a muzzle unless a dog is vomiting, convulsing, has obvious mouth or jaw injuries, or is unconscious. Improvise a stretcher using any flat item, such as an ironing board or removable shelf. If there is no one to help during transport, lightly tie his body, but not his neck, to the board. Alternatively, use a strong blanket to carry the dog. With his back towards you, gently pull him by his chest and rump onto the blanket. Cover him in the blanket to keep him warm and reduce the risk of shock. In cold weather, ensure you turn on the car heater.

If the gums are pink, exert pressure on them with a finger. If they turn white and immediately return to pink when you release finger pressure, the heart is still beating. If there is no pulse and the gums do not refill with blood, the heart has stopped beating. Start heart massage immediately (*see opposite*). After giving 15 seconds of heart massage, give artificial respiration for 10 seconds.

GAGGING AND CHOKING

If your dog has something stuck in its mouth and is gagging, restrain it without using a muzzle. Then open the mouth, with one hand grasping the upper jaw and pressing the upper lips over the teeth and the other hand holding open the lower jaw. Look at the roof of the mouth, the back of the throat, and around the teeth to locate the object. Use tweezers or a spoon handle to gently remove the obstruction as quickly as possible.

If your dog is choking and conscious, put your arms around its belly, make a fist, and squeeze firmly upwards and forwards just behind the ribcage. For a small dog, place your hands either side of its belly and squeeze in the same way. If the dog is unconscious, place it on its side. Press sharply with the heels of your hands just behind the back ribs to expel the blockage.

REMOVING AN OBSTRUCTION

If performing CPR on your own, continue alternating the two until the heartbeat returns, then give artificial respiration alone. Then seek emergency veterinary attention. If two people are present, one gives heart massage for five seconds, then the other gives a breath of artificial respiration. Continue this alternating procedure until the heart resumes beating and it is safe for one person to leave to arrange transport to the veterinary clinic.

EMERGENCY TRANSPORT

It is almost always better for you to get to the vet than for the vet to come to you. If your dog can walk to the car let him do so, otherwise carry him. If his chest is injured, lay him injured side down; gravity keeps blood in the damaged lung. Elevate an injured leg so weight is born on healthy limbs. Keep an injured head higher than the heart to reduce pressure in the skull. Ensure he is restrained and supported.

RESUSCITATION PROCEDURES

Performed promptly and properly, CPR saves lives. Would you be prepared to correctly administer CPR on your dog if you were faced with an emergency? Learn and remember the following steps. They should only be carried out if your dog has stopped breathing.

1 Place your dog on its right-hand side, if possible with its head lower than the rest of the body. Clear any debris from the nose and mouth, and pull the tongue forwards to clear the airway. Close the dog's mouth and ensure that the neck is aligned with the body.

2 Place your mouth over the dog's nose and blow in until its chest rises. If you prefer not to do this, seal your hand around the nose and give breaths through your hand. Lift your mouth away. The lungs will deflate. Repeat 10–20 times until the dog breathes on its own.

3 Check the pulse every 15 seconds to make sure the heart is still beating. If it stops, perform heart massage by compressing the chest with the palm of your hand around 100 times a minute (in large dogs), or by squeezing the fingers and thumb on both sides around 120 times a minute (in small dogs), pushing blood up towards the brain.

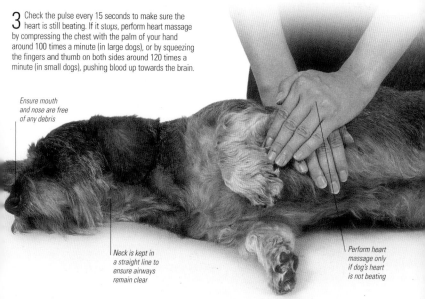

Ensure mouth and nose are free of any debris

Neck is kept in a straight line to ensure airways remain clear

Perform heart massage only if dog's heart is not beating

Wounds and bleeding

As a dog owner, be prepared to deal with the odd graze or wound to your pet. A wound is a break in the skin or internal tissues, and there is usually bleeding from damaged blood vessels. A wounded dog requires medical attention in case of excessive bleeding or the risk of infection.

ASSESSING THE WOUND

The skin may be broken, producing an open, bleeding wound, or it may be closed, producing only visible dis-colouration and swelling. Open wounds look worse, but closed wounds can hide deeper, more dangerous injuries, which should be dealt with by your vet.

Heavy bleeding or slow, continuous, lighter bleeding can lead to dangerous clinical shock (*see* p.305). While internal bleeding is difficult to control, external bleeding can often be controlled by applying pressure. Spurting blood, or arterial bleeding, means that an artery has been damaged. This is more difficult to stop because the blood pressure is higher in arteries than in veins. A wound may not produce much blood at all, but it can still be life-threatening to your dog. Don't waste time treating more minor problems. A dog requires immediate emergency veterinary attention in any of the following circumstances:

■ A penetrating wound to the chest or abdomen, with or without bleeding.
■ Blood spurting from an open wound.
■ Any bleeding that does not stop after five minutes of applied pressure.
■ Bright red blood in vomit or diarrhoea.
■ Profuse bleeding from any body opening.
■ Signs of clinical shock (*see* p.305).

CONTROLLING BLEEDING

Apply pressure at the site of bleeding, preferably using absorbent material, such as medical gauze. If no first-aid material is available, use anything at hand, such as kitchen towels and facial or toilet tissue. When the bleeding stops, don't remove the blood-soaked pad; the clot is controlling the bleeding. Wrap it in place and keep

Rest and recuperation
An injured dog needs care after his wounds have been dressed. He may be in pain, so speak reassuringly and watch for any signs of biting. The tightness of bandages should be checked frequently as wounds can swell.

BE PREPARED

It is impossible to prevent all accidents, but you can reduce risks and be prepared for emergencies.

■ Train your dog in obedience and always keep him under your control.

■ Keep a first aid kit close to hand containing basic wound dressings (non-stick sterile pads and dressings, cotton wool, stretchy roll bandage), scissors, tweezers, washing soda crystals for inducing vomiting, activated charcoal powder for use if your dog is poisoned, and a bottle of clean water for cleansing wounds.

■ Keep both your vet's telephone number and a back-up vet's number in a convenient place.

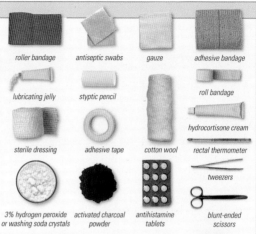

roller bandage *antiseptic swabs* *gauze* *adhesive bandage*

lubricating jelly *styptic pencil* *roll bandage*

sterile dressing *adhesive tape* *cotton wool* *hydrocortisone cream*

rectal thermometer

tweezers

3% hydrogen peroxide or washing soda crystals *activated charcoal powder* *antihistamine tablets* *blunt-ended scissors*

it there until the wound is seen by your vet, at the latest on the same day. If possible, keep the bleeding area higher than the heart, but don't elevate a bleeding limb if there is a possibility of a fracture.

TAKE CARE USING TOURNIQUETS

A tourniquet is a tight band that is applied to a limb to stop life-threatening bleeding. If applied wrongly, it cuts off the blood supply and can lead to the loss of the limb; it should only be used for severe and profuse bleeding. Wrap a tie or similar strip above the bleeding wound and tie with a releasable knot. Slip a stick or pen into the knot and twist until bleeding stops. Release after less than 10 minutes and reapply intermittently if needed.

Use a section cut from a pair of tights to secure ear in position

Keep bandage applied to wound

Dressing a bleeding ear
Immobilizing the ear prevents blood loss when the dog shakes his head. Apply absorbent pads to each side of the ear and secure them in place with a stretchy bandage or a section of tights, taking care not to restrict the breathing.

ATTENDING TO LIGHT WOUNDS

Use tweezers or clean fingers to remove loose dirt or other material from the wound. Flush the wound with 3% hydrogen peroxide, antiseptic fluid, or clean water. Pour the fluid over the wound, or use a clean hand-held plant spray with the nozzle turned to "jet". If the hair is getting into the wound, rub a little water-soluble jelly onto a pair of scissors and cut the hair away; the hair will stick to the scissors. Avoid using oil-based ointments, because these substances are particularly difficult for your vet to cleanse from around open wounds. Always see your vet as soon as possible after administering this kind of first aid – your dog is at risk from infection and may require stitches.

TRAINING A DOG

Training your dog is vital if you are to forge a pleasurable relationship, as an untrained individual will be a constant source of concern. Dogs share a range of needs, feelings, and emotions with us, but they're not people in disguise. To your dog, you and your family are the pack leaders. It's up to you to teach your dog compliance.

THE IMPORTANCE OF TRAINING

I've been in veterinary practice for over 35 years, but it took only the first few months of meeting dogs and their owners for me to realize that answering questions about training is as vital a role for vets as preventing or treating illness and disease. Dogs' behaviour makes or breaks the bond between them and us. I see relationships that are fraught, fraying, or broken, not because the dog is doing anything other than behaving like a dog, but because its owner can't comprehend that problems have arisen because they haven't trained their dogs properly.

The word "training" can sound a little dull, but when you're talking about dog training, nothing could be further from the truth. For a dog, playing is training. When you throw a ball or a stick for Rover, he is unwittingly (or, in some cases, instinctively) learning to retrieve. And those who've mopped up after their puppy for the umpteenth time following another mess in the house won't argue that training is just another chore – housetraining is essential.

Basic obedience is the very least one can expect of a dog owner to instil in their pet. A dog that has never been taught the "Stay" command,

for example, is in very real danger from everyday situations, such as passing traffic or other dogs. Even walking on a lead – something every dog is expected to do – is a skill that canines have to learn, so that they don't surge forwards or jump up or climb and chew the lead.

For the truly gifted pooch, or likewise for the most recalcitrant mutt, advanced training offers something a little extra. Those dogs who have excelled at basic training may benefit from a step-up in learning – beauty contests and agility training, for example. At the other end of the scale, dogs who refuse to act upon your teachings, or those with difficulties in learning, can always be recommended to an animal behaviourist, a personal trainer, or even veterinary help to aid them in progressing.

Good habits to get into
You need to toilet-train your pup from an early age if the two of you are to share a happy relationship.

A little give-and-take
You command and your dog obeys – that's the theory. If it is to work, training demands patience and enthusiasm.

Think dog thoughts

Dogs think in the present. When training your dog, timing is vital. Use both rewards and discipline instantaneously, within seconds, either to reward achievement or to correct bad behaviour. Mistakes should be disregarded, not punished.

UNDERSTAND YOUR DOG'S POTENTIAL

Each dog has its own personality and this affects its ability or, in some instances, its willingness, to be trained. Dominant and confident dogs may disregard or even challenge your commands. At the other end of the personality spectrum, overtly submissive dogs may be so insecure that at the mere hint of a command the dog simply rolls over in trepidation.

Fortunately, the vast majority of dogs are content to compromise. Their natural curiosity, combined with their affinity for people, makes them easy to train. Remember, most dogs have mixed personalities. Some want to please and at the same time can be easily distracted. Others may seem intensely submissive, but in fact control your behaviour by acting in a helpless way. Each dog has greater potential in some areas and lesser potential in others.

He looks up to you
Your dog isn't just asking for a tickle when he rolls over; he is also telling you, through this classic submissive action, that he sees you as a natural leader.

Set sensible goals
Dog training takes patience on your part. Training two dogs at the same time is extremely difficult and is best left to professional dog trainers only.

UNDERSTAND YOUR OWN LIMITATIONS

If you don't have much patience, another member of your family should be primarily responsible for training your dog. Dog training can be frustrating and it is easy to make two common mistakes. The easiest trap to fall into is to treat your dog like a person. All that Sparky hears when you say, "If you do that once more Sparky, I'll get really, really angry" is "Sparky". You're wasting your breath issuing warnings, as dogs don't understand conditional threats. They understand cause and effect. The other mistake to avoid is the misuse of discipline. Discipline should only be theatrical. It's pointless to take out your own frustrations by inflicting pain or retribution on your pet. All you will do is make your dog fear you.

PUTTING IT ALL TOGETHER

Dogs respond best to training through rewards and, to most dogs, the most powerful reward is tasty food. Train your dog before meals when he is hungry using food treats to reward compliance. Chew toys can be equally potent rewards. Touch is also welcome; a stroke to the neck or body is immensely rewarding for tactile dogs, but avoid a pat on the head for submissive individuals. Always give verbal praise with any more potent reward. Eventually your words alone will be sufficient to satisfy your dog.

Only give commands during training if you know you can enforce them. For example, when training your dog to "Come", have your dog on a long line. If he is distracted, you can use the line, not to reel him in, but to regain his attention as you attract him with a food lure and the potential reward of your praising him and stroking him.

Set achievable targets for your dog. For example, don't expect him to bark at "baddies" when they approach your front door, but not bark at other people. Don't expect him to stay off furniture when you visit friends if you allow him on furniture at home. Don't expect him not to beg at the table if you occasionally give him something from your plate. Don't expect more from your dog than you would from a 3-year-old child.

A few well-chosen words
Dogs have a great capacity to understand both words and your tone of voice. Associate words of praise with other potent rewards, such as food or touch.

TRAINING GUIDELINES

In all aspects of your relationship with your dog, including active training and relaxed play, follow these guidelines and you'll have a well-mannered companion.
- Be consistent.
- Give clear, concise commands.
- Give one command at a time and be sure to always reward compliance.
- Use your dog's name when giving a command.
- Always initiate activity. You're the leader.
- Finish any training activity with a spot of fun to leave your dog wanting more.

Train with certainty
This dog is being told to "Come", with the certainty that if she does not respond she can be induced to do so through the training line attached to her collar.

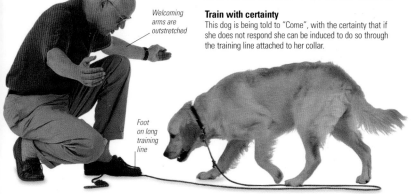

Welcoming arms are outstretched

Foot on long training line

The importance of play

Dogs are honorary members of our families, and playing with them and having fun with them is at the heart of this satisfying relationship. We need to remember, however, that we have our own rules of play, which are different from theirs. Train your dog to play by *your* rules.

PLAY HAS A PURPOSE

By playing together as pups, dogs learn social and hunting skills. They become physically dextrous, adroit at ambush, chase, and tackle. As with humans, a pup's desire to play is perpetuated into adulthood. Both humans and dogs are naturally "neotenized" species: we carry into adulthood a range of juvenile characteristics. Adult dogs continue their playful activity to preserve social relationships and simply to have fun.

Visit your local park and it's easy to see that fetch games are one of the most rewarding activities for dog and owner. Even non-retrieving breeds of dog have a yearning to chase and return objects to their owner. However, make sure you call it quits long before your obsessive friend collapses from over-exertion.

Play is a fine way to train your dog to accept commands from children, asserting their higher ranking in the pack hierarchy, but restrict this solely to fetch games. Avoid tug-of-war games; ensure that your dog doesn't unwittingly feel it owns some of your children's toys; and watch out for inadvertent teasing, especially with food.

Mutual fun
Playful behaviour is a lifelong activity. Playing with your dog is rewarding on so many levels, providing you both with mental and physical stimulation, while at the same time teaching your dog that he plays by your rules.

PLAYING WITH OTHER DOGS

Some male dogs are only interested in play as a prelude to mating, and some insecure dogs are so frightened of canine social activity that they will bite out of fear. The majority of dogs, however, enjoy playing with each other, even on first encounters, especially if they are still relatively young. Play among friends usually involves chasing, shadow boxing, and neck chewing. Just be careful that a tug-of-war over sticks or toys doesn't escalate into possessive aggression.

TYPES OF TOYS

Choose toys that are both appropriate for different types of play and provide a variety of differing rewards.

All dogs, not just puppies, need to chew, and in the absence of prey to gnaw on, they need chew toys. Rawhide is excellent, as are dried pig's ears and sterilized bones, though be alert to the possible danger of fractured teeth. Hard rubber chew toys with hollow insides are also available. They serve two purposes: they are chewable and they can be filled with food rewards, such as spreadable cheese or peanut butter, to make them even more stimulating for your dog.

Squeak toys belong to you, not your dog, and are best played with for only a short time. Soft sheepskin-like material surrounding a squeaker makes an ideal toy. So do very thin-skinned rubber balls with squeakers inside; dogs are less inclined to chew on squeak toys that collapse under the slightest pressure. Give this toy to your dog as a treat.

Canine play
These dogs are innocently playing a favourite game, tug-of-war, but through this activity they learn which is the naturally more dominant individual.

A hard rubber ball on a rope, a Frisbee, a rubber ring, or an erratically bouncing Kong all make suitable fetch toys, and there is a vast selection of purpose-made tug-of-war toys for dogs. Make sure the toy suits the dog: avoid strenuous fetch games for dogs with potential joint problems, and forget about tug-of-war with dogs with dominant personalities – your position as pack leader will be jeopardized if you let them win.

A small, empty plastic water bottle is a great homemade toy. A slight nudge with the nose gets it rolling. Add a little water, and it is more exciting. Don't allow your pup to chew through the plastic though.

Squeak and carry toys
It's probably best not to think too much about why dogs like playing with squeak (or kill) toys! Your dog should learn that these belong to you and are given only as a reward.

SPOILT FOR CHOICE

Don't overwhelm your dog with toys. Initially provide a maximum of three, each with a unique "feel" in the mouth when he chews them. If you give him too great a variety of textures and "feels" he will think he is allowed to chew anything, including your carpets, furniture, and walls.

Housetraining

Housetraining can make or break your relationship with your dog.
Never punish when your dog messes inside. That only leads to skilful
avoidance of you. Housetraining is simple if you are sensible,
conscientious, alert, and – most importantly – consistent.

GETTING DOWN TO BUSINESS

If your dog experiences any difficulties
learning housetraining be aware that it
is almost certainly not your dog's fault.
Dogs are instinctively clean animals,
so soiling their nest is the last thing they
would want to do. Perhaps one of the
first lessons a puppy learns, after his
mother consumes all the waste her
pup leaves in the nest, is the need to
be houseproud. As the new pack leader,
it is your responsibility to teach your
dog that your entire home is "the nest".

WORK WITH YOUR DOG

It is easiest to housetrain your dog
if you have immediate access to the
outdoors. Before a dog even arrives
in your home, choose a toilet area,
preferably a hard surface rather than
grass, away from any activities and
distractions. Have poop scoops available
to clean up immediately after your dog

Ready to go
A dog that puts its nose
down and sniffs intently
is usually signalling that
it is about to eliminate,
so always be alert to
this kind of behaviour.

eliminates. As
a general rule, a
3-month-old puppy needs
to eliminate every three
hours. Plan a house-training
programme, then you'll know that
your dog may want to relieve himself:
- After eating (sometimes within a
minute of walking away from his bowl).
- After waking up.
- After play or exercise.
- Following a bout of excitement, such
as meeting new faces.
Take him to his designated toilet area
frequently and certainly after under-
taking any of the above activities.

Choose the site
This pup has found a place it is happy
to urinate in. Dogs prefer to pee on grass, but
their acid urine often kills it. You may prefer
to train your dog to eliminate on hard surfaces.

URGENT SIGNALS

Your dog will give clues that he has to relieve himself. These include:

- Sniffing the floor.
- Circling.
- Running with his nose to the floor.
- Getting ready to squat.
- Moving in the direction of the door to his toilet area.

If you see him start any of these activities, get his attention and immediately take him outside. Where possible, don't pick your dog up, but let him walk to the door.

Choose a phrase you're happy to say in public and use this every time your dog eliminates. "Do it" is a short, sharp word cue. Your dog will quickly associate these words with his toilet, and this phrase alone will soon induce him to "do it".

PUNISHMENT IS POINTLESS

Accidents will happen. When you see your dog about to squat in the house, get his attention by any means that he finds interesting but not threatening. Pushing his nose in his mess is utterly pointless. It only teaches him to be frightened of you when he messes. Instead, once you have his attention, quickly lead him outdoors to his toilet area and let him finish off his business. If he has already messed in the house, keep him in another room while you clean up after him. Your dog is less likely to mess indoors again if you "neutralize" the affected area with a commercial odour eliminator.

> ### THE IMPORTANCE OF HOUSETRAINING
>
> Lack of housetraining can lead to:
> - Never being fully housetrained.
> - Sex-related urine marking, or lack of sexual maturity.
> - Submissive urinating.
> - Fear, stress, anxiety, or emotional conflict.
> - High excitement.
> - Changes in who is top dog in a multi-dog home.
> - Medical problems.
>
> If your previously reliable dog suddenly starts soiling the house, always contact your vet for advice.

Indoor training
This pup is taken to paper as soon as it awakes or immediately after eating. Paper training is a useful alternative if it is difficult to get outdoors quickly.

CRATE TRAINING

Introduced early in life, a crate is a dog's personal den. A dog instinctively feels comfortable in a crate and is unlikely to mess in it. It is worth training a puppy to eat, play, and sleep in a crate, because it will come to enjoy the reassurance of this container when it is home alone, or when travelling in a car. What's more, crate training speeds up housetraining because your dog is either in his crate, taken out of the crate and eliminating where you want, or safely wandering around your home for a while because both tanks have just been emptied. Using a crate also frees you up to spend time on things other than 24-hour puppy watch. In short, crate training provides the solution to a variety of behaviour problems before they happen.

Ensure the crate is large enough to contain your dog safely

Line the crate with newspaper to soak up any mess

Provide fresh water every meal time

Provide a soft, comfortable bed to sleep on

A toy will keep your dog occupied as it settles in

Basic obedience

All dogs can learn basic obedience, but to teach your dog requires great patience from you. Use consistent hand and word signals, keep the training sessions short, and maintain an upright posture and strong eye contact.

COMING TO YOU

This is the easiest command for a dog to learn. To start with, divide his meals into ten equal portions, and throughout the day entice him to his food bowl using his name and the command "Come". Once he responds reliably, move on to the steps shown below. Never call your dog to you to discipline him: always go to him.

Food treat held up to entice dog

Dog makes eye contact with owner

1 In a quiet area, attach a houseline to your dog's collar. Step back, and with a food treat visible in your hand, speak your dog's name to attract his attention. As he begins to approach, command "Come".

DOG CLASSES

Dog training books, videos, and CDs are fine, but there's nothing better than teaching your dog in the presence of an efficient dog trainer. Dog classes are like pre-school for kids, but not quite as unruly! The pups thrive on the social activity and, at the same time, the owners receive an excellent refresher course in all aspects of dog training.

2 As your dog moves towards you, bend down and hold the food treat out to him. Encourage him with the positive words "Come. Good dog".

Food treat held close to dog's eye-level

Dog shows interest in food treat

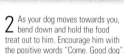

3 As he reaches you, kneel down to get closer to his level. Praise him with words and a gentle stroke, and give him the food reward. To maintain his interest, vary the locations in which the training takes place.

MAINTAIN AN OPEN POSTURE

SITTING ON COMMAND

With your dog trained to come to you on command, proceed to training him to "Sit". It takes only a few days at most for virtually any dog to learn successfully to follow this sequence of commands. To ensure that you are always in control, attach a lead to your dog's collar.

1 Facing your dog, move away with the lead in your left hand and a food treat in your right. As you command him to come to you, show him the food. Stay calm, and do not excite your dog during this exercise.

Owner holds food treat in front of body

2 As he reaches you, begin to slowly move the food treat above his head. The dog will naturally want to sit in order to keep his eyes on the treat. As he begins to bend his hind legs, give the command "Sit".

Dog sits as he watches treat

3 Reinforce the "Sit" command from the front and then to the side of the dog. At first, reward each response with verbal praise and food treats. Gradually reduce the food treats until words alone are sufficient.

REFUSING TO SIT

If your dog does not sit for a food treat, hold his collar with one hand and, while giving the command "Sit", tuck his hind-quarters under with the other. Be careful not to push down hard on his spine, but instead gently squeeze the base of his lower back to settle him. Praise him once he is sitting. If he meekly collapses, encourage him with a toy, then try again later.

Reward with food treat

"Stay"

If your pup has mastered "Come" and "Sit", he has learned to follow a sequence of commands. "Stay" is simply a prolonged variation of "Sit". It is especially useful when you anticipate possible dangers.

Food treat is held up to maintain eye contact

WHY "STAY" MATTERS

Training a dog to "Stay" doesn't just ensure that you can leave him outside safely while you pop into the shops. "Stay" training is a potential life-saver. Busy roads, coastal paths, and even other dogs can be a hazard to your pooch. For this simple reason, "Stay" may be the most important command you ever teach your dog.

1 First, command your dog to "Sit". Hold a food treat in your hand so that the dog can see it. Make sure his head is up, looking at your face, but do not stand too close; he should not be looking up vertically. Choose a location with few distractions so that your dog's attention is fully on you.

2 Show your dog the palm of your hand while you command "Stay". Take a few steps back. If your dog moves, start the exercise again from the beginning. Over several sessions, gradually increase the distance that you move away from your dog, until you are at the limit of the lead.

"Stay" command
Place your hand, palm open, in front of your dog's nose and instruct him to "Stay".

Dog focuses on owner's signals

Owner holds lead without tension

3 Keep the duration of the first "Sit–Stay" commands short. When your dog sits and stays obediently, give the food treat and praise him. Conclude "Stay" by using the release word "Finished". Gradually increase the duration of the "Stay" command on each occasion, making the food rewards intermittent while still praising him.

LIE DOWN

"Lie down" needs only a little more work than "Stay": the action itself is perfectly natural to your dog. Your initial aim is for your dog to comply with your command "Lie down". Once this is achieved, gradually extend the duration until he lies down for as long as you say.

PRAISE AND REWARD

To get the best out of your training sessions, learn how and when to show appreciation for your dog's efforts.
■ Avoid giving your dog excessive praise, especially when finishing training. The excitement may teach him to jump around and be overly exuberant.
■ If food treats turn your dog into a whirling dervish and he can't concentrate, stop the training session. Train him later, on a fuller stomach.

Food treat keeps dog's attention

1 With your dog in a "Sit" position, kneel to his right side, holding his collar in your left hand and a food treat in your right hand. Hold the treat directly in front of your dog's nose, and then start moving your hand downwards.

Ensure control by holding collar

2 As your dog follows the food treat with his nose, sweep your hand in an arc, forwards and downwards. As your dog starts to lie down to keep its nose by the treat, give the command "Lie down".

3 Continue moving the treat along the floor until your dog is completely lying down. Praise him with "Good down", and reward with the treat. Repeat the exercise frequently until your dog responds to words alone.

REFUSING TO LIE DOWN

If your dog refuses to lie down, kneel as before and lift – but don't grip – his forelegs with the palms of your hands. Raise him into a begging position and then lower him into a lying position as you give the command "Lie down". Then immediately reward him both verbally and with a treat. If he won't stay down, apply gentle pressure to his withers, and then reward him for lying down.

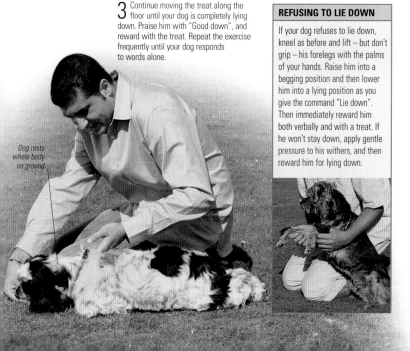

Dog rests whole body on ground

Walking the dog

With careful training, most of us manage to teach our dogs to come, sit, and stay. Teaching walking to heel, with your dog not pulling on his lead, is more difficult. This takes time and perseverance but is essential if you and your dog are to share a happy outdoor relationship.

PLAN AHEAD

Don't expect your dog to understand "Heel" training until he is reliably obedience trained to "Come–Sit–Stay" on command. By now, he should feel comfortable wearing his collar, as well as a lightweight training lead. Train indoors first, ideally in a hallway with no distractions. Slowly graduate to a quiet area outdoors. Build up to more distracting environments only once your puppy is comfortable with "Heel" training. Keep sessions short – between 5 and 15 minutes at a time, and never when the dog is tired. Think about which leg you use first when you start walking: your pup takes his cue from your lead leg. The steps below assume you lead with your left leg; if not, start the dog on your other side.

PULLING ON THE LEAD

Give verbal command "Heel"

Keep only slight tension on lead

Slack in lead provides greater control of dog

Walk forwards with your left leg first

1 Attach your dog's lead to his well-fitted, comfortable collar and, with the lead and a food treat in your right hand, stand to his right. Give the commands "Sit" and "Stay". Make sure you hold the slack in the lead with your left hand, ready to slide down to the collar if your dog decides to make a run for it.

2 Give the release command "OK" and start walking with your left leg first. Let your dog feel only the slightest tension on the lead. As your dog moves forwards, give the command "Heel". If he surges forwards, slide your hand down the lead to his collar and very gently pull back and give the command "Steady".

ALL DOGS ARE TOY DOGS

Sometimes food is too powerful a reward – a dog pays attention only to the food, and not to the training. Less commonly, some dogs are not interested in food rewards. In either situation, use a toy that triggers interest as a reward. Train your dog to value the toy, to want to possess it, by tantalizing him with it before giving it to him.

Food treat tempts dog forwards

Use left hand to gently usher dog right

Reward your dog only after he responds to the command

4 Once your dog heels reliably, you can begin to introduce turns to the right. As you walk forwards, use your left hand gently to guide him to the right, and as he begins to turn, give the command "Heel".

Keep dog close to left leg to maintain control

5 Left turns are a little more difficult to perform. As you're about to turn left, increase your walking speed and slide your left hand down to your dog's collar to control him closely. Keep your dog close to your left leg, and give the command "Steady" as you slow him down before turning.

3 After walking only a few steps, stop and immediately give the command "Stay". Give your dog the food treat combined with verbal praise, then try the procedure again covering the same sequence of events. Repeat the exercise frequently, gradually extending the distance you walk together as you grow in confidence.

Destructive behaviour

Dogs don't bark or howl when left alone, or dig under the fence, or chew your carpets, furniture, or wallpaper, for no reason at all. Dogs don't do these things "to get even". They behave in these ways because they are bored and don't like having nothing to do.

BOREDOM

Prolonged boredom leads to anxiety, which leads to creativity, which produces mayhem. Prevention is always easier and better than trying to overcome a problem. Make your dog's life more stimulating. That's easier said than done, but here are some suggestions.

■ Before leaving your dog home alone, get out a favourite toy and rub it in your hands to leave your scent on it.

■ Make sure your dog has had mental, physical, and social activity before you leave. Exhausted dogs are less likely to bark, dig, chew, or destroy.

Bored, bored, bored
All dogs need stimulation to prevent them from getting bored. A dog with nothing to do is an unhappy dog, so always ensure you leave plenty to keep him occupied.

■ Feed your dog before you depart. Dogs are more likely to curl up and sleep on a full stomach after a good meal.

■ Leave quietly, without fuss. And no smoochy goodbyes. Draw the curtains and leave the television on, especially if there's an animal channel available.

■ Never leave your dog at home all day. Arrange for a neighbour or dog walker to visit and exercise your pooch.

Employ a dog walker
A dog walker is a great help if, on occasion, you're not there to exercise your pooch, but this isn't sufficient when you're away. Consider kennels or a professional dog sitter.

The importance of play
Think of your dog as a coiled spring, crammed full of energy every day. Playing with him releases this energy, conquers boredom, and leaves him feeling relaxed, happy, and thankful for the attention.

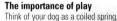

BARKING AND HOWLING

Barking through boredom is a difficult problem to overcome. The best way to turn off barking is to train your dog to "Speak" on command. This exercise takes patience and time on your part; if you can stick to it, you are a marvellous and dedicated dog owner.

1 Attach your dog's lead to a fence and then play with a toy, out of his reach, until he barks with excitement. As he does so, give the command "Speak" and reward him with the toy and the words "Good dog".

2 Once your dog understands the command "Speak" he can be taught "Quiet". Command "Quiet" when he is barking and then give the toy and a verbal reward as soon as he stops. This takes time. Be patient.

3 When your dog routinely responds to the "Quiet" command while barking, increase steadily the distance between the two of you. Reward compliance only with a verbal "Good dog" – stop using the toy now.

4 With your dog reliably trained to stop barking at the "Quiet" command, set up mock departures from home, commanding "Quiet" before you leave. Stand outside the door or garden gate. If he barks, make a noise to startle him to stop barking, then return and praise him for being quiet. It's time-consuming, but it works.

CHEWING

Some pups go through an excessive chewing phase between 6 and 12 months of age. If your dog does, provide him with exciting chew toys and restrict him to his crate (*see* p.317) when you're not able to keep an eagle eye on him. Apply taste deterrents to any objects you do not want your dog to chew.

DIGGING AND FENCE JUMPING

If you have an instinctive digger, lay chicken wire just under the soil where you don't want your dog to dig. Or try channelling his energy into an area of the garden where you have provided a safe, sandy pit for him to dig in. To prevent fence jumping, a line of tin cans strung on a rope around 30cm (12in) from the fence and 1m (3ft) off the ground make a safe, noisy deterrent.

Over-excitement

We offer dogs comfort, security, and a lifetime supply of food. But there are disadvantages to this lifestyle, the greatest being a lack of mental stimulation, leading to over-excitement.

PULLING ON THE LEAD

Dogs seemingly invented one of the basic laws of physics: "For every action there is an equal and opposite reaction." Pulling on the lead is by far the most common problem dog owners experience. What complicates matters is that by pulling back to rein in your dog, you only make him pull harder. To rectify this problem, return to the basics of dog walking (*see* pp.322–323).

Think of the lead as a guide, not a restraint, and remain mentally focused on walking. You want your dog to be aware of you, to feel your presence subtly through the lead. Remember, *you* are in control. Anticipate and interrupt your dog's thoughts of lunging forwards by luring his mind, as well as his body, back to where you want him to be.

PREVENTING PULLING

You want to take your dog for a leisurely walk, not start a frantic game of tug-of-war. Do not attempt to match your strength against your dog's. If retraining your dog in basic obedience (*see* pp.318–319) doesn't improve things, you need to follow the remedial techniques shown below.

Hand pulls back once, gently but firmly

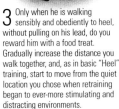

Reward is given

1 In a quiet location, start to walk forwards with your dog on your left, your left hand on the lead near his collar, and the right hand holding the end of the lead. As your dog starts pulling, stop walking and immediately slide your hand down to his collar. Gently but firmly, pull him back to the heel position. Try to avoid pulling on the lead repeatedly.

2 When your dog is back in the correct position, command "Sit" and verbally reward him for doing so. With him once more under your control, start to walk again, giving the command "Heel". After a few paces, stop and repeat the command "Sit". Repeat the procedure every time your dog pulls forwards until it learns to stop pulling on the lead.

3 Only when he is walking sensibly and obediently to heel, without pulling on his lead, do you reward him with a food treat. Gradually increase the distance you walk together, and, as in basic "Heel" training, start to move from the quiet location you chose when retraining began to ever-more stimulating and distracting environments.

Not the leader of the pack
Even a normally well-behaved dog can start pulling when he visits an unfamiliar and exciting place like the beach. However, you must bring him under control; allowing your dog to pull you along undermines your role as pack leader.

PREVENTING OVER-EXCITEMENT

Dogs show they are excited by barking and pulling on the lead (*see opposite*), or by jumping up. Try the following if your dog jumps at visitors:

■ First, ensure your dog is in another room when visitors arrive.

■ If visitors are willing to participate in retraining, put your dog on its lead, use the positive command "Sit", and ensure your dog complies before visitors enter.

■ Instruct your visitors to move slowly and avoid eye contact with your dog upon entering the room.

■ Reward quiet compliance with a food treat and a hushed "Good dog".

■ Allow your dog to be approached or touched by your visitors only after he has responded to your obedience command and shows no signs of jumping up.

Attention-seeker
Nipping at your ankles and clothes is an unwelcome form of dog flattery. Offer him a toy as a distraction as soon as he begins to play a little too exuberantly.

HEAD HALTERS

For some dogs, walking or being trained while on a lead actually incites them to pull. Use a head halter on these headstrong individuals. The lead clips to a ring under the dog's jaw. When the dog pulls forwards on the lead, his own momentum pulls the head down (and jaws shut). Common sense says stop pulling.

Jumping up
Small dogs are particularly prone to jumping up. If someone approaches your dog to stroke him, get your dog to sit so that the person has to bend down to pet him.

Aggression

It's embarrassing, and startling, when a canine member of your family shows unexpected aggression, but we forget too easily that there's a carnivore under that benign dog exterior. Aggression takes many forms. Fortunately, most can be prevented or controlled.

AGGRESSION AWARENESS

There is always a reason, obvious to the dog but sometimes less so to us, why canines bite. Most dogs are skilled at giving body-language warning signs before biting. We fail if we see these signs but do nothing about them. Different forms of aggression should be treated in different ways, but all should ultimately be eliminated.

Understanding aggression

Some dogs are born with a greater tendency to become aggressive, but problems occur only where owners "encourage" the development of a dog's aggressive potential.

DANGER SIGNS TO WATCH OUT FOR

Does your dog:
- Growl at you, other people, or other animals?
- Show his teeth to you, other people, or other animals?
- Snap, growl, or show his teeth when you approach his food or toys?
- Hide when approached by strangers or when you have visitors?
- Nip at your face or limbs when playing with you?
- Chase cats, wildlife, livestock, joggers, or bicycles?
- Give you prolonged cold stares?
- Make you invent excuses, telling people, "It's just a phase he's going through"?

If you answer "Yes" to any of these questions, your dog has the potential to become aggressive.

FEARFUL AGGRESSION

Fear is the most common reason why dogs bite strangers. It occurs most commonly in poorly socialized individuals and dogs with low self-confidence. Fear-biting dogs have usually learned from experience not to trust humans. Aggression is used to make a "threat" go away.

■ TREATMENT: Tell visitors to avoid eye contact with your dog. Equip them with food treats to throw on the floor so that your dog gets a mixed message: strangers are worrisome but, then again, they bring rewards. This will develop trust.

SEX-RELATED AGGRESSION

Mothers suckling their pups may be outwardly aggressive to humans and other dogs. Male dogs may pick fights with other male dogs to assert superiority.

■ TREATMENT: Neutering can eliminate sexual drawbacks, and is a sensible way to reduce sex-related aggression.

POSSESSIVE AGGRESSION

Growling and showing teeth are classic signs of possessive aggression. Some dogs become protective over food or toys and are liable to bite other dogs – or their owners – if their possessions are touched.

■ TREATMENT: Train your dog to be touched while eating. Offer a treat even tastier than his own food, and he will soon learn to enjoy your presence. If he bites to retain possession of a toy, confiscate the toy permanently.

Fear factor
The snap of a fearful dog's jaws may look like dominant aggression, but the reason for it is often low self-esteem. Fear biting is most likely in dogs that as puppies did not have the opportunity to meet lots of people.

PREDATORY AGGRESSION

Dogs are carnivores. They naturally chase and kill animals, especially small ones. This is a basic and primitive form of aggression. Early socializing, and channelling a puppy's desire to chase toys, are the best forms of prevention.

■ TREATMENT: Seek professional help.

DOMINANCE AGGRESSION

Dogs instinctively understand pack hierarchy, but some dogs want to be pack leaders. They assess you and your family members for some time and eventually challenge for the position by biting.

■ TREATMENT: Avoid any form of physical punishment – it is provocative and may make matters worse. Always have a lead or houseline attached to your dog's collar. Use a muzzle if warranted. Through body posture, facial expression, and tone of voice, assert your position as pack leader. At the hint of a challenge, move your dog into isolation for a symbolic minute, then release him and ignore him.

TERRITORIAL AGGRESSION

This is the postman's worst nightmare. A dog is most confident on its own territory, and will potentially protect its home, garden, or car. Many of us encourage our dogs to bark protectively, which promotes potential territorial aggression.

■ TREATMENT: Make a point of rewarding your dog for not being aggressive to delivery people. Leave food treats in a weatherproof box at your gate or door with instructions to visitors to take treats and toss them to your dog when they enter your property.

Barks and bites
Aggression between two dogs is more likely to occur when both are relatively equal – same sex, age, and size. Trouble is more probable in dogs that as puppies were allowed to play rough games without correction.

Advanced training

In virtually all activities we undertake, we learn from experienced others. Advanced training can help the top dogs better themselves, as well as aiding those dogs who find learning more of a struggle. Either way, it's a sure sign of your firm commitment towards your dog.

IN A CLASS OF THEIR OWN

A dog show may appear to be nothing more than a beauty contest, but it's not. Winners are more than just good-lookers. The best in show are superbly trained to behave obediently, confidently, and with panache when being examined or parading in the ring. Unofficial dog shows can be more relaxed events, allowing any dog to compete.

YORKSHIRE TERRIER IN A SHOW

WHAT IS ADVANCED TRAINING?

Advanced training is a set of commands, routines, and exercises developed especially for those dogs who have gone as far as they can with the teaching and guidance available and are ready for another challenge. Whether they are an animal behaviourist's worst nightmare or a rescue dog as intelligent as a canine Einstein, any type of dog can benefit from advanced training.

OBEDIENCE CLASSES

Dog trainers at obedience classes can advise you on the basics of living with a dog, helping you to understand what a dog is and how it functions. While you learn more about your dog, your dog will learn self-control, social skills, and any basic exercises you weren't able to teach it yourself. Your veterinary receptionist will probably know who the best trainers are in your area. Alternatively, contact one of the training organizations listed on pages 334–335.

PERSONAL TRAINERS

While classes are ideal for standard obedience training, there's nothing more efficient and rewarding than one-to-one training. If you can afford one, a personal trainer can individually cater for you and your dog's needs, addressing any particular difficulties and problems.

Gunning for success
This gundog is being taught a highly specialized set of commands. Soon he will be adept at directional control, retrieval, water work, and understanding whistle and hand signals.

In pursuit of excellence
This Rough Collie takes flight as it participates in an organized agility show. The aim of the game is to get your dog around a course "clear" (without faults) and within the specified course time.

RESIDENTIAL TRAINING

There are excellent trainers who offer residential courses for dogs, but sending your pet away for a week isn't the best option for solving routine problems. Most problems occur because of us – either what we do with our dogs, or because of our unwarranted expectations of what we think they can do.

VETERINARY HELP

Most vets today are well aware of the importance of effective training and the negative effects of problematic canine behaviour. Some clinics arrange their own training programmes and many vets have products available such as drugs and pheromone sprays, which may be useful when treating behaviour disorders.

ADVANCED OBEDIENCE

For those dogs who like to be mentally and physically challenged, advanced obedience could be the answer.

Why not try his paw at agility training – jumping hurdles, walking beams, climbing A-frames, leaping through tyres, and so on? Many traditional herding or sledding breeds enjoy the challenge of sheep trials or sledding races. Field trials to test a dog's abilities to point, flush, or retrieve game are a good choice for hunting breeds. Or what about trying Flyball? This popular sport, dominated by Border Collies, pits one team of four dogs against another. The teams are trained to run a course, hit a pad that releases a ball, catch the ball, and run with it back to the starting line in the fastest time.

Agility ability
A Belgian Shepherd Dog learns how to use weave poles as part of its agility training. The course is a test of speed under pressure.

Glossary

ACTION The way a dog moves

ANAL SAC Paired glands on either side of the anus that produce material, deposited on passed faeces, that identifies the depositor to other dogs

BASSET Any low-set, smooth-haired breed of scent hound with short, strong legs and long, pendulous ears. Also known as a basset hound

BAT EAR An erect ear, broad at the base, and rounded at the top

BLENHEIM Chestnut-and-white coat colour

BLUE MERLE Marbled blue-and-grey coat colour mixed with black

BLUETICK A speckled coat colour of a mixture of black hairs on a white background

BRACHYCEPHALIC HEAD A short, flattened, and rather broad head

BREED A grouping of pure-bred dogs that are to a great extent uniform in size and appearance

BREED STANDARDS Description of breeds against which dogs are judged at shows

BRINDLE A mixture of black hairs with lighter gold, brown, red, or grey hairs

BRISKET The part of the body below the chest and between the forelegs

BROKEN COAT Wire-haired coat

BULLDOG Any breed of dog originally bred for bull baiting, having a sturdy, thickset physique with a broad head, muscular body, and undershot jaw.

BUTTON EAR An ear in which the flap folds forwards, with the tip close to the skull

CANIDAE The family of carnivores to which dogs, wolves, foxes, and jackals belong

CANINE TEETH The two upper and lower long teeth lateral to the incisors

CARNASSIAL TEETH The first lower-molar and the last upper-premolar teeth, enlarged and modified for slicing flesh

CARPALS The wrist bones

CAT FEET Short, round, compact feet resembling those of a cat

CEREBRAL CORTEX Region of the brain responsible for hosting complex functions, such as thought and memory

COBBY Short, compact body

COCHLEA Spiral tube forming part of the inner ear

COCKERPOO A cross between a Miniature Poodle and a Cocker Spaniel

COLLIE A silky-coated, often long-haired dog bred for herding sheep and cattle

COONHOUND A hound bred to track and tree raccoon or opossum for hunters

CORDED COAT Coat consisting of separate, rope-like twists of hair formed from intertwined topcoat and undercoat

CORKSCREW TAIL A twisted tail

CPR Cardiopulmonary resuscitation; a life-saving technique involving heart massage to stimulate circulation and artificial respiration to supply air to the lungs

CROPPING The amputation of the ears to enable the remaining part to stand erect. Illegal in the EU

CROSSBREED The progeny of parents of two different breeds

CROUP The part of the back above the hips extending to the root of the tail

CULOTTE Long hair on thighs

DANDER Flakes of skin that are shed naturally when skin renews itself

DEWCLAW The fifth digit (thumb) on the inside of the leg. Sometimes double dewclaws are present

DEWLAP The loose, pendulous skin under the throat

DIAPHRAGM Thin sheet of muscle separating the chest cavity from the abdomen

DISH-FACE A type of face with an upwards slanting, or concave, nasal bone

DNA Deoxyribonucleic acid; a complex molecule in cell nuclei that is the basic structure of genes

DOCKING Amputating the tail. Illegal in most regions of the EU

DOUBLE COAT Warm, waterproof undercoat and weather-resistant topcoat

DROP EAR A folded, drooping ear

DWARF A short-legged dog, originally bred for reduced running speed

DWARFISM A naturally occurring genetic mutation, perpetuated through selective breeding, in which long limb bones shorten and joints thicken

DYSPLASIA, HIP An abnormal development of hip joint tissue, usually leading to arthritis. In part a hereditary condition

ECTROPION A condition in which the lower eyelid hangs loosely, exposing the inner lining, or haw

ELIMINATION The act of urinating or defecating

ENTROPION A condition in which the eyelids turn in, causing the lashes to contact the eye

EPIDIDYMIS A sperm-carrying tube situated at the back of the testis

EPIGLOTTIS A flap of cartilage at the back of the tongue which closes after swallowing to cover the larynx and thus prevent food from entering the lungs

EYE TEETH The upper canines

FEATHERING The long fringe of hair on the ears, legs, tail, or body

FEMUR The thigh bone that lies between the hip and the knee

FIBULA The outer, thinner of the two bones in the leg, between the stifle and the hock

FLANK The sides of the body between the last rib and the hip

FLEWS Pendulous upper lips

FLUSHING The act of driving game from cover, forcing it to take flight

FLYBALL A sport in which teams of dogs race against each other, stopping to press spring-loaded pads that release tennis balls, before running back to their handlers while carrying the balls

FREE RADICALS Atoms or molecules in the body that destroy cell membranes

FRONTAL BONE The skull bone over the eye

FRONTAL SINUS An air-filled cavity in the forehead, connecting to the nose

GAIT The pattern of leg movements, such as walking, trotting, or running, by which a dog moves forward, often specified in breed standards

GASTROINTESTINAL Of, or relating to, the stomach and intestines

GENETIC Concerned with hereditary factors (genes)

GREYHOUND A tall, slender dog of an ancient breed, capable of great speed, which hunts by sight

GRIFFON A type of wire-haired scent hound

GUARD HAIRS The long, thick, heavy hair that creates the topcoat

GUNDOG Any breed of dog bred and trained to work with a hunter or shooting party, especially at pointing, flushing, or retrieving

HACKLES The hair on the back and the neck that can be raised involuntarily

HARE FOOT A long, narrow foot, with middle toes longer than the outer toes, and not too arched

HARLEQUIN Patched colours of black or blue on a white coat

HAUNCH The region that is directly above the hips

HEAD HALTER An arrangement of canvas or webbing straps that fits onto a dog's head, with a lead attached, used to discourage a dog from pulling. When the dog pulls forward, the momentum pulls his head down and shuts the jaws

HEAT The female dog's oestrus period

HEELER A dog that herds cattle by biting or nipping at their heels

HEIGHT The distance from the top of the withers to the ground

HOCK The leg region, formed by the tarsal bones, between the knee and the toes

HORMONES The chemical substances that circulate in the blood, produced by endocrine glands

HOUND Any breed of dog used for hunting

HOUSELINE A long, light leash that can be used around the house to keep control of a dog

HUMERUS The bone of the upper arm

ILIUM The part of the pelvis into the cavity of which the head of the femur fits

IN-BREEDING Mating of closely related dogs

ISCHIUM The hind portion of the floor of the pelvis

LABRADOODLE A cross between a Labrador Retriever and a Standard Poodle

LACRIMAL GLAND A gland that secretes tears. It is found in the upper, outer part of each eye socket

LAUFHUND Any breed of Swiss walking dog, developed to accompany hunters on foot

LEARNING CENTRE Part of the brain that has the capacity to develop consistent responses to situations and stimuli

LENTICULAR SCLEROSIS An eye condition in elderly dogs in which the lenses go cloudy, impairing vision

LIVER A coat colour of brown, bronze, or reddish brown shades – also called chocolate or brown

LOINS The front thigh muscles

MANDIBLE The lower-jaw bone

MASTIFF Any of a group of large, powerful, short-haired dogs related to an ancient breed originally bred for guarding, fighting, and herding. Also known as Molossoid

MAXILLA The upper-jaw bone

MERLE EYE Flecked brown or blue eye, with black iris

METATARSALS The bones between the hock and the foot

MINIATURIZATION A natural genetic mutation, perpetuated by selective breeding, in which all parts of the skeleton are equally reduced in size

MOULT The shedding of the coat

MUTT *see* random-bred dog

MUZZLE The foreface – the head in front of the eyes

NEUTERING Removing the sex hormone-producing apparatus from the male or female. In males, the testicles are removed. In females, the ovaries and uterus are removed

NIEDERLAUFHUND Any of the short-legged breeds of Swiss walking dogs, developed to accompany hunters on foot in mountainous terrain

OESOPHAGUS The tube in the body which takes food from the pharynx (throat) to the stomach

OESTRUS The period during which a female ovulates and mates willingly

OVERSHOT JAW A jaw in which the front teeth overlap and do not touch the teeth of the lower jaw

PADS The thickened cushion beneath the toes and on the soles of the feet

PARIAH DOG Another name for a street dog

PARTI-COLOUR Two colours in variegated patches

PASTERN The region between the hock, or wrist, and the toes

PATELLA The kneecap

PEDIGREE A record of a dog's ancestry

PINNA The ear flap

PINSCHER German for "terrier" or "biter"

POINTER One of many breeds of dog used in hunting, which points to indicate the position of game to the hunter

POINTING Freezing on sight of game and pointing in direction of game

PREMOLAR TEETH The teeth situated between the canines and the molars

PRICK EAR An erect, pointed ear

PRIMITIVE BREED Arbitrary label applied to breeds of dog belonging to a group of breeds that are genetically closest to the wolf

PROSTATE GLAND A gland in males at the neck of the bladder that secretes a liquid that acts as transport medium for sperm

PUREBRED DOG A dog whose parents both belong to the same breed

QUICK The area of living tissue inside a toenail, particularly sensitive to pain

RADIUS The second bone of the foreleg lying parallel to the ulna

RANDOM-BRED DOG A dog whose parents do not both belong to recognized breeds. Also called a mutt

RECYCLED DOG A dog obtained from a rescue centre

REDTICK A speckled coat colour of a mixture of red hairs on a white background

RETRIEVER Any breed of dog bred and trained to retrieve game

ROSE EAR A small, drop ear folding over and back

SABLE Coat colour featuring black-tipped hairs on a background of gold, silver, grey, or tan

SABRE TAIL Tail carried in a curve

SACRUM A mass of fused vertebrae situated between the lumbar vertebrae and the bones of the tail

SCAPULA The shoulder blade

SCENT HOUND A hound that hunts primarily by ground scent

SCISSOR BITE A bite in which the upper teeth closely overlap the lower teeth

SCLERA The white outer layer of the eyeball that surrounds the eye from the cornea at the front to the optic nerve at the back

SEASON A bitch's heat or oestrus period

SEBACEOUS GLAND An oil-producing skin gland that adds waterproofing to the coat

SECOND THIGH The region of the hindquarters from the stifle to the hock

SEMI-PRICK EARS Erect ears, which have tips that break forwards

SEPTUM The division between the nostrils

SETTER One of several breeds of dog developed to freeze on sighting game, indicating the position

SETTING Freezing on sight of game and flushing game upon command

SICKLE TAIL Tail carried out and up in a semicircle

SIGHT HOUND A dog that hunts more by sight than by scent

SOUND Term generally used to describe ease of movement

SPANIEL One of several breeds of usually silky-coated gundogs with long, pendant ears, used for flushing and retrieving

SPECIES A group of individuals sharing common characteristics, with the capacity to interbreed

SPITZ A variety of curly-tailed dog, resembling a wolf, that developed in Arctic regions

STIFLE The joint between the thigh and the second thigh

STOP The depression before the eyes between the skull and the muzzle

STREET DOG A stray dog, without an owner, which survives through scavenging

STRIPPING A COAT The removal by hand of old hair from a wire-haired coat

TAIL SET The position of the tail

TERRIER One of many breeds of small dog, originally used to follow prey underground

THICK-SET Broad and solid

THIGH The region from the hip to the stifle

THYROID GLAND The largest endocrine glands in the dog's body, producing hormones vital for growth and metabolism

TIBIA The inner bone between the stifle and the hock

TICKING Non-solid coat colour, a mixture of coloured hairs on a white background

TOLL To lure (for example, a duck tolling retriever entices ducks to come ashore, capering and leaping in a fox-like manner)

TOPCOAT Coat of heavy, primary (guard) hairs

TOPKNOT The long, fluffy hair that grows on the crown of the head

TOY The smallest size classification of dogs

TREEING Tracking or driving prey into a tree, and then alerting the human hunter

TRICOLOUR Three-coloured – black, white, and tan

ULNA The larger of the lower-foreleg bones

UNDERCOAT The dense, usually short, soft coat closest to the skin

UNDERSHOT JAW A jaw in which the lower-front teeth stick out beyond the upper-front teeth

UVEA The middle layer of the eye, made up of the iris, the ciliary body, and the choroid

VESTIGIAL A part of the body whose original function has been lost or superseded during evolution. For example, the dewclaw

VOMERONASAL ORGAN A sensory organ found in the nose that recognizes specific pheromones

WATER DOG A dog bred and trained to hunt in, or retrieve from, water

WELL-BONED Showing good thickness, quality, and strength in the legs, especially the forelegs

WELL-SPRUNG RIBS Rounded, as opposed to flattened, ribs

WHEATEN Pale yellow or fawn coat colour

WITHERS The highest point on the trunk of a dog's body just behind the neck

WRINKLES The loose folds of skin around the skull

Useful contacts

DOG TRAINING AND ACTIVITY ASSOCIATIONS

Association of Pet Behaviour Counsellors
www.apbc.org.uk
PO BOX 46
Worcester
WR8 9YS
England
+44 (0) 1386 751151

Association of Pet Dog Trainers
www.apdt.co.uk
PO Box 17
Kempsford
GL7 4WZ
England
+44 (0) 1285 810811

The Agility Club
www.agilityclub.co.uk
6 Fane Way
Maidenhead
Berkshire
SL6 2TL
England
+44 (0) 1628 680823

DOG WELFARE

Battersea Dogs Home
www.dogshome.org
4 Battersea Park Road
Battersea
London
SW8 4AA
England
+44 (0) 20 7722 3626

Dogs Trust
www.dogstrust.co.uk
17 Wakley Street
London
EC1V 7RQ
England
+44 (0) 837 0006

The Blue Cross
www.bluecross.org.uk
Shilton Road
Burford
Oxfordshire
OX18 4PF
England
+44 (0) 1993 822651

Royal Society for the Prevention of Cruelty to Animals
www.rspca.org.uk
Wilberforce Way
Southwater
Horsham
West Sussex
RH13 9RS
England
+44 (0) 870 33 35 999

BREED REGISTRIES

The Kennel Club
www.the-kennel-club.org.uk
1 Clarges Street
London
W1J 8AB
England
+44 (0) 870 606 6750

Fédération Cynologique Internationale (FCI)
www.fci.be
Place Albert 1er, 13
B-6530 Thuin
Belgium
+32 71 59 12 38

Irish Kennel Club
www.ikc.ie
Fottrell House
Harold's Cross Bridge
Dublin 6W
Ireland
+353 1 4533300

Index

Author's acknowledgments

Thanks to everyone at the Portman Veterinary Clinic, particularly my colleague Simon Lewi, for creating extra "writing time" for me, and to the delightful people at Studio Cactus, all of whom worked efficiently—dare I say doggedly—to create this book. Special thanks to Candida Frith-MacDonald. Every writer needs a Candida, someone who never forgets anything. Ever. Her freelance help from home was superb.

Publisher's acknowledgments

Dorling Kindersley would like to thank Julian Dams for dtp design, Matt Schofield for design assistance, Rebecca Warren for additional editing, and Francis Wong for jacket design. The quote on p. 5 is from *Man Meets Dog* by Konrad Lorenz, © 1983 Deutscher Taschenbuch Verlag; © for the English Translation, 1999 Deutsche Taschenbuch Verlag, Munich, Germany. Published by Routledge in 2002.

Studio Cactus would like to thank Doghaus Ltd, SHARK GROUP, and Millie and George for providing images of dog clothing; Bruce Fogle and all the staff at the Portman Veterinary Clinic for supplying props; and the following people for their contributions:
Indexer: Zeb Korycinska **Proofreader:** Polly Boyd **Picture Researcher:** Will Jones
Photoshoot advisor: Collette Chase **Models:** Rob Houston, Javier Márquez Marfil, Chamois Rose-Wood, Amy Walters **Photography:** Tracy Morgan Animal Photography, and Damien Moore at Studio Cactus.

Thank you to the owners of all the dogs whose photographs appear in this book, including the following owners for allowing us to photograph their dogs: Sally Aspital for Lottie (Welsh Springer Spaniel); Gloria Brown for Marshmoor (Gordon Setter); Julie Darby and Val Harris for Hermii and Ziggy (Large Münsterländers); Laura Elliot for Oliver (Lhasa Apso); John and Rosemary Griffiths for Raffles Crackerjaane Cello (English Springer Spaniel); Andrew and Janet Holland for Todd (Schipperke); Mrs Lockwood for Monty (Irish Red-and-white Setter); John and Catherine Luckin for Emmy (Flat-coated Retriever); Lynne Luff for Woody and Willow (Italian Spinones); Catherine Maxwell-Miles for Kiri (Lhasa Apso); Sue Morgan and Gill Kennedy-Sloane for Mhairi and Annie (Irish Setters); Jane Morris for Megan and Molly (German Short-haired Pointers); Julie Payne for Angel and Freya (Italian Spinones); Georgina Powell for Ted (English Pointer); Lynne Smith for Shanti (Japanese Spitz); Celia Woodbridge for Crackerjaane Coloratura (English Springer Spaniel); Debbie and Seamus Foster (Bearded Collie pups)

Thank you to the following owners who kindly allowed their dogs to be photographed, which we were not able to feature in this book: Clint Coventry and Anita Scott (Hungarian Vizsla); Desme Daniels and Abbe Marshall-Wyer (German Wire-haired Pointers); Pat Mellish (English Setter); Susan Shenton (Welsh Springer Spaniel); Mike Sweeting (English Setter)

Thank you to the following owners for their permission to include photographs of their dogs: Cara Davani (Kerry Blue Terrier); Benny Lindell (Schillerstövares); Alessio Ottogali (Russo-European Laika); Shelley Ramsay (Siberian Huskies); Shari Stueck (Bourbonnais Pointer); Hedvig Tahlfeldt (Petit Bleu de Gascogne); Ursula Weichler (Russian Black Terriers)

Tracy Morgan would like to thank the following owners of the canine models used in the training photoshoots: Tracy Morgan for Topkyri the Firestarter (English Cocker Spaniel); Stella Carpenter for Warrigal Blue Kookynie at Morrow CD.UDX.WDX.TD. (Australian Cattle Dog); Andrea Page for Exmytom Dandicarroy Maestro (English Pointer); Sam and James Clarke for Fletch (Border Terrier)

Picture credits

The publisher would like to thank the following
for their kind permission to reproduce their photographs:

Key: a = above; b = below; c = centre;
l = left; r = right; rh = running head; t = top

Abbreviations:

Al = Alamy   OSF = Oxford Scientific
Co = Corbis   GI = Getty Images
Ar = Ardea   SS = Shutterstock

1 Al/ImageState; 2 Al/imageshop - zefa visual media uk ltd; 3
Brand X Pictures; 4–5 Al/Bryan & Cherry Alexander Photography;
6 Al/Alt-6; 7 GI/Richard Schultz; 8–9rh SS/Kovalev Serguei;
9cla SS/Matthew Collingwood; 10rh Al/Darren Matthews; 10c
Brand X Pictures 11b Åsa Lindholm; 12–13 GI/Flip Chalfant;
14 Photos.com; 15cra The British Museum; 15br Al/James
Davis Photography; 16tl OSF/Daniel Cox; 16bl Al/Terry Wall;
16bc Premium Stock/Image State; 17tc SS/Matthew Gough;
17tr OSF/Eyal Bartov; 17cr Natural History Museum, London;
17b OSF/Berndt Fischer; 18tr OSF/Digital Vision; 18b
GI/Time Life Pictures; 19r Ar/M. Watson; 19br reprinted from
Current Biology, Vol 15, Issue 5, Byrne, Animal Evolution: Foxy
Friends, R86–R87, 2005, with permission from Elsevier; 20tc
National Geographic Image Collection/Richard Olsenius; 21tc
The British Museum; 21cb Ar/M. Krishnan; 21crb GI/AFP;
22bl OSF/Eyal Bartov; 23cr SS/Peter Guess; 23b Photos.com;
24c Al/Juniors Bildarchiv; 24bl courtesy of Hearing Dogs for
Deaf People; 25d Co/Wolfgang Kaehler; 26 Corbis
Sygma/Clasos Press; 27tr Dogs Trust; 27bl SS/Szabi Borbely;
27bc Bruce Fogle; 27br OSF/Photographic Dan Gair; 31bl
SS/Tina Rencelj; 31background Studio Cactus/Damien
Moore; 35tl Photos.com; 35c GI/Geoff Graham Veer; 37cla
Al/SHOTFILE; 37tr SS/Marily M. Soper; 37cra SS/troy; 37c
Bruce Fogle; 37bl SS/Maria Menshova; 38c Co/Gideon Mendel;
38b Ar/John Cancalosi; 39t SS/Hedser van Brug; 40b Ar/Jean
Paul Ferrero; 41tl Ar/Yann Arthus-Bertrand; 41br GI/AFP; 42
PhotoDisc; 43tl SS/Lancelot et Naelle; 43tc Al/Key
Collection/21 Carrot; 43tr SS/William Batin; 43br GI/Carol
Kohen; 44c courtesy of The Guide Dogs For The Blind
Association; 44bl courtesy of Therapy Dogs of Vermont; 45tc
Ar/John Daniels; 45b Co/SUKREE SUKPLANG/Reuters;
46ca courtesy of www.millieandgeorge.com; 46b Al/Image
Wallace; 47 GI/Time Life Pictures; 48tc GI/Jan Petreshock;
49tr Al/Iain Masterton; 49b SS/Jerome Tisne; 50–51 GI/Lori
Adamski Peek; 53b Al/David McGill; 54 SS/Kovalev Serguei;
55rh Co/Royalty Free; 55bl SS/Peter Darcy; 56 SS/Peter Deal;
57bl SS/Anne Gro Bergersen; 58bl SS/Steven Pepple; 58br
Al/Jeff Greenberg; 59 Al/Pixonnet.com; 60br Ar/John Daniels;
62tr SS/Hurene; 65b Al/Juniors Bildarchiv; 66cl SS/Debra
Ducotey; 68tr SS/Jing Chen; 69 SS/Kristen Drietz; 70cra
GI/Hulton Archive/E. Bacon; 70b SS/WizData, inc; 72tr
SS/Regina Chayer; 72bl SS/Nicholas Peter Gavin Davies; 73b
SS/Tammy McAllister; 76cr SS/troy; 78–79 Al/Juniors Bildarchiv;
80cl AL/BennettPhoto; 81br SS/Carriemore Larmore; 82tr
SS/Vincent; 83crb Al/Hulton Archive; 86 Ar/Bill Coster; 87cl
BAL/Roy Miles Fine Paintings; 88b Bruce Fogle; 89tr
SS/ChipPix; 90 SS/Tammy McAllister; 91tr SS/Chin Kit Sen;
92tr GI/Sean Murphy; 92b SS/Renee Keeton/Simply Focused
Studios; 93br Alice van Kempen; 94b SS/Steven Pepple; 95cr
SS/Parasuraman Nurani; 95b Co/Kevin Lamarque; 98tr
Photos.com; 100 SS/Dan Bris'ki; 101br SS/Steven Pepple; 102
SS/Galina Barskaya; 103rh Co/Royalty Free; 103c Hedvig
Tahlfeldt; 103br SS/George Lee; 105cl SS/Lyn Adams; 106bl
SS/Thomas Polen; 107cl BAL; 110tr Alice van Kempen; 110bl
Alice van Kempen; 111crb BAL/Bibliothèque Nationale, Paris,
France; 112cra Al/David R. Frazier Photolibrary, Inc; 112b
Al/Juniors Bildarchiv; 115cra Åsa Lindholm; 116–117 Åsa
Lindholm; 121b Yves Lanceau Photography/photographers
direct.com; 124cl SS/C. Rene Ammundsen; 124–25b
SS/Aaron Whitney; 125cra courtesy of SARDA (England);
126clb SS/Chin Kit Sen; 127crb SS/Patricia Marroquin; 128b
Andrew Wilson Photography/photographersdirect.com; 129cra
Co/Rob Howard; 131br Alice van Kempen; 132b Alice van
Kempen; 136b Cara Davani; 138b SS/Phillip Alexander
Russell; 138br SS/Casey K. Bishop; 139tr Alice van Kempen;
141tc SS/Erik Lam; 142–43 Al/Dex Image; 144cra Alice van

Kempen; 145br Alice van Kempen; 146tl Alice van Kempen;
150cl SS/Per-Anders Jansson; 151tl Mary Evans Picture
Library; 151b Al/Heather Watson; 152bl akg-images/Walt
Disney Productions/Album; 153tr SS/Tammy McAllister; 153b
SS/Tammy McAllister; 154b NHPA/Yves Lanceau; 155cra Bev
Turner, Small Münsterländer Club of North America; 155b
Alice van Kempen; 157rh Co/Royalty Free; 157c Photos.com;
157b Al/blickwinkel; 159tr Alessio Ottogali; 159b Alice van
Kempen; 160b courtesy of Heather Adeney, www.skidog.ca;
163b SS/Karla Caspari; 164bl SS/Peter Baxter; 165cra Jerry
Shulman Photographer/photographersdirect.com; 165crb
Al/blickwinkel; 166cra Photos.com; 168b SS/Hedser van Brug;
170br Al/Adrian Muttitt; 172br BAL/National Gallery, London,
UK; 175cl BAL/Noortman, Maastricht, Netherlands; 175cr
Alice van Kempen; 176bl Alice van Kempen; 178clb courtesy
of The Advertising Archives; 178br Photos.com; 183crb Animal
Photography/Sally Anne Thompson; 184cr BAL/Whitworth
Art Gallery, The University of Manchester, UK; 186bl
Co/Martin Harvey; 186br Photos.com; 187cra GI/Hulton
Archive; 188–89 Co/Paul Velasco; Gallo Images; 190b
Al/Juniors Bildarchiv; 191clb Al/Craig Steven Thrasher; 192b
Alice van Kempen; 193cra SS/Rosemarie Colombraro; 194cla
Alice van Kempen; 195cla Alice van Kempen; 198tr akg-
images/Kack Wrather Prod./Lassie Telev; 198cl SS/Michael
Ludwig; 199cr courtesy of The Advertising Archives; 201bl Co;
201br SS/Michael Scott Bessier; 202cr SS/David Fink; 203b
SS/George Lee; 205r SS/Steve Sant; 207b Co/Paul A. Souders;
209b Animal Photography; 210cl Mary Evans Picture Library;
210b SS/Joe Gough; 211bl courtesy of SARDA (England);
212–13 Al/Juniors Bildarchiv; 214bl BAL/Private Collection,
The Stapleton Collection, 216b SS/Tina Rencelj; 217tr
SS/Tina Rencelj; 217br Photos.com; 219cl BAL/Kunsthistorisches
Museum, Vienna, Austria; 220–21 Al/Dave Porter; 222bl
SS/Martin Wall ; 223tr Bruce Fogle; 223b Co/Markus
Botzek/zefa; 224–25 Al/Balfour Studios; 231cra Al/Dave
Porter; 231br Al/Janine Wiedel Photolibrary; 233tr courtesy
of Heather Adeney, www.skidog.ca; 234crb Alice van Kempen;
237br Shari Stueck/Rufnit Kennels; 240 GI/GK & Vikki Hart;
241rh Co/Royalty Free; 241br Al/Francisco Martinez; 242b
SS/Kriss Russell/PhotoGen-X; 243cra GI/Time Life Pictures;
243b SS/Bart Goossens; 244tr The Kennel Club/Farlap
Photography; 244b SS/Yan Zommer; 246cb SS/Olga Drozdova;
247tr SS/Thea Reilkoff; 249cl Al/Andrew Harrington; 253br
Alice van Kempen; 256cl SS/troy; 257b Alice van Kempen;
258bl Alice van Kempen; 259b Alice van Kempen; 260clb
SS/George Lee; 261cra Photos.com; 261br Charlotte Stenholt
Kristensen; 262–63 Co/Jim Craigmyle; 264cr Charlotte
Stenholt Kristensen; 264b Åsa Lindholm; 265cr Al/Network
Photographers; 266–67 GI/Picture Press; 268 Brand X Pictures;
270tc Brand X Pictures; 270b Brand X Pictures; 271tl
OSF/Photo Communications Inc – Moni; 272 SS/Norman
Pogson; 273cr SS/Tammy McAllister; 274cra SS/Les Byerley;
274b Co/Larry Williams; 275tr SS/WizData Inc; 275cr
SS/noregt; 276tr SS/Glenn Skanderup; 276cra SS/Paige Falk;
276cr SS/Jennifer Leigh Sellig; 276b SS/Geoff Delderfield;
278cr Al/David McGill; 279cr SS/Felix Fernandez Gonzalez;
280 SS/Joe Gough; 280bc SS/Tina Rencelj; 281cra
Al/Pixonnet.com; 282cra Al/Tina Manley; 282bc Al/Juniors
Bildarchiv; 285br SS/Mary J. Levinson; 286cb Jamie Avery at
Doghaus Ltd; 287cla Jamie Avery at Doghaus Ltd; 287tr Shark
Group; 287cr Jamie Avery at Doghaus Ltd; 288b GI/Neo Vision;
289t SS/Fred Bergeron; 289br SS/George Lee; 290crb
SS/Knud Nielsen; 291c Brand X Pictures; 291br SS/Andreas
Klute; 295t Brand X Pictures; 297tr RSPCA/Andrew Forsyth;
298b Brand X Pictures; 299tl Al/Phototake Inc; 299tr Al/Mark
J. Barrett; 299br OSF/Phototake Inc; 300bl RSPCA/Angela
Hampton; 301t Al/oote boe; 301crb SS/Lucy Ann Dyck; 302bl
SS/Daniel Bellhouse; 303 Brand X Pictures; 305tr AL/Tom
Spalding; 308b CO/LWA-Dann Tardif; 310 Brand X Pictures;
312br Al/Nic Cleave Photography; 313tr Photos.com; 313crb
Photos.com; 314b GI/Ty Allison; 324cra Photos.com; 324clb
SS/Thomas Nord; 324b Photos.com; 326–27 Al/imageshop –
zefa media uk ltd; 328 AL/plainpicture GmbH & Co. KG; 329tr
Al/PhotoStockFile; 330b SS/James R. Hearn; 330b SS/Stuart
Blyth; 331t SS/Rena Schild; 332rh Al/Darren Matthews

All other images © Dorling Kindersley.
For further information see **www.dkimages.com**